Affective Assemblages and Local Economies

Radical Subjects in International Politics

Series Editor: Ruth Kinna

This series uses the idea of political subjection to promote the discussion and analysis of individual, communal, and civic participation and activism. 'Radical subjects' refers both to the character of the topics and issues tacked in the series and to the ethics guiding the research. The series has a radical focus in that it provides a springboard for the discussion of activism that sits outside or on the fringes of institutional politics, yet which, insofar as it reflects a commitment to social change, is far from marginal. It provides a platform for scholarship that interrogates modern political movements, probes the local, regional and global dimensions of activist networking, and the principles that drive them, and develops innovative frames to analyse issues of exclusion and empowerment. The scope of the series is defined by engagement with the concept of the radical in contemporary politics but includes research that is multi- or interdisciplinary, working at the boundaries of art and politics, political utopianism, feminism, sociology, and radical geography.

Titles in Series

Taking the Square: Mediated Dissent and Occupations of Public Space, Edited by Maria Rovisco and Jonathan Corpus Ong

The Politics of Transnational Peasant Struggle: Resistance, Rights and Democracy, Robin Dunford

Sustainable Urbanism and Direct Action: Case Studies in Dialectical Activism, Benjamin Heim Shepard

Participation and Non-Participation in Student Activism: Paths and Barriers to Mobilizing Young People for Political Action, Alexander Hensby

The Crisis of Liberal Democracy and the Path Ahead, Bernd Reiter

Becoming a Movement: Identity and Narratives in the European Global Justice Movement, Priska Daphi

Liminal Subjects: Weaving (Our) Liberation, Sara C. Motta

Autonomy, Refusal and The Black Block: Positioning Class Analysis in Critical and Radical Theory, Robert F. Carley

A Post-Western account of Critical Cosmopolitan Social Theory: Being and Acting in a Democratic World, Michael Murphy

Sustainable Urbanism and Direct Action: Case Studies in Dialectical Activism, Benjamin Heim Shepard

The Confrontational 'Us and Them' Dynamics of Polarised Politics in Venezuela: A Post-Structuralist Examination, Ybiskay Gonzalez Torres

Affective Assemblages and Local Economies, Joanie Willett

Affective Assemblages and Local Economies

Joanie Willett

ROWMAN &
LITTLEFIELD
London • New York

Rowman & Littlefield
4501 Forbes Boulevard, Suite 200, Lanham, Maryland 20706, USA
With additional offices in Boulder, New York, Toronto (Canada), and Plymouth (UK)
www.rowman.com

British Library Cataloguing in Publication Data

A catalogue record for this book is available from the British Library

Library of Congress Cataloging-in-Publication Data

Names: Willett, Joanie, author.
Title: Affective assemblages and local economies / Joanie Willett.
Description: Lanham : Rowman & Littlefield, [2021] | Includes bibliographical
  references and index. | Summary: "This book explores what becomes visible if we
  look at peripheral, deprived rural regions through the lens of a complex adaptive
  assemblage and how we can better support these communities"— Provided by
  publisher.
Identifiers: LCCN 2021032123 | ISBN 9781538150702 (cloth) |
  ISBN 9781538150726 (paperback) | ISBN 9781538150719 (ebook)
Subjects: LCSH: Rural development—Sociological aspects. | Regional disparities—
  Social aspects. | Regional planning—Social aspects.
Classification: LCC HN49.C6 W546 2021 | DDC 307.1/412—dc23
LC record available at https://lccn.loc.gov/2021032123

Contents

Acknowledgments   vii

1   Why the Need for the Complex Adaptive Region Assemblage?   1

2   The Affective Assemblage   21

3   The Evolutionary Regional Assemblage, Becoming and Economies   43

4   Southwest Virginia and Cornwall: Constructing the Complex Adaptive Regional Assemblage   65

5   Southwest Virginia   85

6   Cornwall   115

7   What Do We See? Spaces of Possibility in Southwest Virginia and Cornwall   145

8   Conclusion   159

References   165

Index   179

Acknowledgments

There are many people that I want to thank for your help and support over the past few years of putting this book together. From the Regional Studies Association for their membership research grant to the wonderful residents of Bristol TN/VA amongst whom I lived and who welcomed me into your community so warmly. Thanks too to so many people from all around Cornwall who have been so supportive of this project in many ways. Of course, I also need to thank my family, Donal, Elena, Jayd, Jamie, Holly, and Theo, for their patience, love, and enthusiasm. Last, but by no means least, I have to mention the awesome Angie, who was so much more than a landlady, and became guide, interpreter, and firm friend.

Chapter 1

Why the Need for the Complex Adaptive Region Assemblage?

Although I have been working with the ideas that I explore in this book for many years, the book only really started to take shape in the immediate aftermath of the 2016 referendum for the United Kingdom to leave the European Union. It was at this point that the fragmentation of the human, social, political, and environmental worlds really became evident to me on a regional level. The results of the referendum in certain regions also strongly indicated some of the mistakes that were made because of the atomisation that accompanies that fragmentation, and the wider effects that those mistakes could have.

One of the big puzzles of the time was about why the regions in the United Kingdom who in the past or present had received the highest levels of EU structural funding, should vote for Brexit, or at least, with the exception of Northern Ireland, vote disproportionately highly for it. Structural funding has been a central way for the EU to produce 'territorial cohesion', evening out the inequalities between regions within and amongst member states, a member of the EU, UK regions had benefited from the funding significantly. Regions with a Gross Domestic Product (GDP) of less than 75 per cent of EU averages received the highest levels of funding, with the goal of improving their economic fortunes. Structural funds were also a part of 'Europeanisation' strategies (Dabrowski, 2012), with the rationale that receipt of EU monies would help to build a sense of shared identities and commonalities built around the EU as an institution. The development ethos at the heart of Structural Funds and its associated LEADER project was that they would foster rural development by supporting grass-roots activity. This was about bottom up, endogenous ideas, developing a range of different social programmes aimed at promoting social mobilisation so that individuals and localities could make the most of their potential (Canete et al., 2018; Barke and Newton, 1997). In

1

practice, this is often manifested as supporting the ongoing development of social capital and networks.

In this context, regions in the United Kingdom that had received the highest levels of structural funds (by definition, also some of the poorest parts of Britain in economic terms), should have felt a significant level of loyalty towards the EU as an institution. Technically, from their lengthy experience of the EU's workings, voters should also have been able to witness first-hand the benefits of EU membership. But things did not work out that way. Instead, only two parts of the United Kingdom that had received the highest levels of structural funds voted to remain. One of these was Northern Ireland, which has its own, very specific relationship with the EU post-Good Friday Agreement. The other was the Highlands and Islands of Scotland, which had a significantly lower percentage of Remain voters to the Scottish average as a whole (55% Remain to a Scottish average of 62%). Naturally, this seemingly inexplicable result puzzled many who perceived these areas as voting manifestly contrary to their own interests. To try to understand this a little more, a research team of whom I was a part, conducted some qualitative work with Leave voters in Cornwall, a rural region in the southwest of the United Kingdom which has been in continuous receipt of high levels of EU structural funding since 1999. What made Cornwall's Leave vote even more interesting is that local campaigners had fought vigorously throughout the 1990s to achieve the statistical visibility that would enable it to receive this extra level of support (Willett, 2013). However, seventeen years later, popular opinion had conducted a strong *volte-face*, and 56.5 per cent voted to Leave.

In the research that we conducted (Willett et al., 2019), we were struck by one key fact. Our respondents were able to construct a narrative which said that EU funding hadn't actually helped them because they didn't imagine key, headline projects to have been aimed at people like themselves, nor to have had a direct impact on their lives. However, they enjoyed excellent internet connectivity and significantly improved roads as a direct result of the money. Moreover, it emerged from our discussions that the things that troubled people and made their lives more difficult and precarious than they would have liked (such as access to adequate and affordable housing, healthcare, and education) tended not to be issues which were EU competency areas. Therefore, it was very easy for people to discount EU investment as not having been very significant for the area. What we took from this was not a criticism of the EU *per se*, but we were struck by the realisation that as analysts of regional development, we had not considered questions around how ordinary people, members of the public, separate from those involved in decision-making processes, experienced the projects that were delivered. For all of the endogenous, bottom-up nature of Structural Funds, at no point in the measurement process had we sought to understand the strategic priorities, needs, and requirements of the wider public and how funds had affected people's lives. We knew that investment had had a significant impact on the area, and we knew this because of a number of indicators including GDP and jobs growth. What we did not know is about whether these indicators repre- sented any kind of qualitative improvement to people's quality of life, and it was a real shock to learn, as part of this research, that some of the issues that I remember as making life particularly tricky in the 1980s and 1990s are still a significant problem in Cornwall today. As an example, interviewees often told anecdotes about the extreme isolation of car-less individuals and families, and also the significant difficulties that such people had accessing employment, education, health care, and support networks. There are busses that operate within the locality, but many smaller communities are not on a bus route or receive only patchy service. If they are able to use a bus to get around, the fares for non-retireds (retired people receive a free bus pass in Britain) were often far too expensive for regular commuting whilst on a low income. This was a situation that I remembered from my own pre-car days, but I was very curious why, after 20 years and £1.1 billion of infrastructural and economic support, this was still the case.

From here, I began to reflect on the nature of development and to wonder what we do if we put the priorities of the public at the centre of strategic planning decisions. Clearly, an element of strategic overview is important for exploring transferable ideas, together with an appreciation of national and global contexts within which regions are situated. It is also helpful to have some kind of place to collect ideas, possibilities, and potentialities together. But I wondered what we would find if we started projects by talking to the public first. This was combined by my on-going interest with complex adap- tive systems and drawing on Deleuze and Guattari (2004) asking questions about what would happen if we imagined regions as complex, adaptive, assemblages of pasts, presents, stories, institutions, cultural meanings, prac- tices, economies, and knowledges. I was becoming curious about the ways that knowledge and ideas flow around regions and between disparate groups of people, organisations, and institutions within them. Part of this latter interest was sparked by the observation that despite decades of economic transformation, few people in Cornwall seemed to know much (if anything) about new and emerging sectors. Indeed, I was reminded of a conversation that I had with an old neighbour, who informed me that one of his children had left Cornwall to pursue a career in film-making which he clearly believed was not a career choice that was possible to pursue had he chosen to remain in the area. I found this interesting because even in my non-arts-centred social milieu, I knew of at least two people who had moved to Cornwall pre- cisely for the film-making opportunities that it offered. This is one anecdotal example, but it illustrated to me the massive potential problem for individuals

g3ggffggg

in their decisions about what skills were/are marketable and how well they are able to engage in the new economies. This has a double whammy as it also means that if people do not know what skill sets to invest in if they want to participate in the local economy, then businesses will struggle to recruit adequately trained staff locally, affecting how they are able to grow and adapt (see Willett, 2020). In short, I wondered to what extent a lack of ideational connectivity within the region actively hindered local economic development. In our Brexit research, we realised that many of the Cornish public were unaware of or unable to access the social and economic changes that were transforming the local landscape (Willett et al., 2019). This felt like a very powerful realisation and seemed to indicate how places, in general, and development, in particular, can operate as atomised disparate parts rather than as an organistic whole. The complex adaptive region assemblage felt like an important analytical tool if we were going to be able to address this.

Academic research that incorporates the use of assemblages is not confined to the social sciences. It is used heavily in ecological studies, about topics as diverse as tree communities (Bajpai et al., 2020), fish habitats (Zeni et al., 2019), and Phytoplankton (Giesbrecht et al., 2019). As we will explore in much greater depth in the following chapters, one of the things that assemblage theorising does extremely well is to explore and understand the deep affective interconnections between material and ideational things, natural and built environments, and other things. This is part of its appeal in ecological studies. Following in the well-travelled footprints of Gleick (1987) and Lovelock (2000), if the natural world is a complex and interactive set of evolving connections, the assemblage is a useful analytical tool for exploring that world. Studies of society and regions as assemblages have taken longer to gain traction. A seminal piece is Colin McFarlane's 2011 article, *The City as Assemblage: Dwelling and Urban Space*, which follows an intellectual lineage incorporating Deleuze and Guattari, Jane Bennet, Nigel Thrift, Doreen Massey, Henri Lefebvre, Manuel DeLanda, and David Harvey and makes the case for the city to be imagined as a spatial, processual, relational, and mobile assemblage. In this, and other studies which also use the assemblage as a conceptual tool through which to examine social and political spaces, assemblages enable a rich and textured analysis of the deep complexity of the ways that people, ideas, and institutions interact, connect, break apart, and recombine with regard to the specific environments that they are located in.

One of its key strengths lies in the way that it collapses the Cartesian dualism between mind and body; people and the environment and re-inserts the human world into the materiality of the ecological and built environment (see Prigogine and Stengers, 1985; Smith and Jenks, 2006). This frees the social and political sciences and/or regional studies scholars to be able to imagine the human world in the whole entirety of the material and ideational factors which affect it. For understanding regional development, it enables us to look at the people, spaces, and places which interest us in a much more holistic way. For example, Shand (2018) situates street youths within the assemblages of the city; Calzada (2018) incorporates an analysis of technological innovations into his study of stateless, city-regionalised nations; and Pendlebury (2013) uses the assemblage to explore heritage and conservation planning. Jones et al. (2019) demonstrate to us an additional factor in what the concept has to offer. They look at assemblages surrounding the economies of wool, highlighting the multi-scalar fluidities between assembled matter and ideas, showing how commerce and trade create and maintain deep interconnectivities between places and other places, people, practices, and environments. These relationships are fluid because they are never fixed for all time but are always subject to change in terms of growth or entropy as old multi-scalar relationships crossing regional and spatial boundaries deepen, fade, and new ones are created. This complicates space and the production of place to make visible the ways that places are shaped by a myriad of fluid, mobile affective connectivities inside, but importantly also outside of the geographical place being examined. More on this later.

But there is another aspect to the assemblage which is currently under-studied in regional studies or social sciences assemblages literature. This picks up from Deleuze's interest in the emergence of Bergson (Deleuze, 1991) and is systematised by Latour (2005), DeLanda (2011), Bennett (2010), and Connolly (2002). Here, the fluidity and mobility of the assemblage means not only that it is in a constant state of change but that this constant change means that it is also constantly evolving. The assemblage is an evolutionary, complex, adaptive system (Dovey, 2009, 2012). The story commonly told by complexity scholars, such as Smith and Jenks (2008), Prigogine and Stengers (1985), and Connolly (2002), begins the journey as one where positivistic Enlightenment science won traction over more evolutionary ideas, operating on an unpredictable rather than a predictable linear temporality. Where Positivistic Newtonian science asked for repeatability of experimental outcome, evolutionary theorists knew repeatability to be impossible outside of certain closed-boundary conditions. Instead, the natural, human, and built worlds are in a constant state of change and adaptation, albeit with certain patterns which hold true until entropy or change initiates new patterns. Life is simply fluid. To illustrate, we would never expect a plant to remain in a fixed state, suspended between bud and flower, bloom and seed, never growing. In other words, to quote the title of Connolly's 2011 publication, we exist in a *world of becoming*, always in the process of becoming something new. With a few notable exceptions in urban studies and planning (Dovey, 2009, 2012), this sense of becoming or what will become is currently an under-examined part of the assemblage in the academic regional studies literature although it does infuse evolutionary economic geography (Martin and Sunley, 2007; Boschma and Frenken, 2011) and scholarship on regional resilience (Boschma, 2015; Bristow and Healey, 2014).

The becoming within the regional assemblage needs to be central to all social sciences. Much of our analyses focuses on better understanding spaces, places, and peoples in order to create more socially, politically, economically, and environmentally equitable and sustainable futures. This is certainly the problem outlined at the opening of this chapter. The emerging realisation that this book begins with was that the assemblage of the region had not connected up in the right way to make sure that many people in the regions in question were able to be a part of the benefits that development funding had brought. As a consequence, the futures, or becoming, that emerged was not as inclusive as it needed to be. This meant that it lost popular support, which in turn had its own set of effects. The intention of this book is to redress this balance by constructing a detailed and systematic account of the complex, adaptive, regional assemblage in order to develop a model that can help analysts and practitioners be more inclusive. The book is planned as both a diagnosis and a treatment, of observing the possibilities and potentialities available, connections that are overlooked, and practical steps that can be taken.

This task is particularly important in a post-COVID-19 environment. All of the fieldworks except the final few interviews in Cornwall were conducted in the pre-Coronavirus world, and for most of the work on the book the idea that we would shortly undergo a potentially devastating and transformative global change was never in any of our minds. On the face of it, one might argue that the virus has disrupted our world to such an extent that analytical models developed in earlier times may lack relevance. Moreover, it could be expected that the kinds of questions and priorities that we are asking now are very different from those that engaged us in January 2020 and earlier. However, this would be unnecessarily pessimistic. As discussed in brief above, and as the following two chapters will set out in detail, the complex adaptive regional assemblage is a story about change and an analytical tool to help us to be able to mediate change more effectively. It looks at how societies and groups are connected, how ideas flow between and amongst assemblages, and considers sites of possibility that have the potential to create new and emergent societies and structures. These are factors that are vital to better understand if we are to adapt well as individuals, communities, and regions post-pandemic. At the outset of this project, I envisaged the changes that readers might be considering to be smaller scale, perhaps addressing persistent problems that other models hadn't been able to make visible. However, following the Pandemic, there is an even greater urgency to make sure that regions that are on the wrong side of median distributions of wealth and resources do not fall further behind key regional players.

This book was always imagined as a means for social, economic, political, and environmental analysts to reconceptualise spatial distribution and development. By development, I do not necessarily mean economic growth or even the growth of key statistical measurements of economic indicators. This is not necessarily even about moving towards more well-being (Bache and Scott, 2017) amongst the general population, although well-being and quality of life may well be a part of it. Instead, by development, I mean two things: a qualitative sense amongst regular people that our lives are improving and a more objective measurement that inequalities and inequities between regions in a national context are not getting bigger. It is the contention of this book that inter-regional inequities represent an unfair distribution of resources that, as well as being morally wrong, are also harmful to the national or global assemblages, which complex adaptive regional assemblages are a part of and intricately connected to. If we want to put this into very economic language, we might point out that regional inequality is grossly inefficient in terms of the distribution of resources, with (usually) inordinately expensive core areas and extremely cheap peripheries, imposing significant cost implications on enterprise, innovation, and business (Armstrong and Taylor, 2000). Additionally, we also understand very well that poverty is not just a problem for the individuals that experience it. It is also a social disease that affects life chances, educational possibilities, and health outcomes (Alcock, 1997). Poverty, whether individual or regional, affects the public purse in terms of increased spending on health and welfare programmes. The impacts on life chances are devastating on a personal level, meaning that lives are literally blighted by being poor (Black et al., 2018). On a collective level, such blighted lives mean that individuals and affected regions are unable to contribute as efficiently and effectively to national economies.

In this book, my case studies are two rural regions. Again, this does not mean that the ideas explored in this publication need to be limited to the rural. Instead, the complex adaptive regional assemblage can be applied to a whole range of regions and at a whole range of different community scales—from the village, town or city, local authority, county, state, province, or even nation. The fact that the case studies are rural does not preclude scholars of metropolitan regions from finding the material to be of interest. Whether these metropolitan areas are at the core of national or federal economic activity or whether such metropolitan regions are imagined as economically, culturally, or socially peripheral, trying to stave off decline and further peripheralisation (Gormar and Lang, 2019). Indeed, many of Germany's 'Shrinking Cities' have been proud socially, culturally, and economically dominant communities for centuries but have struggled to adapt effectively to a reunified Germany (see also Burke et al., 2012; Lang, 2012). Detroit, Michigan, is another example of a city that once held a central or core position in the U.S.

economy, but which over time the collapse of its manufacturing industry has led to it becoming increasingly peripheral.

The case studies were selected carefully. As I outline in chapter 4, constructing a complex adaptive regional assemblage from the ground up requires a deep understanding of, and engagement with, the localities in question. An obvious starting point was to use Cornwall as a case study. This is a place that I know extremely well as a researcher and as someone who grew up there and still lives within its borders. However, sometimes such an intimate knowledge and understanding of a place can give us blind spots, where we fail to see the deeply familiar. For this, I wanted another case study, which was the opposite—somewhere with which I was entirely unfamiliar. This meant in another country and for reasons detailed in chapter 4, I selected the southwest of the U.S. state of Virginia in the southern Appalachian mountain range.

Rural or urban, the peripheral region is part of a fluid, mobile, evolutionary process whereby some towns, cities, or regions are more or less peripheral at different points in time (See Görmar and Lang, 2019). This also notices how regions and cities which once found themselves at the centre of national or even global social, political, and economic activity also need to be able to adapt to changes in the world around them if they are to retain and maintain their central position. We cannot assume that London, New York, or Paris will remain dominant global centres for all time, unless they are able to evolve in accordance with local and global natural, social, political, and economic environmental conditions. This does not mean that the peripheral or peripheralising region (whether rural or urban) is at fault or somehow to blame for its failure to adapt. Sometimes, of course, decision-makers at all levels make bad decisions and/or fail to spot possibilities and opportunities. Sometimes places are not able to find or build the talent pool required by a particular cultural, environmental, political, or economic moment or for some cultural reason people are unable to take advantage of opportunities and potentialities. But as we have noted already, and will observe in more detail in chapter 2, complex adaptive regional assemblages do not exist in isolation but are also part of national and global assemblages which may initiate changes beyond regional control or influence. The decisions of political and economic actors in other assemblages can have an inordinate effect on the possibilities and potentialities available to others, meaning that adaptive flourishing is not about value statements surrounding individual 'success' or 'failure'.

Neither is it about finding 'one size fits all' policy initiatives which, after working well in one region, can then be implemented in other areas. As I shall discuss in chapter 3, the creative industries development discourse is one such dogma, which, although written as an example by Richard Florida (2002) of how a (city) region managed to harness its adaptive capacity, became interpreted and re-interpreted in both policy and academic studies as a set of tools to be copied elsewhere, regardless of circumstances. Rather than taking away a greater understanding of the *processes* involved in evolutionary, adaptive development, the key message received by many scholars and practitioners was more of an 'add creativity and stir' approach, where a vibrant creative economy would necessarily help to create a new version of silicon valley, or similar (see also Willett, 2016). Instead, and in the vein of Latour (2005), the suggestions and analyses offered by this book are about understanding fluidity, processes, and movement rather than the creation and maintenance of fixed and solid, ideational, and physical objects.

THE RURAL COMPLEX ADAPTIVE
REGIONAL ASSEMBLAGE

In part, this book aims to address a real need for additional policy and academic attention to rural areas (see DeSouza, 2018). There is a large and vibrant academic discipline of rural studies, offering analysis of rural communities, practices, and economies globally. However, this does not mean that the rural always receives the attention that it deserves or requires. Indeed, Morgan and Shepherd (2020) argue in their report for the New Local Government Network that the United Kingdom has a 'policy corridor' where most activity happens, but where rural and peripheral areas are excluded from; Reimer et al. (2016) note the waning political influence of rural regions in the U.S. metropolitan areas, with their huge populations, are much more statistically and socially visible than rural areas. To illustrate, the southwest of Virginia (SWVA) (Virginia Growth and Opportunity Area 1) is home to 389,173 persons in a geographical area that takes approximately two hours to drive from the north to the south, east to the west. This is a large physical space, containing few people. The nearest big city is Roanoke, with a population of 96,714 persons, in a compact geographical space, roughly 10 miles from north to south, east to west. This is one quarter of the population of GO VA Region 1, in a fraction of the space.[1] To take this theme about the dispersed nature of rurality to a U.K. context, in Britain in 2014, 17 per cent of the population live in rural areas (Department for Environment, Food, and Rural Affairs, 2020), whereas the built-on and green urban environments only account for 3.25 per cent of the landmass (BBC, 2017). In the United States, these figures are reasonably similar with 19.3 per cent of the population being rural dwellers and 97 per cent of the landmass being rural.

Within the designated 'rural' landscape, we will find a significant variation in types of rurality. Frequently, this is shorthanded into 'remote' and 'accessible' rural, which describes the distance of a rural area from the nearest significant metropolis (Shortall and Warner, 2012). There is a degree of relativity here though. For example, from the position of SWVA, Roanoke is the most significant city for several hours drive. However, at over 3.5 hours drive from Washington DC (its next appreciable city), from the perspective of the urban core, Roanoke is a distant, small, country city, well outside of the metropolis and with easy accessibility. Therefore, it is both urban *and* rural in how it is interpreted, imagined, and connected. Clearly, there are further differences in experiences between the smaller cities, towns, and hamlets moving well beyond Roanoke, and for whom Roanoke is the distant big city. We discuss the 'rural' as a discrete category, when a more accurate portrayal would be to put it on a kind of spectrum between accessibility and remoteness with regard to metropolitan core areas. Although the problem with this characterisation is that it begins from a starting point where there is something 'wrong' with the rural, which needs to be contrasted with its urban counterpart (see Cloke and Edwards, 1986).

The amount of countryside that we have highlights strongly how important it is as part of the geographical spaces that we occupy. However, carrying such a small fragment of the population has implications for the countryside. In what Bennett (2010) or Latour (2005) might call indicative of our anthropocentrism, it is the places of largest population rather than of greater environmental import that occupy policy attention most deeply. There are some rational and logistical reasons for this. Clearly, it is much easier to deliver policy and social programmes in the city rather than in the widely dispersed environment of the sparsely populated rural area. Indeed, this was the finding of Canette et al. (2018) with regard to Spain, where they found that projects tended to focus on the metropolitan areas of otherwise rural regions, because a more concentrated population had denser and more easily accessible networks and a greater quantity of businesses to work with. From a comprehensive review of the literature, Deller et al. (2019) explain that many of the requirements that traditionally are used to imagine a vibrant economy – such as population density, investment, and human capital – are typically urban rather than rural characteristics. This carries some severe implications for regional inequalities, as demonstrated by Faulker et al. (2019) in their study of household vulnerability in Ireland, where they found that recovery from the 2008 financial crisis has been significantly slower in rural areas, expanding rural–urban divides.

This is not to say that businesses in rural regions work less, or less efficiently than their urban counterparts. On the contrary, rural enterprises can suffer from the 'liability of rurality' whereby the higher the degree of rurality, the higher the penalty incurred. In part, this boils down to infrastructural issues, including less up-to-date social technology, and affects businesses right from their start-up phase (Hoyvarde Clausen, 2020). Employees in rural parts of the United States are more likely to do informal work, such as growing food, as a way to literally make ends meet. This is borne out of economic distress rather than a desire for a particular type of earthy rural lifestyle (Jensen et al., 2019). Unemployment is growing in rural America, alongside in-work poverty (Thiede et al., 2018) and even a temporary period of economic hardship can have important long-term implications. In a study of a rural community in northern England, Black et al. (2018) find that when parents and older persons in a support network are in crisis and therefore unable to provide adequate support to younger people, the effects of the crisis becomes intergenerational affecting the life chances of younger generations. Taken together, this all presents a bleak picture of rural spaces, but the commitment and attachment to a place held, by the sense of permanence and rootedness of some rural peoples, is in itself an asset and one that helps to drive resilience and adaptation (Paniagua, 2013). We could also read this as being indicative of an enormous missed opportunity to explore and utilise the capacity and potentiality of rural areas, in order to develop an environmentally conscious shared prosperity (Morgan and Sheperd, 2020). Nevertheless, we are left with a rural space which is subject to a policy emphasis on addressing populations rather than geographical space, combined with the greater ease of policy delivery at an urban level (especially when 'success' metrics, such as jobs and GDP growth, are predicated on more urban characteristics). Consequently, rural areas maintain their statistical invisibility and are increasingly 'left-behind'. The United States has the additional problem, whereby rural policy tends to be dominated by the agricultural sector, meaning that this is how rural policy tends to be imagined and framed, minimising the voices and lobbying power of other elements of rural communities from policy discourse (Reimer et al., 2016; Honadle, 2011). This can also lead to a rural policy that is much more fragmented and fractured than it needs to be (Kleinschmit and Clausen, 2012; Drabenstott, 2001).

For global post-COVID-19 recovery, this implies a risk that policy will continue to focus on the areas of high population density, which are much easier and cheaper to access and work with and which are quite literally able to reach a far higher number of people. This will feel particularly urgent as global and national economies shrink with near unprecedented speed, and there is much less money to go around. With mounting national debt and a smaller-sized pie, policy-makers will be trying to make tax-payers money stretch as far as it can. In this urgent situation, it is far too easy to (continue to) overlook the needs and capacities of the rural, which can tend to feel important mostly to (the relatively few in number) rural dwellers themselves. But this would be a mistake. We have already outlined above the inefficiencies brought to bear by regional inequality. But by incorporating the notion of

rural–urban divide, we can also see how these inefficiencies can have significant and important consequences on the broader body politic. At the beginning of this chapter, I opened by mentioning the 2016 referendum for Britain
to exit the European Union. Aside from a realisation that for a then unknown
reason, EU development programmes had not won the loyalty of high benefi-
ciary regions, it was also evident that there was a largely metropolitan versus
rural divide in terms of the Leave/Remain vote (Brooks, 2019). Polarisation
by population density is not a new phenomenon to British politics. If we take
voting patterns as a very blunt measurement tool, with the caveat that it masks
a significant proportion of the population who vote differently, pre-2019,
English and Welsh politics has tended to be characterised by a largely Labour
metropolis and largely Conservative countryside (Johnston et al., 2018).

This polarisation is far from confined to the United Kingdom. Only a
casual glance at Republican versus Democrat voting patterns in the United
States demonstrates a stark urban rural differentiation (Roddern, 2019).
Away from the First Past, the post-voting systems of the United Kingdom
and the United States, in mainland Europe, Germany's rise of Alternative
Fur Deutschland (Stecker and Debus, 2019), and France with regard to support for Marine LePen (Ivadi and Gombin, 2015) also demonstrate clear
rural/urban divides. France is a particularly interesting case here, because
in 2018 the tensions largely between the rural and the urban spilled out into
the mass popular protest and civil unrest of the Gilet's Jaunes (Bruneau
et al., 2018). This latter example demonstrates loudly the implications that a
divided society can have on the body politic and the cultural distinctions that
separate many dwellers of rural spaces from their urban counterparts. We
might even say that cultural divides are so large that they represent two different assembled cultural groups within the same nation state. Furthermore,
there is evidence that right-wing populist parties utilise the conservatism of
traditional rural characterisations in order to create an imagined 'authentic'
rurality (Mamonova and Franquesa, 2020).

This is not to say that the goal of development should be to try to close
this gap by making rural lives more like the urban, or generally evening out
the differences between the two. Neither is it the intention of this project to
argue that there are aspects of rural culture that are 'wrong' and need to be
fixed. On the contrary, this book is designed as more of a celebration of all
things that are wonderful about rural regions and the people who live within
them. However, it also seeks to strip away the rural idyll (Lowe et al., 2012;
Shucksmith, 2018) through which ruralities are perceived and imagined, and
also understand what they are *really* like to live in. The rural idyll represents
an idealised version of rurality that imagines the countryside as a kind of
pastoral utopia and balm to the weary urbanite. Part of the problem is that
this overlooks the quite considerable issues and inequalities that rural areas

can face in terms of poverty, life-chances, and ease of going about one's life (Willett, 2016).

More difficultly, the rural idyll can also carry with it a flip-side set of perceptions about rural dwellers that is far from complimentary to countryside populations. For example, many scholars have noted how people who live in rural areas are frequently characterised as slow, backward, awkward, difficult, and/or inept with old-fashioned/regressive values, attitudes, and beliefs (Eriksson, 2008; Willett, 2016). This takes place as a form of 'othering' (see Said, 2003) through which certain internal others (See Jansson, 2003) are imbued with layers of stereotyped characterisations that mark rural dwellers as 'different' to the metropolitan core population and imbue them with negative characteristics which the cultural core also shares, but does not want to own. These stigmatisations (see Burke et al., 2012; Meyer et al., 2016) are then able to mean that economically and socially poorer rural areas can be explained as the agents of their own misfortune and victims of their own ineptitude. To see the impact that this can have we only need to witness the backlash and bitterness between Leave and Remain voters (UK), Republican and Democrat (US), as both sides demonise the cultural differences underpinning the different voting decisions of each. Because these differences are often shorthanded to those of between urban and rural areas (with the caveat that these are popular stereotypes rather than universal truths), this situation deepens frustrations and resistances between rural and urban areas, as each struggle for access to cultural, economic, political, and social resources. I contend that one way through this, collapsing the binary distinctions between the urban and the rural, is to explore the differences between cultural groups, in the hope that this might lead to a better understanding of rural dwellers and what we/they have to offer. If we can collectively do this, we might be able to create a fairer society and break down some of the tensions and frustrations epitomised by the Gilet's Jaunes, the U.K. vote to Leave the EU, and the rise of populist figures in many parts of the Western world. In order to do this, this book presents a version of rurality and place which enables better understanding of cultural groupings, with which we may be unfamiliar, and strips away some of the old and extremely harmful stereotyping through which rural dwellers can be characterised.

This task is more than just a cultural endeavour. Instead, the dark side of stigmatising regional characterisations (See Burke et al., 2012) is that they deepen the processes of peripheralisation within affected regional assemblages, entrenching the social and economic divisions between core and periphery and rural and urban (Willett and Lang, 2018; Meyer et al., 2016).[2] Part of the reason behind this is because if rural stigmatic stereotypes are taken literally, who would want to do business with a company staffed predominantly with potential idiots and who clearly will not be anywhere near the cutting edge of innovative new ideas in that sector. Furthermore, in human capital terms, 'innovative and dynamic' potential members of the work force are more likely to imagine their future in the dichotomous thrusting innovation of the metropolis rather than the pedestrian backwardness of the stereotypically rural (see Willett, 2016; Williams and Harrison, 1995). With regard to the United States, Crabtree (2016: 619) puts this as 'If Americans think of rural areas simply as economic dead zones, filled with people waiting to leave oppressive conditions, that idea could become a self-fulfilling prophecy'.

INNOVATION

However, it would be grossly inaccurate to imagine that all innovation happens in urban, metropolitan areas, or to think that rural settings lack innovation. To start with, most primary physical and natural resources come from rural areas, and this is also where food is grown (Shucksmith and Brown, 2016; Kleinschmit and Clausen, 2012). Moreover, as we have noted in our sketch complex adaptive regional assemblage, and as we will see in considerable more detail in chapter 3, assemblages are continually adapting, and part of that adaptation necessarily involves innovative ideas and working. Part of the issue was beautifully articulated to me by a business development leader many years ago. He said we have a tendency to imagine innovation as involving test tubes and radical ways of bending bits of metal. This is a high science model that positions innovation as something that happens in laboratories, using highly trained individuals. But like the debates over what constituted 'knowledge' in a global knowledge economy (see Bruckmeier and Tovey, 2008), Paniagua (2013) implies that there is something about a rootedness in place, the intimate local knowledges that go alongside that rootedness, and a desire to find a way through potentially challenging situations that can foster and encourage innovation. More contemporary academic languages are now starting to acknowledge the importance of distinctly local practices and identities (Tuitjer and Steinfuhrer, 2019) and are beginning to discuss this in terms of the utilisation of 'place-based' resources. Studies have shown that rural and peripheral regions have many intangible, ideational resources of their own from which to draw innovatory potential, and many rural enterprises and projects are able to understand and employ local resources and networks in order to innovate and adapt (Galliano et al., 2019). Much research in the early 2000s considered how local and traditional cultures were resources which could be treated as an endogenous economic development asset (Jenkins, 2000). Tuitjer and Steinfuhrer (2019) show how an interest and emphasis on endogenous factors can help to value and place importance in local cultures, knowledges, and practices. Supporting individuals and enterprises to be better embedded within the place from which they work is a key part of endogenous growth strategies, aiming to help to enable local businesses to grow from the inside out, better able to access and utilise local resources, knowledges, and networks. This is at the heart of the LEADER part of EU Structural Funding programmes, enabling greater local participation with the goal of facilitating grassroots, endogenous participation, and social and economic adaptation (Barke and Newton, 1997; High and Nemes, 2007; Canete et al., 2018). It also underpinned regional branding campaigns across European regions, which aimed to create a set of shared values, attitudes, and meanings from local identities, in order to foster embeddedness, and therefore endogenous development (Dominguez Garcia et al., 2013; Donner et al., 2017).

In other words, in a European framework, adaptation and innovation are fostered by encouraging enterprises and organisations to be better embedded within the complex adaptive region assemblage, facilitating greater connectivities between ideas and knowledges. The general population comes into this with regard to creating capacity. Community participation has been a popular tool for this, increasing the flow of information around regions as the public interacts more, develops stronger, wider, and deeper networks, within the region assemblage, and increasing levels of social and human capital (High and Nemes, 2007). There are other factors that also impact on connectivity within the region assemblage, and therefore affect innovation and adaptive capacity.

Although this book emphasises and focuses on a deeply endogenous approach, there is a risk of overlooking the significance, benefits, and rationales behind other methods. Exogenous tools, such as those emphasised in U.S. policy (Deller et al., 2019), have an important role to play in injecting resources into places that might otherwise be badly underserved. Moreover, some degree of spatial redistribution at a national level is important (Margarian, 2013) and investment from outside sources play a role in local economies. With caveats around embeddedness, manufacturing relocation can be a useful part of the regional development arsenal. Regional industrial recruitment strategies include using tax breaks and the lure of cheaper operating costs in terms of wages and real estate to encourage large factories to relocate to the locality (Deller et al., 2019). Nevertheless, there has been an overlay between exogenous approaches and a perception about the (stigmatising and peripheralising) 'backwardness' of rural regions.

Over recent decades, access to the internet has played an increasing role in ensuring an adequate flow of knowledges and information within regions. Again in Europe, the EU has had a target to ensure that all households have access to high speed internet by 2020 and 79 per cent of EU citizens use the internet at least once a week (Raisanen and Tuovinen, 2020). Although the Rural Utilities Service is allocating grants and loans in order to make rural

U.S. communities better connected (Ali and Duemmel, 2019), rural U.S. is generally not so well served by internet provision and many individuals do not have any internet access in their homes. Consequently, libraries have emerged as key places where rural Americans are able to get online (Strover et al., 2020). Although having internet capacity does not mean being able to *use* the technologies, because sometimes people's IT skills levels need additional support (Raisanen and Tuovinen, 2020), and there are further questions about inclusion of all social groupings (Striker et al., 2017). Poor connection speeds can also be a problem (Bowen and Morris, 2019). Nevertheless, good fast internet connection speeds is becoming increasingly important for the well-functioning regional assemblage, and indeed, a lack of internet connectivity makes it even more difficult for rural areas to innovate at pace with their urban counterparts. Soft-tech, such as social media, is an important tool for businesses to connect with consumers and other businesses (Bowen and Morris, 2019) and studies have shown a strong positive link between access to broadband, economic performance (Strover et al., 2020), and adaptability (Roberts and Townsend, 2015). That said, merely having the capacity to share information throughout the region does not mean that it is being utilised effectively to ensure that the broader public is familiar with new changes or that the public is able to find ways of ensuring that their hopes and priorities are taken on board by decision makers. Indeed, if information was flowing well in regions that are well-connected, then situations such as that outlined in the opening pages of this chapter would have been less likely to occur. Rather than feel alienated and distant from funded projects, voters in regions in the United Kingdom, which had received the highest levels of development support from the EU, might have had a stronger working appreciation of how investment had impacted their lives and communities. The indicators, therefore, point to some important blockages in the connectivities which bind the complex adaptive region assemblage, regardless of acquisition and use of new technologies.

Even if knowledges were flowing freely within the region, this also would not necessarily be sufficient for strong levels of innovation. Earlier, we considered how an assemblage cannot be imagined in isolation from other assemblages, which provide a contextual, environmental backdrop. This also means that knowledges need to flow outside of an assemblage, between it, and others. Regional knowledges cannot remain only in the region but must extend outward, and new knowledges from other areas need to be explored. Indeed, research has shown that the better connected rural regions are the better performing ones economically (Shortall and Warner, 2012). There are overlays here with the Social Capital literature, which takes Putnam's (2000) distinction between 'bridging capital' and 'bonding capital'. Above, we have largely discussed the flows of information that come from intra-assemblage bonding capital. But this risk means that the assemblage operates as a closed system, not taking in any new information. In turn, an absence of new ideas risks repeating old patterns, and therefore not being innovative. Even worse, at times existing patterns and relationships can become so deeply entrenched that an excess of bonding social capital can be quite harmful to regional economies (see Atterton, 2007).

One way of trying to develop bridging capital is by encouraging commercial counter-urbanisation. Here, partially also to combat ongoing issues of rural population decline, persons from core urban regions are encouraged to bring their enterprises to rural locations to help stimulate local economies (Bosworth and Bat Finke, 2019). The idea is that commercial counter-urbanisers will be able to bring new ideas and knowledges into the region and with it the benefit of their out-of-region networks contributing to bridging capital and external knowledge flows. Kalantaridis et al. (2019) add that they are also able to bring fresh eyes, unencumbered by local frustrations about the supposed disadvantages of doing business within rural spaces. These are valuable tools, up to a point, and need to be interwoven and balanced by an appreciation of the multiplicity of other factors affecting rural regional assemblages such as perceptions of the rural idyll, stigmatising and peripheralising discourses (Burke et al., 2012; Willett and Lang, 2018). Not all commercial counter-urbanisers *want* to be a part of the regeneration of the rural region that they move to, and many have made a specific choice to privilege quality of life over financial acquisition (Bosworth and Willett, 2011). Some counter-urbanisers want their businesses to stay small, providing employment for the owner only, on what Deller et al. (2019) calls a 'survival' basis. Moreover, there is also the risk that a rural narrative heavy with placing faith in others from the outside reproduces peripheralising perceptions of place by focusing on the inadequacy of locals (See Erickson, 2008). It also does little to ensure that older residents and counter-urbanisers are able to share information and networks in an open manner or whether external networks are hoarded and utilised by counter-urbanisers for comparative advantage in a competitive market.

Counter-urbanisation also raises some interesting general questions. For example, the fact that it is required in order to address rural population decline indicates at the outset that there is something about living in rural areas, and the amount of opportunities that particularly younger people feel are accessible to them that induces younger people to leave. Although it would be a mistake to assume that the people who choose to stay are not in themselves making a dynamic choice (Stockdale, 2018), this is often imagined as a kind of brain drain. Bright and ambitious young people, with much to offer the region, believe that 'to get on, they have to get out' (Williams and Harrison, 1995). Largely, this is about the amount and type of employment opportunities open to them. Of course, some people will always want to move away from the places that they were raised in and explore the world beyond. But others also feel the draw of family and friendship networks and are more reluctant to outward migration. At the same time, these regions are imagined as attractive places for older people. Pre-retirees tend to have more inclination to start their own enterprises (Deller et al., 2019); retirees in the United States in particular are seen as attractive for the taxation that they contribute (Poudyal et al., 2008). With echoes of the rural idyll (Lowe et al., 2012), the amenity value of the countryside is a key draw, with in-migrants keen to enjoy the enhanced lifestyle offered in a more nature-based environment (Sampaio and King, 2019). Acknowledging the ways that amenity feeds in to a general commodification of nature (Higgens et al., 2014), it also (re)produces a very specific set of post-productivist and arguably peripheralising stories about rural places (Erikson, 2008; Willett and Lang, 2018). Moreover, whilst an economic emphasis on amenity value might work for some places, this is by no means universal. Some research finds that significant small-town business growth can be better fostered by developing businesses which specifically address the social, economic, and political realities of area, especially if combined with investment in transport accessibility (Powe, 2018). This latter insight brings us back around to the conundrum of counter-urbanisation and large-scale outward migration. Whilst recognising the benefits of the inward migration of (often) wealthier, older people, it is as important to ensure that ambitious younger people feel that they have a choice about where they have a future and that future does not necessarily have to mean that people leave. But for this to happen, younger people and the adults, advising them and supporting their decisions, need to believe that opportunities exist within their communities and feel that these opportunities are accessible to them. In short, maintaining the situation outlined in the opening of this chapter, whereby many voters were not aware about/did not feel that investment had made any tangible benefit to their lives, is not going to help rural areas to become more socially and economically sustainable. And yet, addressing these inequalities in access to information, opportunities, and resources is essential if we are to be able to create vibrant, innovative, and cohesive communities and regions in a post-COVID-19 world. It is to addressing this task that we now turn.

The book is organised as follows. Chapters 2 and 3 set out in detail what the complex, adaptive region assemblage looks like: first, by examining what we mean by a region assemblage, and then in chapter 3, by introducing the evolutionary economy into the complex, adaptive region assemblage. Chapter 2 examines closely Deleuze and Guattari, DeLanda, Connolly, Ahmed, Bennett and Latour to draw the region as an assemblage. The chapter foregrounds the deep interrelationship between people, environments, objects, organisations, and processes that we find in the region and argues that if we are to understand the region, we need to understand these affective interactions and the different ways that knowledges and information flow around territorial space.

Chapter 3 begins by making the case for why the examination of the economy is important for understanding the regional assemblage, arguing that the region assemblage is an evolutionary complex adaptive system, operating in response to a vast array of different stimuli in its environment. This relies on an understanding of time and temporality that is based on emergence rather than linearity, meaning that it is full of the potentiality to become something new. In the second part of the chapter, I take the complex adaptive system and apply it to the regional economy, examining the particulars of what it looks like and the important roles and functions of various aspects of the economy assemblage.

The next three chapters focus on the empirical research. Chapter 4 provides some background about the two case study regions, Cornwall and the southwest of Virginia, and examines what kind of inquiry is needed in order to understand the societies, economies, and challenges of the complex adaptive region assemblage. Chapters 5 and 6 takes both case study areas in turn and uses the concepts developed in chapters 2 and 3 to examine the ethnographic interview data gathered in both case studies. It considers how participants talk about the region, their lives and experiences within it, and the kinds of things that they feel are important to their worlds. From this emerging view of the complex adaptive region assemblage, it is then possible to see some of the sites of possibility, potentiality, and becoming for the region moving forward.

The final two chapters seek to understand what examining the regions as complex adaptive assemblages means for regional development in both of the case study areas (chapter 7), and in the concluding chapter, what the region assemblage can do for wider studies of rural, peripheral, and regional development. It begins by asking what the complex adaptive region assemblage makes visible and how this can address some of the fragmentations and tensions within region assemblages. It goes on to consider extra-regional relationships and connectivities, including those manifest in core–periphery rural–urban divides.

NOTES

1. It should be noted here that Roanoke does not sit within the GO Virginia region 1 boundaries.

2. Although it should be noted that not all rural areas are poor, and not all are peripheral.

Chapter 2

The Affective Assemblage

The purpose of this chapter is to explore regions and territories as affective assemblages. In order to do this, we need to adopt a much more fluid understanding of what the region is, what it does, and how it does it. We also need to think more deeply about the interconnections among objects, organisations, and processes that we find in the places within which we live, work, and observe. Bruno Latour (2005) in his book *Reassembling the Social: An Introduction to Actor Network Theory* makes the argument that we need to look not at the objects of our inquiry but at the networks, impacts, and connections that make up that object. The logic is that if we look at the region, town, city, business, corporation, or the university, we are only examining a very brief snapshot in time of the thing that we study. Our observations hold well for the moment at which we made them, and if the world was not subject to constant processes of change, these observations would be true for much longer. However (and as we will explore in the following chapter), all objects, things, physical or ideational organisms, eco-systems, and institutions are subject to constant processes of adaptation or entropy, which modify the thing that we examine. This means our investigations can only uncover a snapshot of a particular moment in time. Just as the temporal moment that the photographer captures starts to become out of date as soon as the activated shutter seals that exact array of reflected and absorbed light particles, so the truths of even the best piece of research about an object start to decay as soon as the fieldwork has been made and interpreted.

So if we want to understand more about our world, what can we do? According to Latour (2005), we need to consider the processes and connections that make these changes happen. For Latour, objects are actually interconnected networks. For example, the region (rural or otherwise) is a complex interaction between the people living in that place: their relationships with

their natural and built environments, the cultural meanings and understandings through which inhabitants interpret and make sense of their world,
and the kinds of activities through which people sustain themselves bodily
and which make up territorial economies. The physical things that people
do contribute to the kinds of institutions and organisations that exist in a
given territorial space (such as businesses, networks, sports groups, and
civic organisations; see, for example, Putnam, 2000) and the political bodies
that regulate, govern, and support the social, environmental, and economic
activities in which inhabitants participate. None of these things (or actors)
determines the region (although some may dominate), but each contributes
towards the distinctly unique character of each place. Neither does Latour
imagine a distinction between human and non-human actors: the hurricane,
the fertility of the soil, the (human and non-human; sentient and non-sentient)
life. Or the physical structures in the region *all* are actors which have the
capacity to affect each other, and thereby impact on the networks that bind
together the activities and cultures that occur within the space. If we are to
fully understand the region, we need to understand the way that the people,
practices, and organisations listed above connect, interact, and impact each
other and the ways that different kinds of information and knowledges flow
around the territorial space. These connections are fluid, dynamic, and mobile
eco-systems, representing and depicting how places change or might potentially change. In practice, this means that as social scientists and regional
analysts, we are examining flows, rather than objects, and becoming, rather
than being. Moreover and as we will see in chapter 3, becoming (or what we
will become) emerges out of a myriad of interacting, intersecting material
and ideational things, incorporating present realities and past histories.

But if we are to do or be able to analyse this effectively, we need to have
a conceptual architecture through which to examine places and regions.
In this chapter, we build this through a framework that relies on Deleuze
and Guattari (2004), DeLanda (2011), Bennett (2010), Ahmed (2004), and
Connolly (2002); exploring how we might imagine the region as a (complex, adaptive) affective assemblage. We consider what this means and the
concepts through which we can understand our emerging region assemblage.

AFFECT

The concept of affect provides us with a language through which we can
trace the complex dynamic impacts that things have on other things – and
indeed, the way that objects and ideas that might seem completely unrelated
and distant and are connected or intertwined through affective processes.
Affect is based on the post-Epicurean philosophy of Spinoza (1996) who

posited that material or ideational bodies collide and that this alters their trajectory in some way. This literally refers to the capacity of some things, ideas, or practices to affect or impact others, leaving an imprint of itself (see also Damasio, 2004). We might imagine it to be similar to a sticky sweet paper that transfers a residue to whatever surface it comes into contact with. Unlike the sweet paper, there is no mechanical relationship between the capacity of a phenomenon to create (physical or emotional) impact or affect. Sometimes, a tiny thing can create a huge impact that ripples and amplifies throughout immediate and distant environments, whereas other much larger affective impacts might have minimal consequences. This is the phenomenon of the small thing that sparks a revolution. In December of 2010, a fruit and vegetable seller in Tunisia unwittingly did this when he set himself on fire following a long-running and humiliating dispute with the authorities. Mohammed Bouazizi could not find work and for years had had to sell his wares in the street in order to support his family. However, he did not have a license to do so, and his produce was often confiscated. On the penultimate occasion, it was reported that he had to borrow money in order to re-stock his cart. It was also reported that part of his humiliation had been that he had been struck in the face by a female official. His self-immolation was a terrible act of personal frustration and desperation borne of extreme vulnerabilities. But desperate acts by frantic people happen all around the world, all of the time and mostly occur and disappear without a trace. Mohammed Bouazizi's action, however, chimed, rippled, and echoed with the experiences of many other Tunisians, who had seen joblessness climb to 850,000 people (in a country of 10 million). Within a month, the president had fled (France 24: 2017) and the Arab Spring was borne, sparking revolutions throughout the Middle East and literally transforming the face of the region.

The affective impacts of Bouazizi's terrible suicide amplified beyond all proportion from the original event. In order to understand how this could happen, we can look to the phenomenology which Deleuze and Guattari take from Bergson (2004), borrowing from a thermodynamic rather than mechanistic perspective of power (Prigogine and Stengers, 1985). Here, because of particular historics, some affects 'resonate' (Connolly, 2008), whilst others do not. The key to understanding this lies in the relationship between time and affect. Affective impacts do not only work on a temporally horizontal plane, functioning across whatever is happening at a particular snapshot moment, but also operate on a temporally vertical one, incorporating histories into our interpretations of the present. This is not to say that the past determines the present and the future, but it does shape it. Bergson (2004) describes time as being like a cone. At the point of the cone is the point of the present, whereby in the present moment an individual or group of people, community, nation, or culture has to make a choice about how to act to a familiar or unfamiliar stimulus. We do this by taking things that have happened from our individual and collective memories (which, in Bergson's metaphor, are situated in the main body of the cone) and use them as a guide for how to act in the present. But in order to select the appropriate interpretive memory, we look for points of similarity which can help to guide us toward the most effective available support. As a consequence, we are actively seeking affective resonances and reverberations in order to select the appropriate memories to help to mediate our day-to-day existence, interpret our worlds, and the options that we feel are available to us when we consider what we need to do. This means that according to Bergson, the past never actually passes because it remains active at all times. An example of this might be that of what is considered good manners whenever we meet a person that we haven't met before. If I am in a work situation in the global north, I have culturally embedded memories which inform me that if the other person holds out their right hand, that is an invitation to greet with a handshake (See also Goffman, 1959; Mead, 1934). Equally, I might feel that it is appropriate for me to initiate the handshake greeting in order to help to create a good impression of myself. In some professional situations, however, this becomes a little more complicated, and it might be considered more normal to greet with some form of air-kiss on one or both cheeks. In order to determine what is the right course of action in this situation, I have to make an appeal to my memory. I have to consider the people that I am meeting (are these persons that I have worked with before or that are from a place where it is culturally more normal to air-kiss), and do I read their body language as if they are expecting to air-kiss or to shake hands. For this, I look to memories that resonate or echo with the situation in which I currently find myself. Finally, if I select the incorrect memories in order to choose my course of action, do I have anything which can help me to extricate myself from a potentially embarrassing situation? For this latter, I might have to make an appeal to resonating memories from a much broader available repertoire than that of a professional encounter, incorporating a range of social situations.

Some memories are more readily available to us as interpretive schema than others or are more accessible to ourselves at some particular moments in time than others. The degree to which an event will have an impact on us individually or culturally depends to a large extent on how we are able to situate it within our cone of memory and the particular emotional affects that we are experiencing at any given point in time. Bouazizi's death, for example, may have resonated with the physical and emotional hardship, fear, vulnerabilities, frustration, and anger of how contemporary Tunisians (and people in the wider region) were experiencing their lives. This meant that affects were better able to resonate and amplify disproportionately. Furthermore, Bergson also talks about how the ways that a thing affects us is also about how it is perceived by us as individuals, communities, organisations, or nations. Quite literally, the interpretive effect of memory means that our pasts – or the parts of our past that we return to most frequently – help to shape or 'cloak' how we receive, perceive, and chose to act on affective stimuli. This helps to create what Ahmed (2004) calls 'affective economies' whereby ideas, beliefs, and emotions become readily transferred and dispersed around a particular physical or ideational space, providing a backdrop for the kinds of responses that are engendered to particular stimuli.

For our regional assemblages, affect helps us to consider the particular cultural knowledges, values, beliefs, and ideas which arise within a territorial space, how these transfer around the locality, how ideas become produced and situated, and how new physical and ideational material are (or are not) absorbed into territorial culture. It also helps to make visible the complex interactions between people and our physical, ecological, built, environmental, cultural, and economic environments. Through affect, Latour's (2005) Actor Network Theory provides a language that can consider the affective impacts of non-human and non-sentient beings and matter within regional spaces. In *Vibrant Matter: A Political Ecology of Things*, Jane Bennett (2010) takes this a step further. Whilst asking the question about whether non-humans have political agency, Bennett constructs a world whereby affect closes the anthropocentric gap that distances humans from the ecological and built environment, setting people apart and above the other beings and objects on our planet and in our localities. Instead, Bennett uses affect to re-insert humans and human activity into and inside of natural and physical ecologies, by showing that we are all a part of the same environmental organism. She shows how non-human things affect human activities, possibilities, and potentialities in a multiplicity of different ways. For example, using the earthworm, Bennett explains how this tiny, often disregarded being has an enormous and considered impact on the kinds of lives that people are able to live, the ways that people are able to sustain themselves, the ways that the immediate environment looks, and the ways that human civilisation becomes preserved. Bennett shows that in processing organic waste, the earthworm enriches the soil as well as helps to ensure that decaying vegetable matter (for example, fallen leaves and fruits) are cleared away, burying (and thereby potentially preserving) human artefacts. This process turns organic material into a form that can again be re-incorporated and re-utilised in a local or regional ecology, which includes the activities of all matter, living or apparently inert. As a consequence, the activity of the earthworm ensures that soils become fertile and vegetation is able to grow more productively. This then means that a food chain originating with insects and herbivorous species is able to develop, and people can sustain themselves by cultivating crops or capturing animals. Resultantly, the humble, tiny, often neglected earthworm has a disproportionately large and important impact on the ability of people to be able to live in a particular place. Therefore, the natural ecologies and ecosystems of a region are crucial to both how a region has developed and how it sustains and maintains itself.

Channelling Spinoza and the ancient Greek Atomists (of whom Epicurus was one), we can recognise that whilst we might experience the sentient and non-sentient, living or inert bodies in our regional localities to be fully formed objects, if we look a little deeper and a little closer, at an atomic level these bodies are made up of other bodies. To take the 1970 Crosby, Stills, & Nash song literally, we are stardust, composed of an endlessly circulating and finite pool of molecular material that has existed since the Big Bang and has followed a journey which, over the intervening billions of years, has formed part of countless and diverse organisms. When we look at the world in this way, we see that as human beings we are not only culturally formed from the environments and regions within which we live and have lived or have consumed ideas, but that we are also *physically* formed from the spaces from which we absorb matter. To illustrate this, recent studies examining the fall in violent crime rates over the past few decades have found a tight correlation between a reduction in both criminal behaviour and atmospheric lead in the environment (BBC, 2013). The hypothesis is that the shift to unleaded petrol meant there was less lead in local environments. They also find that high concentrates of environmental lead alter the physiology of the growing human brain, contributing to a reduction in information processing skills and a tendency towards violent behaviour. In this example, the airborne matter experienced by a person in their formative years literally became folded into their physiological make-up and affected their behaviour. Consequently, our regional built, ecological, and physical environments are intricately bound to our bodies, and the possibilities and potentialities that we can experience. As a result, we can see that the affects of Latour's actor-network go far beyond the cultural or ideational impacts that non-living, non-human, or non-sentient beings might have on human memories, perceptions, or understandings of our past, present, or future worlds. Instead it extends to our very molecular construction. We might even go so far as to make the claim that the region, its physical, biological, human, and infrastructural eco-systems, and indeed the world is one flesh, or one whole, bodily organism of which human activity is only a small part.

Therefore, affect can help us to better understand the impact of new infrastructures, enterprises, procedures, structures, and dynamics within local economies and regional ecosystems. It also opens up possibilities for examining political, economic, and cultural ecologies and provides assistance for examining the mobilities and fluidities of knowledge and ideas. However, we need something else to bind all of this together. If we are to maximise the utility of affect as a tool of regional analysis, we need to find a language that can be situated in the complex interactions and intersections within our localities, move us beyond and outside of the structured fixidity of the physical region and move it into a conceptual space. The concept of affective assemblage will help us to do this.

THE REGIONAL ASSEMBLAGE

In many respects, there are a lot of similarities between the affective assemblage of Deleuze and Guattari (2004) and the discourse offered by Foucault. This is not entirely surprising, given that both were engaged with exploring and understanding power as coming from a multiplicity of different sources, capable of being harnessed by a range of political actors and not just those who are traditionally conceived of as 'powerful'. This means that their ideas can be valuable for conceptualising how social and political spaces become shaped by all actors, including those that we might otherwise imagine to be 'marginalised'. Similarly, both discourse and the assemblage is a way of imagining the complex interactions amongst and between all aspects of our lived experiences. Consequently, they are made up of (amongst other things) institutions, practices, ways of speaking about, economies, physical and conceptual structures, thoughts, and knowledges. In fact all that we encounter, know about the world, how it works, and our place in it can be located into either the assemblage or discourse. This is one of the places in which discourse stops being as useful to our later inquiry. The word 'discourse' is linked in our minds and practices to words, and also the analysis of words. As a result, in the popular imagination, we often end up overlooking the many other factors that contribute to Foucauldian discourse. Indeed, discourse analysis has come to be heavily used within the academic toolkit, usually emphasising the forms and patterns of speech and the exclusionary practices contained within (Foucault, 1998). The assemblage provides a better tool for us here, with fewer cultural baggages which over-determine how we use it, and a more intuitive use of words which provide us with a ready-made language that allows us to better conceptualise the region as an assemblage. Finally, and as we will explore further later, the assemblage has developed a ready path through Deleuzes' engagement with the evolutionary emergence of Bergson (2004), and in later use by theorists, such as Connolly (2002, 2008), which helps us to consider the region as more than purely a geographical space and its economies as being more than the financially sustaining activities which occur there. Instead, the organistic metaphors of the region that we have begun to explore through Bennett and Latour help to provide us with an imagination of the region as an evolving, adapting being, operating in a close interaction with all of its parts, and which we will explore more fully in the following chapter.

The assemblage is a series of nested, complex, intertwined, and interactive networks linking ideas, concepts, structures, practices, and institutions in particular ways, at particular times and around particular things. None of the connections and linkages from which it is formed are fixed for all time but are subject to shifting patterns of mutating power relationships that change as a direct effect of the activities which occur within an assemblage or the assemblages that it is connected to or affected by. Let's illustrate this by imagining the region as an assemblage. In geographical terms, the region assemblage is comprised of many other geographical assemblages of varying sizes. These include large and small towns, villages, and cities each with similar but different histories. In some spaces, these community assemblages might occupy a shared geological and environmental topography. Others might vary quite considerably despite a relatively small physical difference. For example, the environmental variations between a coastal community and one just a few miles inland might be quite stark. The layers of rock might be very different which will have affected the soils and historically what forms of agriculture are or were (or were not able) to be cultivated in that place. The topography will have had an affect on the flora and fauna that were able to exist there, which will have impacted not only on the capacity of the territory to sustain human life but also on how it appears, its capacity to be affected by extreme weather conditions such as storm winds or flooding. Some communities will have been formed on a geological strata that contained minerals or rock that was or is useful to other people – whether this is rock used in aspects of construction, or precious or semi-precious stone, or mineral deposits that are later processed and used to make important products. Many of such communities will have or will continue to have some form of extractive industry based around removing rocks or minerals for sale in the local, national, or international market. These will be industries that will employ and sustain some people in that locality, others will have made their living in industries which provide services for others, and yet more will have or continue to be employed in some completely different activity.

This complicates place-based assemblages and highlights that they are in a continual, ongoing process of being produced (see Dovey, 2010, 2012). The ways that coastal communities were formed and continue to be sustained will also have had a significant impact on the way assemblages were formulated and on what they have become in the present. Perhaps a thriving fishing town was developed, or maybe the location was ideally placed for major sea-faring trade routes. Perhaps the previous inhabitants were peaceful and industrious and managed to transform their town into a major commercial location, or maybe the topographical characteristics of the surrounding area meant that land access was difficult, shipping had to avoid too many half-hidden rocks, or the populations were content not to expand their enterprises. However, maybe the geological aspects which compromised the development of the fishing town meant that in more recent times, it became appealing to visitors who delight in its small community and facilitated the development of a tourism industry. However these spaces developed, and whatever they became, it would also be impossible to picture these separate communities in isolation from each other. It might well have been that the produce from farming, mining, quarrying, or hunting was sold and transported through the neighbouring coastal community. Therefore, although each community formed its own assemblage made up of their own particular industries, institutions, governance, people, practices, cultures, and natural environments, their community assemblages needed (and continue to need) to be connected with other community assemblages in order to survive and thrive. They need to form part of a complex and interactive network, incorporating many different communities, across a particular territorial space. This territorial space is the region.

Furthermore, whilst predominantly in the following pages we are considering the spatialised geographies of assemblages, examining how they are connected to particular territories; to imagine them as *only* connected to place would be fallacious and inaccurate. As Zygmut Bauman intimated in his 2000 book *Liquid Modernity*, the interests and activities that people pursue—the businesses, industries, materials, practices, and processes underpinning economic activity; the institutions of governance; the natural environment of flaura, fauna, and organisations designed to maintain it all—have their own system of assemblages. At some point(s), these assemblages of interest or practice attach themselves to a particular place or places. However, this spatial attachment is certainly not defining to the non-spatial assemblage, just as this activity or interest might not be defining to the region assemblage. For example, some people in the region may enjoy reading comic books, and as a consequence, participate in wider national and global assembled communities around this. The comic book assemblage(s) may consist of virtual communities through online forums and informative websites or physical communities brought together at comic conventions and other organised activities. These bring geographically located individuals into contact with people, thoughts, cultures, and ideas from a diverse range of places both inside *and* outside of the nation assemblage. Moreover, this assemblage will incorporate the varied activities which create, promote, and sustain comic books and the people that buy them, which itself incorporates disparate activities such as the production and processing of paper, paints, and industrial printing. As we can see, the region assemblage intersects and interacts with this global and dynamic community through the activities of the number of local residents or employees who are plugged in to both, and even what appears to be a deeply localised and tiny club or associated practice will be directly or indirectly plugged in to many others.

A further example might be that of a crafting or sewing group. Whilst seeming to exist in isolation from the rest of the world, it is actually consti-tuted of the people that make up its active or inactive members. These mem-bers will have some form of job or role through which they economically support themselves, and these roles will (probably) be separate and different from their outside interest in crafting or sewing. This makes them part of a particular workplace and industrial assemblages. The deep interconnected-ness between these working practices and the members of the club means that our club assemblage might actually find that it has deep and long-lasting flows, interconnections, and influences with other assemblages seemingly far outside of the remit of the club. The club will also have strong linkages with cultural assemblages within the particular environment in which they are situ-ated and with the cultural environment which has developed around needle-work as a hobby. This might incorporate recent emerging trends which have developed similar crafts as newly fashionable – which in turn might affect the type of membership that are attracted to the group. A further assemblage which plays off the position of needlecraft in broader society will also shape the kinds of products available to members in the practice of their craft and how information about such products is disseminated. This creates a close interrelationship with both the global economic environment, and members' personal relationship with the global economy, which impacts their affluence (and therefore willingness to purchase products), and the amount of time that persons have to commit to the club and their craft. Finally, the club will be deeply interwoven into assemblages around the particular space within which they are located. The infrastructure available will shape possible meeting locations, the governance of the community feeds into locations, but also the broader environmental context (and perhaps time constraints of members), and the types of individuals that live and are active in a space will affect the types of activities perpetuated and the kinds of social capital (see Putnam, 2000) that can be developed.

Through this example, we can see some of the interactions and intercon-nections within the community assemblage, the smaller assemblages of which it is comprised, and (some of) the external assemblages that these interact with. We can also begin to see how knowledges and ideas become shared and transferred between individuals, groups, and assemblages. This helps to make visible some of the mobilities and interconnections of which Latour (2005) spoke and which provides some of the spaces for Ahmed's (2004) affective economies to be initiated and become situated, amplified, or reduced. Invoking DeLanda's use of Weber, we see also that assemblages are social, involving much more than mechanical relationships of cause and effect, but which invoke the motivations and meanings which underpin social action and interaction, the complex web of cognitive and pre-cognitive understandings, and cultural learned behaviours on which these interactions are based.

Whilst this study primarily concerns itself with the region as an assemblage, it is important to appreciate and be aware that the region is only one assemblage out of many layers – or what Deleuze and Guattari call 'plateaus'. The region is comprised of assembled communities, cultures, practices, natural and physical environments, activities, and industries. These are all assemblages in and of themselves. Consequently, a business is an assemblage of people, practices, spaces, and things which might (or might not) be intricately bound up in the fabric of the community in which it is a part. It extends links and connections through trade and collaborations with individuals and organisations that operate far beyond the boundaries of the community, region, or nation but might be part of very global networks. The governance of the community assemblage also will be local but with strong connectivity to other communities and to the region assemblage. In turn, and as an additional plateau, the region interacts in some way with other levels of government, and even with governance at a supra-national level through institutions, such as the European Union, North American Free Trade Association, World Trade Organisation, and the United Nations. We might also describe the global capitalist economy as a vast and complex assemblage, incorporating an incomprehensibly vast array of practices, processes, organisations, and culturally embedded meanings and interpretations.

At this point, the scalar nature of the way that we have described assemblages can make it appear as if assemblages and plateaus operate on a hierarchical network. Whilst at one level, we certainly seem to be discussing the local, community level as being much smaller and less powerful than those of the national or international, this perspective within the framework prepared for us by Deleuze and Guattari would be inaccurate and perhaps the example of the environment can show how this is so. Our local immediate natural environments undoubtedly are deeply connected to the geological strata which create the conditions for natural and human environments to flourish or otherwise. But our local environmental systems are deeply interconnected to the affective wider world far beyond the locality or the region. James Glieck's (1987) butterfly effect is of help to us here. Gleick relates how as a young scientist running computer models, he set up a programme to forecast weather. The models being utilised were accurate to a .0000001 decimal point. However, forecasting the weather has to take into account an enormous array of complex dynamics. One day, he rounded up a figure by 0.001 per cent, which dramatically altered the weather predictions that he developed.

In a world of such complexity, the level of accuracy that Gleik and his team utilised was not enough. Even infinitesimal differences in the model led to wildly different modelled results. From this observation, Gleik posited that in a complex interdependent system, the merest affective impact of a butterfly beating its wings could trigger a chain of causality that could culminate in a hurricane on the other side of the world. This provides us with an example of the way that power functions within the amplificatory nature of affect. Power is not linear or mechanical, and as we know from our example of Bouazzin, in the right conditions, the smallest thing can have a disproportionately huge impact. Consequently, regional assemblages and local, community assemblages cannot be imagined as at the bottom of a hierarchical layering of the plateau, but as one part of a much bigger, universal whole.

Whilst communities and regions might be small, we are reminded of the questions raised by Aristotle in *Nichomachean Ethics* regarding the relationship of the citizen to the city. For Aristotle in what we now might consider as an evaluation of the relationship between parts and wholes, it is illogical and inconceivable to consider the citizen in isolation to the city, just as it does not make sense to discuss a disembodied hand. If I was to remove my hand from my body, my body would still be able to exist but with reduced functionality. My hand, however, would not be able to support itself in isolation and would quickly be drained of all life. Whilst we might want to debate whether a particular region could be likened to a hand or whether its loss to the broader whole might be more comparable to an arm or conversely to a finger tip, the point is that regardless, its loss or reduced functionality is *felt*. Therefore, it is in the interests of regions and nation states that even the smallest communities are able to continue to be vibrant places where people feel able to live a happy and productive life (howsoever they might define it) in some kind of coherence with their physical, natural, and institutional environments. It is important to remember also that the poor functioning of one or two towns or villages might not impact the national assemblage too greatly (perhaps being comparable to a few small scars on the skin, serving as reminders of some past or present malaise). However, the cumulative effect of community decline can have a dramatic impact on the capacity and potentiality of national and supra-national spaces. The community or the subnational region might be comparatively small in size, population, and scale, but its affects are important, and as we already know, affective impacts tend not to remain localised but ripple and vibrate throughout associated assemblages.

Does this mean that we should care about regional inequality for utilitarian reasons? In one version of utility, small or sparsely populated regions take second place behind places that house many people. Metropolitan areas and cities, housing the lives and activities of so many more people than rural spaces, simply means that an investment in areas of dense population impacts more people and so therefore can be judged to be better at meeting improval targets. But this notion of impact is an interesting one that the assemblage problematises, making visible as it does the way that affective impacts have an indirect, transferrable effect within the 'whole' of the bigger assemblage.

WHAT KEEPS THE REGIONAL-ASSEMBLAGE TOGETHER?

Up to this point, we know that the assemblage is vast, interconnected, and made up of multiple and layered assemblages and plateaus. The region is just one of these plateaus. We also appreciate that assemblages are assembled around particular things, places, ideas, and practices, producing a system through which affects resonate. Finally, through Bergson and Connolly, we understand that affective actions rely on some aspect of memory to ensure that affects resonate, that particular memories are called into interpretive action at particular moments, and that this forms an important part of the fabric of contextual backdrop through which regionalised cultures develop. What Foucault (1998) calls 'claims to truth' do not get made and accepted in a vacuum, but need to be able to be situated within individual and/or cultural memory in order to be able to be accepted as such. Therefore, if I was to make a claim that rural regions across the world are dynamic and innovative, I would have to expect this claim to be heavily questioned or rejected by others at best, or laughter and derision at worst. This is because culturally, we 'know' that innovation happens in metropolitan areas and that the rural has an 'out of time' quality whereby temporality is slower and people and industries have a tendency to be more 'backward' (Murdoch et al., 2003). As a consequence, the idea that rural areas might be places where innovative and interesting things happen (beyond the leisured consumption of countryside) can be difficult for people to accept (Bürk et al., 2012; Willett, 2016; Erikson, 2008). This is because as individuals and cultures, we rely on our cultural framing of material in order to be able to assess the veracity or otherwise of claims to truth. We need to have something within our Bergsonian (2004) cone of memory in order to be able to situate the knowledges that we encounter (see also Connolly, 2002, 2010).

Furthermore, the available cultural knowledges, our need to communicate with others, and our need to be able to situate knowledges and actions within collective cones of memory means that we select shared available narratives in order to recognise the similarity between ourselves and others and initiate shared communicative spaces (see Bergson, 2004; Mead, 1936; Merleau-Ponty, 2002). For example, as a British person, I always know that I can usually initiate a light and gentle conversation based around observations about the weather, and as a parent, the available narrative that 'kids grow up too fast' can usually be used as the basis of some form of conversation with other parents. These available narratives can be deeply, generationally entrenched and help to shape culture in very specific ways. For example, in his 1983 book *Hooligan, a History of Respectable Fears,* Geoffrey Pearson relates how the moral panic around the 'decline of young people today' is a story that can be traced as far back as Elizabethan England in the early 1600s. In this story, the past is a nostalgic golden age where people worked together in some form of harmony. However, we have (apparently) witnessed a significant moral decline in recent years, which means that the youth of today are degenerate and crime-ridden. Culturally and in order to enjoy an unchallenging conversation whereby both interlocutors can recognise each other's similarity, it is much easier and more pleasant to be able to use this available narrative as a means of finding a shared discursive space based on this collective memory of a story. In the process, it creates a feedback loop which reinforces the narrative or cultural affective responses (see also Ahmed, 2004). To challenge this story or feedback loop means that the individual or group demarcates a line between them and the person(s) they are speaking with, risking setting themselves as in some way outside of the group. This can create consequences for the degree to which they are later able to be included. On the converse, a challenge made in the 'right', or a sensitive way might enable individuals and groups to question the available cultural repertoire of knowledges and ideas, weakening problematic feedback loops and developing new ones.

This is of significance because it can help us to understand *why* some communities develop particular strong sub-cultures (e.g., around comic books) around some topics and not others and why this may vary from other communities. Or why at a particular moment in time, a strong actual and affective economy has developed around the sewing club, and whether this happens at the expense of the comic book assemblages, or whether it spills over into them. What we are talking about here is about what DeLanda calls the 'territorialising' effects of the assemblage. By this, he means the things, events, physical and social structures, and processes which bind the assemblage together into some form of whole, connecting the collective. It is important to note at this point that the assembled ideas, objects, and things can never be totalising or essentialising. Assemblages are mobile and fluid, never fixed, so their borders are always fuzzy and flexible. As a consequence, the 'truths' that they contain will shift, grow, and evolve (see Connolly, 1995; Bennett, 2010), meaning that whilst the assemblages of which we are a part *shapes* the things that constitute it, never defines it. This also means that the assemblage necessarily includes a diversity of things, objects, and ideas around a particular topic, so we can never say that because we draw a boundary around a grouping and call it 'this' that everything within that grouping will conform to a specific set of norms, ideas, and values. To do otherwise would be as ludicrous as to make the claim that everyone in a particular regional space conformed to a pre-defined set of identities. We know that this is not so even though sometimes stereotyping of people(s) from specific places would try to claim otherwise (see, for example, Jansson, 2003; Ericksson, 2008; Willett and Lang, 2018). One of the things that Deleuze and Guattari's assemblage helps to make visible is that identities are multiplicities. They are clustered *around* some objects, places, ideas, and values, but they are not defined by them, and they are not fixed for all always but are subject to change and adaptation over the course of time.

Nevertheless, and as DeLanda (2006) makes clear, some practices, processes, institutions, values, and knowledges act as territorialising factors, articulating the assemblage, and pulling it together in the first place, and then helping to maintain it longer term. DeLanda describes how part of the content of the assemblage functions as codes that bind it together (and may even attempt – ultimately unsuccessfully – to be totalising). To illustrate, language operates as a code, increasing homogeneity amongst the assembled matter. In the most extreme examples, two different (and yet contiguous) regions will utilise completely separate languages. For example, in the United Kingdom, Wales and England are situated right next to each other. English reflects the turbulent and complex history of England over the past two millennia, incorporating Germanic Saxon, French from the centuries-long after-effects of Norman conquest, and Latin as a reflection of the geographic mobilities of the nobility and clergy and its role as a pan-continental elite language. The story of the Welsh language is much different. At root, it reflects that of the ancient Britons prior to Saxon invasion and links Wales to Brittonic Celtic regions, such as Cornwall and Western Scotland. Over centuries, the language went from being symbolic of defiance and resistance to English Assimilation (Day, 2002), to becoming threatened and almost dying out in the early twentieth century. However, over the latter twentieth century and onwards into the twenty-first, the Welsh language became a way of coding a regional resistance to the ongoing processes of English cultural assimilation. If we are to put this in the framework of the assemblage, the assemblages around 'Wales' and 'Welshness' had begun to deterritorialise, become more heterogeneous with boundaries and borders that became increasingly fuzzy, risking assimilation into the assemblage around Englishness. This sparked a period and process of resistance, which emphasised the narratives, emotional affects, institutions, histories, interpretations, cultural practices, and of course the language, which acted as coding mechanisms and processes of territorialisation which stabilised Welsh assemblages. As a consequence, assemblages around Welshness have become strong and clearly defined, visible to local and global observers. We see also that processes of territorialisation and deterritorialisation can be both passive *or* active, imbued with intentionality or subject to the whimsical nature of chance.

The example of language provided here operates as an extreme instance of how territorialising factors connect an assemblage internally, differentiating it from other spaces. Dialect also operates in this kind of manner, providing a distinct way of talking about the immediate physical, natural, and cultural environments which help to produce a set of shared cultural meanings and understandings, whilst it is also developed from those same shared meanings. Sometimes the territorialising factor is an object which becomes a metaphor for something, such as Boris Johnson's (2008) mayoral election campaign where he pledged to bring back London's red double-decker Routemaster busses (Mulholland, 2011). Johnson was seeking to capitalise on dissatisfaction with the then-current London mayoral incumbent Ken Livingstone's road transportation innovation of the 'bendy-bus'. Johnson's gamble was that the iconic nature of the Routemaster made it a territorialising metaphor, symbolic of a particular version of the city, which he could collect support around. To some degree, this paid off for him electorally, although unfortunately for him the vast expense and inefficiency of the new Routemasters meant that his busses were also able to become totemic metaphors for territorialising the assemblage of resistance to his Mayorship.

In the 1990s and early 2000s, and as epitomised by Bauman's (2000) *Liquid Modernity* and Manuel Castell's three-volume collection *The Information Age: Economy Society and Culture* published between 1996 and 1998, much of the scholarships problematised the role of spatial identities by emphasising the deterritorialising effects of globalisation. In this thesis, identifications based around attachment to places were likely to become less and less relevant over time as communication revolutions, such as the internet and mobile telephony, fused with how easy it is to travel long distances by car, train, or plane. As a consequence, spatial difference has become radically re-constituted, and people can now take in information from a range of sources and from places far beyond the relatively small territories in which we live most of our lives. According to theorists, such as Bauman and Castells, this meant that we were going to see more and more people forming identities and communities virtually, around shared interests rather than physical contiguity. The reason for this was because new forms of global communication would foster what DeLanda calls 'relations of exteriority' – or easier communications and interactions with people, places, things, and ideas from beyond the region assemblage. This expansion in the range of information, activities, and assemblages with which individuals are now able to engage was expected to blur the edges of territorial assemblages and leave them less and less relevant. Consequently, some scholars concerned with preserving regional cultures asked questions about how to maintain territorial distinctiveness in an era of the deterritorialising effects of pervasive relations of exteriority (Kneafsey, 2000; Askegaard and Kjeldgaard, 2007). In the event, we now know that this has not happened. Instead, regional assemblages have found ways of incorporating the fast pace of informational change whilst also maintaining strong relations of interiority and processes of territorialisation (see Willett and Tredinnick-Rowe, 2016; Jones et al., 2018). Indeed, in some spaces, this has led to a challenge to the nation-state in the opposite direction as territories, such as Scotland and Catalonia, seek independence based on the strength of assemblages around these spaces. However, what concepts such as interiority and exteriority, territorialisation and deterritorialisation do for us is to help to illuminate some of the fluid processes and connections through which assemblages remain assembled and connect to other assemblages. For the region assemblage, it helps to make visible how the region is connected externally and internally, and to help to facilitate exploration about what these connections look like, and how they are changing over time.

The social, political, and economic interconnectedness of the activities and processes which maintain the integrity of an assemblage has a utility. Assemblages change, however, and they are assembled. Even if they were left to operate as what Prigogine and Stengers (1985) describe as a closed system, incorporating nothing new over the course of their lifespan, they would still be subject to change, in the form of entropy. To illustrate, if I let my car sit in my garage for several decades, I will not be able to inure it from this process. It will still rust, the metals that it is made of will start to fatigue, and insects and other creatures will make a home in it, further impacting on the material integrity of the vehicle and degrading the objects from which it is constituted. All of these actions will mean that over the course of time, my car will deterritorialise, degrade, and will no longer function as a car. The important thing is to ensure that the affective changes that happen within the assemblages that matter to us help to shift the assemblage in a helpful direction. We will cover this more fully in the next chapter, but the social action and interaction through which humans navigate the region assemblage has an additional affect, and to explore this more fully, we need to turn to Robert Putnam's 2000 work *Bowling Alone*. In this book, he develops the concept of social capital, taking it away from Bourdieu's (1991) interpretation of it as the means through which class becomes upheld within communities, to describe how the activities, which people do within their community assemblages, share and create territorial knowledges and networks. For Putnam, being a part of an active community helps to create and maintain the Bergsonian shared knowledges and understandings through which people culturally navigate their environments, and it helps to share and disperse these understandings. Finally, the social, political, and economic networks that community participation engenders help to provide support during good and bad times.

What this means is that the things which take place within regional assemblages not only help to actively (re)create meanings within the assemblage
but also help to keep knowledges, affects, and ideas moving, mobile, and
fluid. As a result, the region assemblage is able to change and adapt. More
than this, Putnam's bridging and bonding capital overlays the relations of
interiority and exteriority that DeLanda provides us with. For Putnam, and
similar to relations of exteriority, bridging capital brings together different
networks (or assemblages), whilst bonding capital embeds relations of interiority. What this demonstrates is how being a part of the comic book club or
sewing group, or being involved in the council or a business network not only
bonds and/or extends the community assemblage, but it also keeps it mobile,
active, and therefore open to new amplificatory affects. Although not using
the language of the assemblage, Putnam argues that the strong interconnections and networks (derived from active community participation) help to
build strong regional economies.

THE ECOSYSTEM OF THE ASSEMBLAGE

Part of the reason behind why the mobilities underpinning Putnam's (2000)
social capital and active communities provide more of what Deleuze and
Guattari (2004) call 'spaces of possibility' for becoming is linked to their
metaphor of the wasp and the orchid and relations of exteriority. Here, the
orchid imitates a female wasp, tricking the male wasp into believing that
instead of a flower, it is a potential mate. The male is drawn to the orchid,
attempts to copulate, and then moves on to other orchids. The orchid is invit-
ing a relation of exteriority with the wasp, making connections between two
apparently disparate species. The result of this extension of the orchid beyond
itself is that the wasp tracks pollen between plants, enabling the orchid to
reproduce. Consequently, by looking outside of itself into assemblages from
beyond itself, the orchid also is able to re-territorialise, sustain its own species assemblage, and become something new through the reproductive process. The orchid, wasp, and pollen illustrate to us how looking beyond our
own community, interest, or region assemblage can bring in new ideas and
material to cross-fertilise that which already exists. The incorporation of new
material creates a space of possibility for new things to emerge – or become
– which wouldn't have existed if the orchid had been embedded inwards,
towards relations of interiority. A failure to connect itself outwards would
also bring the death of the orchid species.

   What this does for the assemblage is to demonstrate how even a thing as
clearly defined as a species is in reality only a part of an affective eco-system.
Similar to Aristotle's relation between the hand and the body, the orchid

would not be able to continue to exist if it was not part of bigger assemblages. And it is in the connections that emerge within the ecosystem of assemblages of which the region is a part that new material and ideas are introduced, creating spaces of possibility for regions to consider how to adapt to changes within the ecosystems into which they contribute. Indeed, this process is so intricately interwoven and connected that we need to imagine regions as eco-systems rather than species and demonstrate how species, assemblages, regions, and communities are only contingent in relation to matter around them rather than being fixed for all time.

This process also illustrates Deleuze and Guattari's metaphor of the rhizome and the root. The root is unilinear, consisting of a single power source connecting the plant to its nutrient source underground. Like the root, the rhizome also exists below the earth's surface, but it is at the same time both fragmented yet connected with what Deleuze and Guattari call middles (or plateaus), but no obvious centre. Unlike the tree root which will stay in the same place always, the 'middles' of the rhizome can spatially move over time. It is like couch grass, or Japanese knotweed, it spreads quickly and easily along 'lines of flight'; new flows and connections between middles, or shoots off along a nutrient source, which may become populated and embedded into a new plateau, or might burn out its energy and dissipate. Eventually, it is impossible to tell where it started or where it's going, you just know that if let be, it will get everywhere. We can overlay the rhizome onto our region assemblage. It also is comprised of multiple plateaus and dispersed assemblages. Lines of flight can be likened to new ideas which take off or become newly embedded into the ideational fabric of the region. Perhaps these ideas might have arisen from relations of exteriority or maybe they will be something that has been generated from the territorialising effects of interior processes. An example would be the predominantly pre-teen 2014 craze for Loom Bands (BBC, 2014). For a few weeks only, U.K. shops could not stock enough packs of these multi-coloured elastic bands to satisfy demand. People made the bands into bracelets, toys, and even in one case, a dress (Daily Mirror, 2014). This line of flight quickly fizzled out, however, and the dress failed to sell for months. Other lines of flight also erupt into view, transform the landscape, but remain. Perhaps the smartphone is an example here of a thing which emerged, was discovered to be essential to how global societies were now developing, and became deeply embedded into daily lives, impacting assemblages and creating new spaces of possibility.

The concept of affect is crucial to helping to understand why some lines of flight take off in the first place, capture the imagination, and articulate new things, ideas, or ways of being, or fade, and for this we need to turn to Connolly's (2008) concept of resonance. Drawing on phenomenologies and Bergson's cone of memory, some affects just resonate with a particular

cultural moment in time when individuals or societies are ready for or receptive towards new objects or interpretive schema. It might create previously
unimaginable connections, entirely re-shaping the contexts, emphases, and
practices within nearby assemblages, transforming the ideational landscape.
For example, for years, environmental campaigners have been raising the
problem of over-consumption of plastics and the issues that we have with
its uncompostable nature. However, it was British broadcaster and natural
historian David Attenborough's TV series 'the Blue Planet' which in autumn
of 2017 sparked awareness of the plastics issue and launched many 2018 new
year resolutions to reduce or cut out plastics from people's lives (see Canavan,
2018). Previous campaigns had played a valuable role in keeping the idea of
reducing plastic alive in popular discourse. But it was Attenborough's bringing attention to the pollution of plastic in the oceans that arrived at culturally
just the right time to resonate and light the spark that energised a line of flight
around plastics and spilled out into a cultural assessment of waste and con-
sumerism in the United Kingdom. It amplified later analysis about the impact
of fast fashion and initiated a new line of articulation around consumer
awareness of the environmental impact of twenty-first-century living which
has provided environmental campaigners with many spaces of possibility to
try to reduce the burden that humans place on our environmental eco-system.

What we are witnessing here is an enormous diffusion of power and energy
throughout the rhizome/region/assemblage, which enables it to create and
re-create itself anew. This rhizomatic nature is also the key to its resilience.
The tree root can be easily cut down and destroyed, but this is not the case
with the rhizome, whose lateral power structure and lack of centre means that
there is no obvious place or way of getting rid of it beyond removing every
last piece of it. And even when this is achieved, there is no way of knowing
quite what new sites of vegetation may come from its dispersed seeds (lines
of flight). It cannot be broken, shattered, or ruptured, or it will start up again
on one of its old lines of flight, or might just grow a new line. To illustrate,
to destroy the Japanese Knotweed that is considered an invasive species and
has spread particularly throughout the southwest of the United Kingdom, it
is necessary to remove or poison every last fibre of the rhizome or it will
return. Deleuze and Guattari hold this as an example of the sustainability and
resilience of power and knowledge sources that come from a multiplicity of
points, dispersed throughout the organism rather than from one centralised
location which can be readily dismantled.

If we apply this to the region assemblage, a rhizomatic structure with
sites of power and the production of knowledge dispersed throughout the
region means that it is more resilient to changes that happen in any part of
its assembled natural, social, economic, cultural, and ideational spheres. The
communities, economies, institutions, and organisations that make up the

region assemblage are connected by feedback loops which ensure ready and easy communication between the various parts of the structure, and which helps knowledge to flow readily around it, and for new knowledges to be created, adapted, and dispersed. Similarly, feedback loops act as conduits connecting the rhizome-region assemblage to other assemblages, exterior to itself. As a loop, this movement is a two-way process whereby information and ideas flow from one place and back again, mutually affecting each other, in a co-production of knowledges.

The power source or centre of the rhizomatic region assemblage comes from within itself, from the interwoven interactions of the parts of its structure rather than from any one particular source or sources. On the converse, perhaps a root-region might be overly dependent or reliant on an external space to shape its economy, governance, and the knowledges about the region that affect how people think about it. This is not to say of course that the rhizomatic region exists independently of other assemblages – including that of the world or the nation. This would be undesirable and impossible, especially given the extent to which other assemblages amplify regional capacity. Moreover, external assemblages at the very least help to create the natural, physical, and ideational environments in which the region assemblage is located. But the happenings within a root-region would be much more controlled or determined by external assemblages or plateau and would struggle to find the political agency to create its own structures and spaces for possibility. Furthermore, destruction or the loss of dominant or controlling assemblages can have a detrimental affective impact on the ability of the region assemblage to continue effectively. Finally, and as we will discuss in greater depth in the following chapter, the dispersed nature of the multiplicity of interior and exterior assemblages which constitute the region assemblage means that the region assemblage is an organism, operating as a spatial, ideational, and natural evolutionary eco-system.

The region-assemblage provides us with a way of understanding the region which takes account of the deep levels of interconnections, interrelationships, and networks between people, things, institutions, and infrastructure. Second, it offers an analysis which considers the ways and means by which these interconnections circulate throughout the region, what these flows look like, incorporate, coalesce around, and how they change and affect each other. In the following chapter, we take this a step further to consider how processes within the ecosystem of the affective assemblage facilitate adaptation to social, political, and economic niches. Third, in emphasising the importance of interconnectivity, it makes visible what from other perspectives may be overlooked. In this book, we examine what we see if we look at the region from a different starting point and through the model of the complex adaptive system of the region assemblage.

Chapter 3

The Evolutionary Regional Assemblage, Becoming and Economies

Economies might be only one part of the region assemblage, but they are a part which allows people to subsist and keep themselves alive in that space. These economies might be complex, or they might be simple. At a most basic subsistence level, economies relate to the means through which individuals sustain themselves through selling or bartering food or basic equipment which they themselves have grown, caught, or made. In more complex societies, an economy relates to the intricate network through which people make, trade, sell, and buy the goods and services which make up the real and culturally constructed needs and wants that fuel processes of exchange. From the previous chapter, we understand that economies and economic assemblages do not exist in isolation. On the contrary, they are reliant on and contribute to local biological, infrastructural, governmental, and social environments and assemblages. It is not the aim of this book to claim that economic assemblages are the most important ones within a region. Indeed, as should be clear by now, economies can only be imagined as one part of the region assemblage. Neither can we perceive them as the only assemblage within the plateau of the region assemblage which directly interacts in some way with most of the other aspects of the region assemblage. Therefore, we do not claim that economies are 'special'. Assemblages are far too deeply interconnected for this. However, economies make many of the differences which exist between regions immediately visible. We can see which areas rely on which forms of economic activity and have a series of measurements to consider how productive these economic activities are. We can find ways to visualise how many people are incorporated into each form of activity and where, and what percentage of the local labour force this is. We can also witness the level of skills and education that local people bring to the economy, how this is employed, what kind of financial reward this brings to workers, and how this compares to the costs of living in these areas. From this information, we are able to observe how differing region assemblages compare to others nearby or covered within shared national or international boundaries. From here we are able to see where regional inequalities lie, where they are at risk of emerging, and so consequently consider how we might be able to develop policies and practices which ameliorate the widest difficulties.

In turn, this has implications for the cohesiveness of the body politic however we choose to construct it. It is widely accepted that regional inequalities do not only have a detrimental effect on the individuals who are subject to a mis-match in life chances from the well-documented effects of absolute and relative poverty (Alcock, 1997; Townsend, 1979; Hallerod and Larson, 2008). Additionally, inequalities contribute towards an array of societal problems and pathologies akin to Durkheim's (2002 [1897]) 'anomie', which can amplify the difficulties that individuals and communities have in being able to flourish and play an active and beneficial role in local and regional economic assemblages (Shucksmith and Chapman, 1998; Armstrong and Taylor, 2000). If not adequately addressed, the consequence of this is that social and political divisions and resentments begin to build up, fragmenting and fracturing the body politic. Indeed, Gest (2016) makes the claim that the economic (and thereby social) inequalities experienced by middle England and middle America have created the situation whereby communities have become pushed to the political extremes. Indeed, other studies agree that inequalities have helped to create the space whereby some individuals and communities have become fearful about a future which feels very uncertain. Moreover, the vulnerabilities experienced by those on the sharp end of unequal societies means that people feel ill-equipped to be able to navigate this uncertain future and so seek support from a real or perceived imagination of the 'nation' (Willett et al., 2019; Arzrout and Wojcieszak, 2017; Polyakova and Fligstein, 2016). Not only does this negatively impact on local, regional, and national social and political cohesion, but this also can have an amplificatory affect on the ability of struggling regional economies to be able to catch up with other, more prosperous territories, creating a difficult cycle and negative (and indeed, destructive) feedback loops. Clearly, regional economic inequalities need to be addressed. In this chapter, I seek to create a model of the regional economy which helps to look at them in a different way, making new phenomena visible and helping to create new ways to try to tackle the problem. I am going to make the claim that region assemblages and their economies are adaptive, evolutionary organisms. In the first part of this chapter, I will argue that the region assemblage is a complex adaptive system, operating in response to a vast array of different stimuli in its environment. This relies on an understanding of time and temporality that is based on emergence rather than linearity. In the second part of the chapter, I take the complex adaptive system and apply it to the regional economy, examining the particulars of what it looks like and the important roles and functions of various aspects of the economy assemblage within the region.

TIME AND TEMPORALITY

Popularly, discussions about emergent, evolutionary time and temporalities juxtapose themselves with the ordered and predictable linearities of scientific time (see Smith and Jenks, 2008; Prigogine and Stengers, 1985; Coole and Frost, 2010; Connolly, 2002; Bergson, 2004). In this story, scientific time runs as a neat line connecting the past, present, and future. According to Bergson, Gallileo and Kepler, time is divided up into moments which count equally and are of equal weighting and importance. This turns time into a magnitude which can be measured. These moments are virtual stopping places along a given trajectory, and positive science is the study of the movement of an object along this trajectory (e.g., the movement of the planets). Through an accurate-enough knowledge and understanding about each of these moments, it is then possible to be able to predict what will happen at future points along this line, like making an accurate assessment about the location of the planets in the solar system at various points in the future through the knowledges about orbits and bodies within the solar system which have been constructed over extensive studies over a long period of time. These paths are unchangeable – and this is necessarily so because if they were subject to change, then we would not be able to predict what is going to happen along a given trajectory. This predictability means that the link between actions and outcomes is repeatable, so the same elements along the same timeline will always lead to the same outcome. It is interesting to realise that this version of time means that we are literally able to foretell the future if we know enough about the properties of the elements that we input. Here, the goal of knowledge is to seek predictable patterns. Equally, just as repeatability means that the exact combination of the exact same elements in exactly the same conditions will lead to exactly the same outcome, so actions in linear time are reversible. Literally, if we are to remove all of the different elements that we have inputted, we will be left with the same building blocks that we began with. Life becomes like a lego village that can be reduced to its foundational building blocks and re-built in exactly the same way, with the same inputs, and culminating in the same results.

Perhaps another way of understanding linear time is to borrow Bergson's (1944) metaphor of the film. Here it does not matter how many times a film is watched, or a book is read. The crucial moments or turning points within the plot will always be the same, with the same main and peripheral characters, and the same consequences, arriving at the same outcome (Connolly, 2002; DeLanda, 2011; Kaufman, 1995; Prigogine and Stengers, 1985). In fact, it would be astonishing to imagine that it might be possible to watch the same film and at each time be presented with a different story. Instead, the film is the ultimate closed system (see Prigogine and Stengers, 1985) representing a (sometimes quite complex) chain of causality which never introduces anything new, and so therefore arrives at a different ending. It is completely repeatable *ad infinitum*.

For regional assemblages, and particularly for any form or development of regional assemblages, we might imagine this in terms of gaining the ability to know what the outcome will be from a certain set of stimuli. For example, Richard Florida (2002) is widely read as claiming that being attractive to creative people was the crucial element behind the success of San Francisco and Silicon Valley. He argues that creative people are motivated by living in a nice place and having a high quality of life. This spawned an entire and very popular strand of economic development research and practice where regional assemblages sought to manage their image and branding in order to present the impression that theirs is a place where a person can enjoy an excellent quality of life and a great lifestyle with lots of cultural opportunities. Following popular interpretations of Florida, researchers and planners hoped that 'dynamic entrepreneurs' from a geographically mobile 'creative class' would be motivated to relocate to their region (see Bell and Jayne, 2010; Herslund, 2012; Nathan, 2005; Stam et al., 2008; Lee et al., 2005; Willett, 2016). In adopting a linear causal model, the assumption was that an injection of such individuals would replicate and repeat the conditions identified by Florida (2002) in San Francisco and would re-boot the local economy and kick-start the trajectory that will lead to this region becoming the next silicon valley. However, although he was read in this way, this was not the temporal perspective that Florida utilised. Instead, his argument was that it was the creativity of the local inhabitants which allowed them to best adapt to the environment around them, which in that place, and at that point in time, led to the development of what was to become the global centre of the information technology revolution. His point was that rather than being the closed system like Bergson's film, life follows a more open system with a constant flow of new material and stimuli. This means that change is inevitable and what's more, that individuals, groups, and communities need to be able to navigate it. This was the skill that Florida (2002) saw in his Creative Class. Here, he found a group of individuals whose creativity meant that not only were they able to best find solutions to new and emerging problems but that they were able to best adapt to the changes that they saw in the world around them. They had the ability to 'think outside of the box', break closed system like linear repeatable circuits, and create new knowledges.

To understand this better, we can look again to Bergson's cone of memory and his concept of Elan Vital and becoming. We already know that through the metaphor of the cone, Bergson (1944, 2004) describes an interdependent relationship between the past, the present, and the future. Rather than the past being something that is gone and is now inoperative, instead it is actively used in order to create something new out of an interaction between an interpretation of the present and the present moment. But this movement is a compulsion. The organism has a life force which compels it to move on into the future. Memory *forces* itself into the present (the point at the base of the cone), which is merely the most concentrated point of the past. This contraction of memory is *pushed* into the future by this impulsion which Bergson calls *élan vital* and which creates the future. This process is unpredictable, and it is creating something entirely new. It is a 'becoming' which could not have been expected even with a really strong understanding of the properties of the cone, because it is not linear time. Although at some points, things will follow some form of pattern, the creativity underneath *élan vital* ensures that becoming is interwoven with the spaces of possibility that we discussed in the previous chapter (see Deleuze and Guattari, 2004). This is the opposite of the predictability imposed by positive science as things don't have a telos (an endpoint), or even a next point that they will automatically move on to. Instead, things only have the potentiality to become something or be something different. The unpredictability and uncertainty behind becoming and possibility are *good* things, because it allows the space for the emergence of new and potentially exciting phenomena and multiple possibilities for becoming (Bergson, 1944; Connolly, 2011; Merleau-Ponty, 2002). Indeed, Bergson argues that without *élan vital* and the capacity to create something new, things are rendered dead, sterile, lifeless, and passive.

For regional development, viewing time in this way means that there is and can be no over-arching model which can be used to fix the problems or inequalities experienced within regions. For some time, a dominant policy response was to do this through attempting to improve the capacity of regional assemblages to be a part of and contribute to national and global knowledge economies (Kok, 2004; Cooke, 2002; Crone and Roper, 2001; Hewitt-Dundas et al., 2005; Marz et al., 2006). The idea was and is to reduce inequalities through improving economic growth by raising competitiveness and productivity. It was hoped that improving the sophistication of the knowledges held and utilised by individuals, firms, and industries operating within regional assemblages would help to facilitate research and development and innovation, and thereby lead to 'convergence' between rich and poor areas. The idea was that whilst once extractive processes and resource exploitation might have been enough to provide a good standard of living within the classically industrial economy, this had now changed and knowledge economies presuppose a highly educated workforce that is able to process and add value to commodities extracted or created. For example, the minerals gouged out of the soil or the vegetation cultivated and sold are worth significantly less in their 'raw' state than they will be by the time they have been re-worked into a sophisticated piece of technology, or food product, and packaged and marketed. Therefore, whilst the extraction of the raw material is very important, it is what is done with it that generates larger amounts of capital, and this can only be achieved through a highly skilled, knowledge-based workforce.

What does this have to do with time? Well, there are a number of different perspectives about how to best achieve knowledge economies in what are often referred to as 'underperforming' regions. Popularly, planners seek to do this by encouraging exogenous growth – or the inward migration of highly skilled individuals and companies (Dargan and Shucksmith, 2008) which are imagined as filling knowledge gaps by introducing human and social capital (see Putnam, 2000; Shortall, 2004; Evans and Synett, 2007). Not dissimilar to the example provided above with the popular interpretation of Florida's (2002) creative class, it is imagined that an injection of the 'right' kind of thing that is currently missing from the regional assemblage will be able to fix the problem. This imagines there is a mechanical relationship between the performance of the region assemblage and the things that it lacks. This follows the linear, reductionist model described above where a particular future can be reached by knowing enough about the present in order to be able to identify and correctly add the missing parts. However, as we already know, the region is a very complex assemblage, comprised of a vast array of an intricate series of connectivities, feedback loops, and affective relationships. The more elements that are introduced into a system, the more complex and unpredictable it becomes. It might be helpful there to think about the interactions between groups of people. It is easier to make a guesstimated assessment about how two people might interact, work together, and produce something. However, the more people that you add to the group, the more complex these interactions become even though it also means a degree of sharing workload and task specification. Consequently, we talk about the *art* of putting together a good team rather than the science, because we recognise that bringing together a large group of people to work together on a project is an affective judgement rather than something that is infinitely repeatable based on following a particular given set of parameters.

As Kim (2008) writes in Bedau and Humphries (2008: 127), 'as systems acquire increasingly higher degrees of organisational complexity, they begin to exhibit novel properties that in some sense transcend the properties of their constituent parts and behave in ways that cannot be predicted on the basis of the laws governing simpler systems'. The more complicated the series of actions and interactions that occur within a system, the more difficult that it becomes to be able to predict the affective responses between individuals, groups, institutions, and environments. Partly, this can be explained by the fact that some phenomena interact in emergent rather than linear ways. For example, by knowing how acids and alkalines respond to each other, I can guess beforehand that mixing baking soda with vinegar will result in some form of reaction. However, even in science, this is not always the case, and Bedau and Humphries (2008) provide us with the example of water. Even if I had an extensive prior knowledge about the properties of hydrogen and oxygen, I would not have been able to predict that by compounding these elements in a certain way, I would end up with a substance with the properties of water. This is because the reaction between hydrogen and oxygen is *emergent*. It could not have previously been imagined but emerges as a consequence of the interaction. However, once we know that this is how these elements respond, we are then able to repeat the experiment and get the same results every time.

However, this kind of neat chain of causality and repeatability has eluded scholars of regional and peripheral development (Bristow and Healey, 2018) because of the complexity of causality in a non-linear world. Indeed, the linear perspective of causality is further compromised by the problem of downward causality. Here, the emergent properties of an interaction go on to have an effect on the chain of causality in the future and a new piece of knowledge acts on the present and future in ways that couldn't have been predicted at the outset. For example, if I take an academic paper that I really was proud of to a conference and got an unexpectedly bad reception, that experience will have some kind of affect on my psyche the next time that I introduce this paper to the wider public. However much I try, and however receptive future audiences, the echoes and reverberations of the affective experience with the initial audience will continue to have an impact on the causal chain embedded in how I present my work and anticipate it being received. It is impossible to undo this experience and take how I view my work back to pre-bad conference days because a fundamental change has occurred. In this respect, it has created a bifurcation point (Prigogine and Stengers, 1985; Connolly, 2002) that has initiated a new timeline which is entirely different from the one that it grew from and represents a break from the past that has gone before. As social researchers in the region assemblage, we see evidence of this in how we are received by communities that we want to study. Sometimes previous experiences with scholars impact in a variety of different ways on how receptive people are to our questions. We are told of 'consultation fatigue', or how a study in the past had raised people's hopes that something would change, but in the eventuality, they never saw or experienced anything out of it. Or the ways that the data was used confused or saddened the community in some way, which went on to affect how receptive they would be in

similar situations in later years. At other times, we find that the ways that our
research findings are interpreted, used, and operationalised are affected by
some prior piece of information or experience which completely alters (either
positively or negatively) how effectively we can get our new research across
or the implementation strategies that we envisaged.

Prigogine and Stengers (1985) explain that this type of non-linearity exists
in the biological world because it is characterised by a lack of structures that
are fixed for all time. Instead, they use an ontology based on thermodynamics,
rather than mechanics, to claim that life – or Bergson's *Elan Vital* comes from
chaos, disorder, and disequilibrium (see also Kaufman, 1995). Whilst disci-
plines such as physics see non-linear systems only very rarely, for living matter, unpredictability is the norm. This is very important as it provides a role
for life, or the life force, as the thing that creates instability and unpredictability and collapses hierarchies of power within the system. It means that there
is something unpredictable about life which operates on a non-linear time
and which creates self-organising structures (see also Kaufman, 1995). They
write 'In biological or ecological systems, the parameters defining interaction
with the environment cannot generally be considered as constants. Both the
cell and the ecological niche draw their sustenance from their environment,
as well as humidity, P.H, salt concentration, light, and nutrients from a permanently fluctuating environment. The sensitivity of non-equilibrium states,
not only to fluctuations produced by their internal activity but also to those
coming from their environment, suggests new perspectives for biological
enquiry' (Prigogine and Stengers, 1985: 167). Here, life exists in an environment that is 'permanently fluctuating' on both the inside and on the outside.
As a consequence, change and new material are constantly being added to the
system within which life exists.

From this instability and uncertainty, life and order starts to emerge,
and with it reasonably stable, structured (more linear) systems. However,
even apparently fixed and stable, living structures are only ever temporarily so. In a linear system, the structure would be 'closed', meaning that the
phenomena operating within the system use *only* matter within that system.
Nothing new gets in and nothing within the system gets out. It is limited by
the state imposed by its boundary conditions and will remain this way until
something new breaks through the boundaries of its closed form and injects
change into the previously fixed and predictable structures. Far from equi-
librium, structures are the opposite. Although over time, they may develop
a linearity and predictability as new emergent structures become fixed and
the boundary conditions become more closed for a time. What happens next
is that something new and different occurs, which disrupts the stability that
had previously been present. An interaction with the environment beyond the
boundaries of what had been closed may become the starting point for new,

dissipative structures – spontaneous, self-organised structural forms which embody the transformation from chaos to order. Kaufman (1995) helps us to understand this a little better with his version of evolution that challenges Darwinian models based on miniscule, incremental changes. He uses the Cambrian explosion to illustrate how once the environmental conditions are exactly right, life explodes into a multiplicity of potential variations, some of which will be able to survive, and some of which will not. Over the next period of time, the organisms that are least able to exist in the environments within which they are situated decline and vanish, whilst the viable organisms remain, following the Darwinian incremental adaptation model. Eventually, over an extended process of sifting, only a few species initiated in the Cambrian explosion remained. Kaufman uses this as an example of how out of an initial chaos (the Cambrian explosion) life begins a process of simplification until some form of order is created. Or in other words, to borrow from the title of Prigogine and Stengers (1985) book, the patterns of order are created over an extended period of time, out of an initial chaos.

How does the idea of a tendency towards unpredictability square with social and political theorists that find structures throughout the assemblages of human organisation? The key thing is that structures emerge out of the initial chaos – although we also have to be aware that structures themselves are subject to changing conditions in the environment within which they operate. Therefore, structuralist sociologists, like Emile Durkheim and Talcott Parsons, or structuralist anthropologists, like Claude Levi-Strauss, could find regularities and enough path dependency to make predictions about society and the way that it operates. But crucially, this is limited to systems operating within at present unbreached boundaries. The concept that is important here is that of time. For example, for Connolly (2002), the speeding up of time is something that can assist the move towards a more radical democratic pluralism, because it means that encroaches on the structural boundary conditions happen more frequently. This disrupts what had previously been more regular, fixed structures and allows the space for what Connolly perceives as more democratic forms of political discourse. Indeed, new forms of emergent structures and what they mean for society in a time of rapid technological and social change have troubled postmodern sociologists for decades (Bauman, 2000; Castells, 2000). Moreover, we still live in a period of rapid technological change. We don't need to go into a lengthy discussion about how the internet and mobile communications have revolutionised social and political practices over the past few decades in order to do this. We also don't need to become embedded in the kind of nostalgia observed by Pearson (1983), whereby the structures of the past were a safer, better, more pleasant place. However, we do need to recognise that structural changes to familiar patterns of living can be experienced as some kind of societal 'breakdown'. And it is indeed a breakdown of structure, but it is also a natural change in response to a changing world.

We need to view these structural changes with regard to the cone of memory, feedback loops, and path dependencies discussed in the previous chapter, if we are to understand and appreciate the affects that they have on our region assemblages. To begin, we can start with Durkhiem's (2002[1897]) concept of Anomie. Durkheim developed the concept when he was trying to understand the problem of suicide. What he found was that there were higher rates of suicide in societies or groups that had experienced a period of rapid social, economic, or political change. He hypothesised that the reason for this was what he called 'anomie', or a state of normlessness. Here, the norms acted as culturally available patterns of behaviour which individuals had ready access to within their Bergsonian cones of memory. Any time that the individual encountered a new phenomenon, they were able to affectively situate it within a particular feedback loop, which consequently was able to provide information and guidance about the appropriate way to respond to situations that might actually be quite new or unusual to the person or group in question. Over a period of time, these particular present stimuli/memory/action affective feedback loops create patterns or social structures that initiate a sense of order and familiarity. In some instances, this can even go so far as to bring about path dependencies, whereby the structured patterns are so deeply embedded that it is difficult to step outside of them either individually or collectively. Whilst particular feedback loops may begin as the best available response to a problem at a particular period of time, we also know that time does not stand still, and the environments to which we respond are constantly changing. This means that even patterns and structures, which were excellent or necessary at one time, lose their efficiency as times change and may even eventually become harmful. Indeed, Florida (2002) is addressing just this question when he notes that the ability to step outside of path dependencies or 'think outside the box' is really useful for ensuring that societies can best adapt to new situations and stimuli. However, even if old orders no longer work effectively, Bergson shows us the safety and familiarity of the old. It is for this reason that Connolly (2002) notes how rigorously some societies guard against societal change and police the boundaries of their environments to try to restrict new material which might initiate this. Ultimately, however, such action can only be unsuccessful.

We know from Prigogine and Stengers (1985) that environmental change is inherent in life, which as a complex adaptive system, is continually needing to navigate, adapt, and evolve to the systemic changes that it encounters. At some points, these changes are small, requiring a minor adaptation. However, at other times, the changes are so huge that they break down the old structures and patterns of behaviour, representing what Prigogine and Stengers call a moment of chaos, from which order is yet to emerge. At this point and as Durkheim observes, the old norms, values, truths, practices, and patterns no longer achieve satisfactory results, and the individual is cast into the state of normlessness that he describes as Anomie. Quite literally, people do not know the way to respond and act toward the phenomenon that they encounter. Moreover, these patterns also represented temporary temporal linearities, which meant that as long as they held, individuals and societies were able to foresee a little of what the future holds. The end of the structure signals the end of being able to hold this security over what will happen next and a bifurcation point or a rupture which renders the future as yet to emerge and entirely unknowable. Whilst this might be interpreted as an exciting opportunity or space of possibility and becoming, it can also be perceived and experienced as a frightening time, hence Durkheim's observations about a concurrent rise in the rates of suicide at these moments. Indeed, anomic chaos has later been utilised as a way of examining and explaining criminal behaviour and the societal breakdown caused by poverty and inequality. It is also this state of vulnerability that was observed by Gest (2016) and Willett et al. (2019) in their studies of regional inequalities and the way that various regional assemblages have responded to them.

Over the preceding pages, we have created a temporal model of living matter which argues that life is a complex adaptive system. This means that the regional assemblage, composed as it is of a rich interaction of living matter, is also a complex adaptive system – or we might say a complex adaptive assemblage. We appreciate that life and our assemblages adapt and evolve. Sometimes this is an incremental process and other times it is more radical – what Deleuze and Guattari might call a 'line of flight'. We also know that both assemblages and complex adaptive systems operate in response to a vast array of environmental stimuli and that each aspect of these environments affects each other in a multiplicity of different ways. We know too that our region assemblages have emerged from divergent historical processes, which provide us with cultural variations and different structures of order which evolved as a response to questions about how best to navigate the plateau of assemblages within which they find themselves. As a consequence, the identities of assemblages are the product of extensive emergent, unreplicable processes that make each one unique in how it has become, as a response to its particular societal, environmental, cultural, economic, and historical conditions. In the next part of this chapter, we will look specifically at the economy as an adaptive assemblage, exploring the concepts and knowledges that we need in order to understand the evolutionary economy, what it means, how it grows, and the implications for the region assemblage.

EVOLUTION AND THE ECONOMY

The neo-classical economics that dominates much economic analysis of contemporary society is only one way of imagining how economies operate. Founded on an ontology drawn from Newtonian mechanics, it attempts to explain and predict phenomena through a sophisticated use of mathematical calculations (Boulding, 1981). However, as we learned from the failure of traditional approaches to predict the financial crisis of 2008, often these explanations or predictions are elusive, including for uneven development and methods to create more equal societies. The problem lies in the knowledge about how the world works that is inadequate at appreciating, understanding, and explaining the complexity of the social world (Boulding, 1981) and which underpins a particular mode of production at a given time (Marx, 2005). As an evolutionary economist, Boulding has an interesting thesis about why this might be, claiming that if Darwin's work had predated that of Smith, Ricardo, and Malthus, that these classical giants would have adopted an evolutionary viewpoint and founded the discipline of economics on the emergent properties of life.

Nevertheless, evolutionary economics is a strong discipline of its own, and evolutionary economic geography plays a significant role within the analysis of regional economics with a strong theoretical tradition. According to Witt (2008), there are two main approaches to Evolutionary Geography. First, there are analyses founded in neo-Schumpetarian ideas, which often use Darwinian biological metaphors, particularly with regard to natural selection. This recalls the work of Kenneth Boulding (1982) who likened business to biological organisms, adapting to and creating their own specific environmental niche, (multi)parenting new products. The second approach is based on evolutionary game theory. Witt might also have added a third framework, not entirely dissimilar to the first, which used complex adaptive systems as a means of understanding the organism of the economy within a newly emergent evolutionary economic geography (Martin and Sunley, 2007). Perhaps part of the reason that complex adaptive systems was starting to work for regional economists was in the way that it enables the region to be imagined as an organism that is bounded, but also connected to the socio-economic and political environment outside of the particular space or territory that is being examined (Meekes, 2017). In other words, it speaks to a way of understanding the region and the regional economy that imagines it in terms of assemblages and plateau.

Frequently, evolutionary economic geography scholars connect complexity theory with an evolutionary interpretation of resilience (Bristow and Healey, 2018; Boschma, 2015; Bristow and Healey, 2014; Dawley et al., 2010) using conceptual tools which intersect with those of complex adaptive systems, resilience, and Schumpetarian biological evolutionary economics. For our complex adaptive regional assemblages, this means that words such as 'knowledge' do more than connote perceptions, representations, and truths, but also are frequently paired with 'innovation', to denote sophistication and productivity within the regional economy (Moreno et al., 2005; Ozturk, 2018; Corradini, 2017; Malerba and McKelvy, 2018; Antonietti and Gambarotto, 2018; Bristow and Healey, 2018, Markey and Taylor, 2018). As we have already observed above, economic assemblages based on a high level of knowledge will be more productive and hopefully more innovative than the opposite, based on primary labour. Moreover, it will require a more skilled workforce in order to be able to service the industries developed and to facilitate innovation. Innovation better enables the adaptation which is essential if the economy is to be resilient and flourish (Bristow and Healey, 2018; Boschma, 2015; Bristow and Healey, 2014; Dawley et al., 2010; Pike et al., 2010). To this end, regions seek to improve the connectivity between these aspects of regional assemblages, developing feedback loops and affective interactions which spawn innovation systems (Corradini, 2017) and knowledge networks (Boschma, 2015). The aim is that these will facilitate lines of flight which will be able to create innovative economic knowledge and embed them into the regional assemblage, maintaining innovation systems.

An important facilitator – or on the converse – inhibitor of knowledge development and innovation within regional assemblages is the role of regional and industrial histories. Innovative regions need to have an open rather than a closed system (Meekes, 2017; Boschma and Frenken, 2011; Dawley et al., 2010), which allows new knowledges to enter, disrupt previous orders, patterns and structures, and as a consequence are able to develop new growth paths. In other words, creating the spaces of possibility for new ideas and innovation to be able to emerge (Boschma and Frenken, 2011; Martin and Sunley, 2006; Boschma, 2015; Dawley et al., 2010). As we have already learned from Prigogine and Stengers (1985), path dependency inhibits new ideas from taking shape and being implemented, which in turn has a deleterious effect on the production of new economic knowledge systems.

Taken in isolation, this could be interpreted that histories are harmful, but this is not the case at all. Actually, regional and peripheral context is vitally important as a way of explaining differential spatial development (Boschma and Frenken, 2011; Meekes, 2017) and the particular identities that have emerged around particular regional assemblages. It is the *path dependencies* derived from these histories which threaten to lock regions in to harmful practices (Boschma and Frenken, 2011). In short, regional specificities help to shape the distinctive knowledges (and therefore economies) that regional assemblages are able to use in order to amplify their economies. The temporal non-linearity at the heart of complex adaptive systems means that the best forms of peripheral development are those that emerge from within the region and from regional context (see also Prigogine and Stengers, 1981; Bedau and Humphries, 2008; Smith and Jenks, 2008). To bring this back to our earlier discussion about complex systems and the Bergsonian cone of memory, the identities and experiences of the individuals and communities within regional assemblages and which develop individual and collective feedback loops, within the cone, guide action and activity. The patterns and order that this action creates have an important function in as much as it helps to make the world within the assemblage intelligible, for individuals and communities to be able to understand how they can contribute, and then to be able to actively participate. To introduce economic knowledges within regional assemblages which are completely beyond and outside of the experiences, understandings, and identities of the people living there means that it becomes difficult for existing inhabitants to be able to work out how they can engage with these new knowledges. As a radical example, building a silicon-valley type of technology company in the middle of an agrarian, pre-industrial region (even if the infrastructure permitted it) might dramatically improve the gross domestic product (GDP) of the area, however it is highly unlikely that existing inhabitants would be able to participate in any meaningful way. If sharp and damaging inequalities were to be avoided, much work would need to be done (possibly over several generations) in order to construct a cultural backdrop within the collective regional Bergsonian cone which could create the requisite knowledges for existing inhabitants to be able to take up the new jobs on offer. In the meantime, there would be a considerable risk of the anomic dislocation and frustration of individuals and communities which have become forced to construct a new interpretive schema entirely from scratch. The new structures which emerge from such a radical disruption might indeed help to create a new order which is beneficial to all. But this is by no means a pre-given and carries enormous risks to vulnerable societies and communities. Following these ideas, a more productive (albeit potentially slower) way to economically transform region assemblages is to explore the existing cultural norms, identities, and affective meanings and consider what from these can be supported in order to improve the life chances and outcomes of individuals and communities in regional assemblages which are considered to require some support. This is an approach which embraces the emergent non-linearity of the complex adaptive assemblage and appreciates that whilst the eventual results might be unpredictable (so we have no way of knowing what we will eventually end up with), that with the requisite support to amplify regional strengths, that we might find a way to help region assemblages to flourish. Even if (as in the case of rural regions) we do not yet know quite what a flourishing rural economy actually looks like. This is the task to which this book is dedicated.

THE EVOLUTIONARY ECONOMIC ORGANISM

In order to understand this process more fully, we next can turn to a deeper examination of what Boulding (1981) meant when he described the economy as an organism. 'Knowledge' is created not, or not only through straightforward invention, but in the successful identification and exploitation of, and adaptation to, market 'niche'. We might also consider innovation to mean successfully building or maintaining a niche despite how the environment is evolving. For example, although there have been some modifications in the product over the years, the real innovation behind the longevity of Coca-Cola is arguably in their ability to maintain and expand their consumer loyalty through innovative marketing techniques and an excellent knowledge and understanding of their market. It is this level of intimate understanding of the structures, connections, flows of information, and institutions: the assemblages underpinning societies and economies which Boulding advocates, as opposed to expending effort attempting to predict future developments. This is because he likens economies, products, services, and objects to biological organisms which need to be able fit within and adapt to their niche.

Boulding begins in his discussion of evolutionary economics by likening the reproduction of 'social artefacts' or commodities, to biological reproduction, with the primary difference being that social artefacts are multi parental, involving many people in their (re)creation rather than the two parents of biological organisms. It is this 'multi-parental' nature which, unlike in nature, allows social artefacts to evolve as quickly as they do. The input of many different sets of knowledges (genes) into the production of a thing means that it can change (adapt) much more rapidly than a thing with only two parents or sets of genetic/knowledge input. The main difference between Bouldings biological species and commodities is that commodities do not contain their genetic code internally. Instead, for reproductive purposes, it is held elsewhere, in an interaction between the minds of the people that have worked on the commodity and the materials out of which it was made. Moreover, the interaction of commodities within their ecological system is mediated through price structure, which is governed by reciprocity, or what one party is willing to give for that object in the belief that it will be a reasonable exchange. In other words, whether a social artefact or commodity is able to either reproduce or adapt and evolve is dependent on the extent to which it is able to be sold in the market for a price that it is both cost effective and for which people are willing to pay.

'Knowledge' or 'know how' is likened to the genetic information structure of biological organisms and makes up one factor of production alongside energy and materials. It is this knowledge that is used to make commodities and sell them at prices where people are willing to pay which leads to constant mutations in the commodities themselves and also in their processes of production. These mutations lead to a rapid evolution in the development of social artefacts, facilitated by the market mechanism. This is understood as being like biological evolution with the primary difference being that that capital rather than biological survival determines economic development and emergence. The survival of social artefacts or their longevity depends, as with biological species, on finding a 'niche'. Darwin's (1910) theory of evolution is frequently miscommunicated in the shorthand that it is about the survival of the fittest. In actual fact, this phrase was first used by Herbert Spenser after reading Darwin's *The Origin of the Species*. Darwin's evolutionary theory actually observes that survival is founded on being *the best adapted*. This reminds one of the Aesop fable about the lion and the mouse, where the lion for all of its strength (or 'fitness') was unable to break itself free of the ropes that bound it. The mouse, on the other hand, despite being small and apparently weak and much more vulnerable, had equipment that was best adapted to the situation and so was able to use its tiny sharp teeth to nibble its way through the ropes and set the lion free that way. This is not a story about strength, it is one wherein the strengths of a biological or non-biological organism are able to find a niche in which to become situated, or exploit, and flourish.

In terms of assemblages of non-biological organisms, social artefacts, or commodities, we can take the example of Cornish mining engineer and pioneer of high-pressure steam, Richard Trevithick. On Christmas Eve 1801, Trevithick succeeded in turning an engine using 'strong' steam into a 'travelling engine' that carried six passengers through his home town of Camborne (Nuvolari, 2004). This event is immortalised in the song 'Camborne Hill', and as the inventor of the steam locomotive, which was to revolutionise early nineteenth-century transport globally, Trevithick should have been able to capitalise richly on his invention. Moreover, as is evidenced by early interest from mining companies, there was a ready market niche available without having to construct a new one based on an as-yet non-existent passenger market (Nuvolari, 2004). However, Trevithick died in poverty, having failed to make any money from his endeavours. The reason for this was twofold. First, used on the road, the locomotive was more expensive to run than a horse-drawn carriage. In order to maximise efficiency and make the locomotive cost-effective to run, it needed to run on metal rails. However, Trevithick's locomotive was invented before there was adequate metals technology to make iron of sufficient strength to carry the locomotive. Every time someone bought the technology, the rails buckled under the weight of the machine. It was not until several years later that metallurgy caught up, George Stephenson was able to capitalise on the available technology and take the credit for the invention of the steam train.

To return to Boulding, despite that Trevithick had the best (or earliest) know-how, he did not have an adequate available niche within the assemblage in which he operated, within which his work could survive and flourish. Not only was he ahead of his time, but he himself was not able to find a way to create that available niche. If Trevithick had been a metallurgical as well as an engineering genius or had been able to have brought together a team that included compound metals experts, then he might have been able to assemble all of the elements together in order to make his own niche work for him. This is because niche is not necessarily merely the passive consequence of chance, but the activities of people and things can actively work to create that space of possibility and potentiality that is represented in Boulding's niche. We can therefore best describe it as a gap within which an organism or social artefact can exist and develop, evolve and flourish.

THE EVOLUTIONARY REGIONAL ASSEMBLAGE

We currently imagine underperforming regions in very specific ways. This might be as spaces that need to develop clusters of innovation (see for example Bramwell et al., 2008) or where improvements should be made to local levels of skills (Lee et al., 2005). This might be achieved through the inward investment of capital and skills (Pike et al., 2006) or by finding ways to increase the competitiveness (Herrschel, 2010) of regional economies such as through endogenous growth (Rodriguez-Pose and Crescenzi, 2008) which broadly means supporting and developing local strengths. To tackle these inequalities, we might advocate improving some aspect of infrastructure, such as transport or communications (Crescenzi et al., 2016) or making investments in social and human capital (Shortall, 2004). We might also observe that rural regions are fundamentally different from metropolitan, 'core' spaces (De Souza, 2017) and that this is a large part of the problem. They lack population density, economies of scale and agglomeration, and apparently economic dynamism. Regardless of the diagnosis and potential cure, these approaches imagine that 'underperforming' or peripheral regional assemblages are 'lacking' in something which needs to be fixed and that global cities represent the standard of successful regional economies. However, another way of looking at the situation might be to imagine them as regional assemblages whose niche has altered with the passage of time and which have been unable to find a way to best adapt to the new social, political, and economic environment or plateau, within which these assembled communities now found themselves to be situated.

If we examine this 'problem' from the other way around, we also observe the struggles that economic development scholarship has frequently had, in considering the strengths of rural and/or peripheral regions. Consequently, we learn how countryside assemblages are frequently constructed as 'traditional', pastoral rural idyll (Lowe et al., 2012) which negatively impacts on the kinds of capacities, capabilities, and potentialities that rural regions are imagined to possess (Görmar and Lang, 2019; Willett, 2016; Eriksson, 2008; Jansson, 2003). All of these respond to a construction whereby the rural itself is the mal-adapted object to a metropolitan-centric contemporary global economy. The problem with this perspective is that first, in focusing on the negatives, it overlooks what rural economies might have that is special and which might be able to contribute in different ways. Second, it is (wrongly) assuming that the relationship that regional assemblages have with the niche within which economic plateaus operate is passive, and not something which might, through strong assessment of the spaces of possibility and potentiality within it, be shaped. Following on from this, we might also make the claim that inequalities between assemblages arise from inequalities in the kinds of knowledges that a society or group of people has related to their niche. Therefore, it is really important for the evolutionary adaptive assemblage to be able to have the capacity to be able to transfer (appropriate) knowledges around the region assemblage and for regions to be able to create the skills that are required in order to make, adapt to, and exploit emerging niche and spaces for possibility. This means that connectivity is vitally important in order to ensure the adaptations of region assemblages.

We have witnessed this in part with the economic development scholarship about innovation clusters (Bramwell et al., 2008; Cooke, 2002), communications and accessibility (Rodriguez-Pose and Crescenzi, 2008), the need to connect knowledge systems within sectors (Malerra and McKelvey, 2018; Antonietti and Gambarotto, 2018) or between policy and other actors (Bristow and Healey, 2014; Dawley et al., 2010). However, what current studies tend to miss from their analyses about knowledge transfer and communications is attention paid to the general public and ensuring that the wider population has a strong understanding about the opportunities, possibilities, and potentialities within regional economic assemblages. As the wealth of literature which focuses on the importance of human and social capital for regional economies helps to show (Casey and Christ, 2005; Evans and Synett, 2007; Lee et al., 2005), skills and the capacity to use those skills in local employment is really important. But what we don't yet see is how the regular public is to obtain accurate knowledges about the kinds of skills that are required in their localities for when they make decisions about what personal skills to invest in. However, as we have just observed above, the regular public are largely overlooked in analyses of regional economic assemblages and the transfer of knowledges. Moreover, popular perceptions about the impact of development programmes (see Willett et al., 2019) do not form part of impact assessment strategies which tend to be weighted more heavily towards employment statistics and GDP. Nevertheless, from our understanding of the affective interconnectivity of assemblages from the previous chapter, we also appreciate that regions are assembled from the interactions and interrelationships of *all* of their assembled parts. This means that even if regular publics are inadequately understood as contributors to the region, we need to have a strong appreciation of the dynamic interactions, capacities, flows of information, and knowledges across the entirety of the plateau developed around regions, people, organisations, and institutions.

The key to this argument is that it is not about having the fittest, strongest, or best economy, which can triumph over all competitors. In other words, rural regions are not just mal-adapted to contemporary twenty-first-century economies. Instead, survival lies in finding a place within the natural world or the market where the complex adaptive system of the rural regional assemblage can fit in and the way that this might occur is compromised by imagining rural or peripheral regions as lacking the attributes of our global cities. Instead, we need to be much better at finding the individual niche for rural regional assemblages. Knowledge in this sense has to include the ability to develop a knowledge and understanding of what the assemblage is, where this niche might be, and how the region might utilise that niche. Unlike the brutal notion of the 'survival of the fittest' which resonates with the market supremacy of neo-classicism and a growing emphasis towards stronger and more powerful cities, it means that actors within the socio-economic environment have a high degree of agency regarding their survival. They are able not only to make technological changes to the organism or social artefact but also to actually alter the environment within which they sit. This is a supply-side system whereby knowledge and innovation helps to produce new niches for a product. Therefore, if the existing market environment for a product weakens, people and businesses have the ability to evolve, explore new markets, and adapt to the changes required to take part in them rather than to begin again in a whole different environment. This means that there is also an intimate relation between the complex adaptive system, knowledge, and the environment.

The key (and recalling Bergson's cone of memory) is that things mutate, developing incrementally according to changes in the environment and building on the technological advances that have gone before, utilising memory or previously acquired knowledge which is located within the identity of the generating assemblage. Histories are important because of their role in downward causation, underpinning (although not determining) what the region assemblage and its economies can become. This is a perspective to which both Darwin and Boulding concur. For Darwin, once an evolutionary change has been made, its effect remains within a species for many generations, meaning that past changes remain in the DNA of present and future organisms. To deny this past inheritance or mutation, or to ignore it, is to suggest that a biological organism should alter a part of its physical make up. To expect to be able to radically alter the regional economic assemblage, invoking a complete break with what has gone before and adopting an entirely new strategy is as incongruous as expecting a herd of elephants to exist wild in the middle of a city. Adaptation to emerging niche needs to come from within the region, by facilitating, developing, and growing the lives and capacities of the people that already live there.

What this example enables us to see is that regional development can be viewed as a negotiation between the social (in terms of available workforce), available technologies, and the economic (in terms of structures and economic practices) that already exist. Economies and enterprises grow incrementally, and the successful developments are those that evolve into a complex negotiation with all of the differing aspects of the social, political, and knowledge environment. Conceptualising the region as an evolutionary organistic assemblage can allow us a means to explore how to improve peripheral economies whilst paying attention to the dynamic interconnectedness that is at the heart of regions as economic spaces. Moreover, this redefines what we mean by a 'periphery'. Rather than being an economically poor area at the fringe of the global economy, we can here conceive of it as a space which, for whatever reason, has at this point in time not been particularly successful at adapting to changing global economic and political conditions. This nuance is what we mean by 'successful' development. We might add that as well as creating a more equal society between core and periphery, and within the periphery itself; successful development is that which is able to evolve and adapt its niche to shifting environmental conditions.

IS THERE A ROLE FOR POLICY?

Looking at regions as complex adaptive assemblages poses two problems for policy. First, that in a world of unpredictability, what kind of policy solutions can be offered, and second, if struggling regions and economies are the ones that are failing to adapt, is supporting them counterproductive? That the evolutionary process simply weeds out the biological or ideational organisms which are no longer suited to the contemporary world? I am going to argue that there *is* a role for policy, but that we need a different kind of approach, and also that we *should* support regional assemblages which are struggling to adapt because to do otherwise carries important affective impacts on the wider assemblages within which regions are connected.

In what Connolly (2011) calls 'a world of becoming' and as evolutionary economic geographers know (Bristow and Healey, 2018; Boschma, 2015; Bristow and Healey, 2014; Dawley et al., 2010), it is not possible to alter the futures of regional assemblages by simply adopting success stories from elsewhere as a model and expecting to be able to create replicable triumphs. Instead, developing complex adaptive regional assemblages needs to embrace non-linearity and know that the small changes made in the present will lead to emergent, unpredictable, but hopefully improved outcomes. It is also to accept that we have no way of knowing if these outcomes are ones to which we might now consider desirable. However, whatever outcomes do occur, they will be embedded in places, identities, and how people in those places understand the world. Changes that people make in these identities can then happen on the basis of realising how to adapt in order to meet contemporary challenges rather than by force. In order to do this, we first need to ensure that knowledges and ideas are able to flow freely inside, outside, and between assemblages and that the assemblage then has the capacity to be able to act on this information. It is of crucial importance that people, organisations, institutions, and businesses have a thorough and accurate appreciation of what the interior and exterior environments look like, in all of its complexity. This requires systems of affective feedback loops connecting assemblages within the plateau and connecting them to sites beyond the region. As we know from Boulding (1981), it is this kind of accurate understanding that creates the conditions for evolution to occur in the first place. To give one example, it means that when changes do occur – for example, a new line of flight creates an exciting space of possibility – that people, organisations, industries, and businesses know enough to be able to get involved, participate, and amplify. As a consequence, a line of flight that might once have withered away, for lack of affective resonance drawing people in, might be able to embed itself, develop itself into its own assemblage, and contribute to the evolving region organism. But knowledge flows on their own are not enough, and here the people involved in the region assemblage need to be able to bounce off of spaces of possibility, have the capacity to take them forward, and the willingness to take on any emerging new ideas. Policy can have a role in all of these places.

But *should* policy get involved? This is a nod to the fact that unlike the ideas of 'progress' underpinning enlightenment thought and all positions that arise from it, there is no guarantee that the futures that become will be futures that we now consider to be in progress. Perhaps an example here can be found in the debate raised by New Zealand Prime Minister Jacinda Ardern who in 2019 announced that economic statistics would no longer emphasise economic growth but well-being (Young-Powell, 2019). This poses a direct challenge to orthodoxies over what has traditionally been considered to be 'progress' in economic development. This illustrates how notions of 'progress' in themselves need to be considered as an open system that allows for adaptation to contemporary questions. The trick is in ensuring that the version of progress being used is one that can broadly be supported by the assemblages within which such knowledges emerge from, and are situated. In some respects, this also underscores the problem of linear, teleological policy. By the time that we have steered the ocean-liner and changed our direction, our goals might out of necessity have had to change for a whole range of environmental reasons. Perhaps the COVID-19 pandemic serves to illustrate that, for example, a 10-year plan developed in 1997 would have had to navigate the extraordinary rapidity of the technological revolution which in this period alone went from the internet being the preserve of a relatively few people, through to wireless connectivity, and the birth of the smartphone.

The other reason why we might question the need for policy's involvement relates to the fact that we might choose to take a more *laissez-faire* approach and argue that regional-organisms that flop have failed to adapt or recreate their environments, and therefore display themselves as evolutionarily unfit. Aside from the moral questions that this poses (such as is it acceptable to our version of civilisation to allow people to suffer on an individual level, on this basis), it also poses problems for the assemblages which are connected to struggling region assemblages. This was the question that we considered at the beginning of the chapter and to which we now return. Struggling regions affect the environment within which all connecting assemblages operate. This affects everybody's possibilities, potentialities, and adaptive capacities. As a consequence, it is in everyone's interests to ensure that we are all able to move forward together.

Chapter 4

Southwest Virginia and Cornwall

Constructing the Complex Adaptive Regional Assemblage

The previous two chapters draw regions as complex, adaptive assemblages, operating like an organism in an intricate and ongoing communication between the region, all of its connected parts, and the environments within which it is situated. The complex adaptive region assemblage seeks out ways that it can flourish within the niche that it is situated – or looks for a new niche within which it can participate and, hopefully, thrive. Different regions prioritise things differently, will have divergent ideas about what this flourishing looks like, and the balance between the lives of people in the location, the economies, and the natural and biological environments within which communities are located. These divergent ideas are founded on their different histories, as well as different environmental conditions. For example, as we saw in the introduction, the U.S. rural policy environment has tended toward a more individualistic approach than in the United Kingdom and mainland Europe, who for reasons of historical development have evolved a more community welfare-based approach (Shucksmith et al., 2012).

As we appreciate from the previous chapters, supporting the rural and peripheral complex adaptive assemblage is an important space for policy involvement, because regional inequality is bad for everyone. It is destructive for communities which experience troubled lives whereby people are unable to realise their talents, and it is problematic for the wider assemblages to which they are connected for the lack of the contribution that struggling regions are unable to make to the collective. Moreover, such regions also require additional tangible and tacit support from other assemblages, and the problems of regional inequality can spill over into connected assemblages. But in the adaptive world of evolutionary rather than linear temporalities, policy solutions need to be able to embrace the emergent unpredictability of the complex adaptive regional assemblage, facilitating 'becoming' through a deep understanding of the region. From a research perspective, this means that before we can explore what needs to happen within rural or peripheral regional assemblages that are struggling over how to best adapt to the contemporary economy, we need to be able to develop an in-depth understanding of such regions starting from the bottom up. We appreciate that innovations and support need to grow from strengths that already exist if new developments are to be inclusive. But first, we need to understand what these regional strengths might look like. We also need to be willing to accept that these strengths are likely to vary from region to region and that at the beginning of our inquiry what emerges as strengths might be very different from what we might previously imagine to be strengths. In short, we need to be able to see and accept regions for what they are, clear of our own personal assessments of value.

This is the task which the remainder of this book explores. It asks what we see if we look at rural peripheral regions as complex adaptive assemblages and use this as a basis to consider how complex adaptive regional assemblages might evolve. Although I use two case studies from two nation states, this is not a comparison in the strictest sense of the word but is more of a juxtaposition (Hantrais, 2009). It is simply an examination of what is made visible if we look at two similar spaces through a novel lens. Perhaps contradictorily in an approach which borrows from an ethnographical, anthropological tradition for its cultural enquiry, in order to celebrate regional differences; this book finds some points of similarity and overlay which could almost be considered to be tentative universalisms (see also Hantrais, 2009). However, it is for other studies to examine any causal or correlatory links between, for example, excellent rural public transportation and communications. Indeed, other remote or peripheral locations may have very different sets of contexts and cultures which raise different sets of issues. The point of this study is to provide a new way of seeing, which might be able to lead to new ways of doing things.

In this particular study, I place people and people's lives at the heart of the research. This is not to say that I think that people are the most important actors within rural assemblages. Far from it, as explained in chapter 2, regional assemblages are a complex interaction between people, natural, physical, institutional, and ideational environments, and the histories that each location has experienced. All of these things interact with the cultural frameworks through which people navigate their worlds and through which regions are both constructed and produced. The study will consider environmental, cultural, and infrastructural assemblages, too, but will place people's lives at the heart of the project. This signals another point of divergence with more traditional analyses of regional economies in as much as that this research focuses on the lives of ordinary people and how they connect with economies. It is the contention of this book that the ways that people navigate their natural and cultural environments is at the heart of the complex adaptive region assemblage. People use their knowledges of the region assemblage in order to assess possibilities and opportunities, which have a disproportionate impact on many other parts of the economic assemblage. To illustrate, whilst a region might have a (quietly) thriving sector with much potential to develop new and exciting lines of flight, if people don't know about it, they might still imagine that regional fortunes are best served by an environmentally destructive extractive industry which has become folded into their culture through having been a part of their economy for decades. In this hypothetical example, the newer industry might then begin to struggle for lack of input, because the role of cultural memory will have had a disproportionate impact on how people are – and are able to engage in new and emergent opportunities which are happening in the locality.

Consequently, the research that forms the remainder of this book sought out to understand better the phenomenological meanings through which participants in the case study areas understand their worlds (Bergson, 2004; Mead, 1934; Goffman, 1959; Blumer, 1969). By this I mean that I tried to understand how participants situated the things that they told me within their contextual worlds of meaning. As an example, sometimes in the United States I was told that President Obama was a communist. To someone from a European background, this felt like a very unfamiliar conjunction. In fact, the idea that *any* of U.S. politics might possibly be able to be equated with communism, as Europeans imagine it, is quite a stretch. However, it made sense to the people that I was speaking to and so it was important to explore that. It transpired that this statement relied on the conflation of communism with totalitarianism.

To understand this better, we already appreciate from chapter 2 that assemblages are 'affective' or that the things, ideas, objects, and meanings within assemblages impact or affect other things, ideas, meanings, and objects. Words are part of this affective activity. For example, as an academic, I imbue the word 'paper' with a set of meanings associated with academic publishing. Part of the affective attachment incorporates *feelings* or the emotions that stick to the surfaces of words and transfer to others (see Ahmed, 2004). As a consequence, as an academic, when I imagine a paper (the object), I might experience a whole range of emotions including excitement, fascination, curiosity, and even stress. A non-academic might attach a whole other set of meanings to the word 'paper', maybe locating it in terms of news periodicals and the feelings that they associate with newspapers rather than a scholarly research article. Unless an observer explores deeper what is meant by the object, 'a paper', they will understand none of it.

More than this, the transfer of words, emotions, and meanings surrounding objects is described as an 'economy' in a state of a constant flow of movement which means that words, ideas, and meanings impact on each other; 'stick' to each other; and continue to transfer between each other, developing new constellations of meaning. Sometimes, particular meanings literally become embodied in certain literal or ideational objects. Consequently, perhaps the biggest affective marker that I might feel is connected to the concept 'communism' would be an extreme form of 'socialism' based on a probably inaccurate interpretation of Marx. In my mind, I imagine 'socialism' as part of an affective economy which incorporates ideals such as equality, justice, and fairness, with the aim of producing a classless society and a more fair distribution of resources derived from the abolition of capitalism. From this perspective, therefore, whilst Obama might be imagined as having been motivated by social justice, it is a long way between social justice and communism, with many variants of social democracy in the middle. Bearing this in mind, when people expressed to me the opinion that Obama was a communist, they were not drawing on the same (or even a similar) affective economy or set of meanings to the one that I imagined. Instead, the tight affective linkages that they made associated communism with totalitarianism.

This is understandable if one remembers how especially in the Cold War times, communist states linked to the USSR were juxtaposed against the liberal democratic freedoms of the 'West'. The imaginary around the totalitarian dictatorships of the USSR involved a central system of planning which meant that ordinary people were unable to shape or have any input into decisions made around them. The liberal democracy, on the other hand, ensured that the freedom for the individual to do as they pleased was at the heart of their polity, and as a part of this, citizens could shape governmental decisions. For this particular group of people, Obama was discursively constructed as creating a heavier regulatory environment. Regardless of the rationale behind regulation or its necessity, this was able to be imagined as something which impinged on libertarian freedoms, and which consequently was able to neatly slide into totalitarianism, and from there to communism. Whilst an observer might or might not agree with how this set of meanings was produced, it at least enables an understanding of the rationale rather than an outright rejection of a statement that might otherwise appear to be strange. What this example shows us is of the importance of doing much more than simply listening to the words that people tell us, but also to understand the contextual worlds that individuals within their communities utilise to give meaning to these words. To relate back to our complex adaptive systems of affective assemblages, it is important to be able to situate the things that people say into the individual and collective cones of memory from which they draw (See Bergson, 2004; Connolly, 2006) and the assemblages which these objects are situated. In this way, we can try (as much as is possible) to develop an accurate and sensitive set of understandings based on the subjective position of people who participated in the research rather than to impose a set of meanings from my own world on to those that I observe.

If this study was going to be able to meet its aims therefore and explore peripheral, rural regions as complex adaptive assemblages before considering how these assemblages might best adapt to twenty-first-century economies, then first the research needed to get as close as possible to understanding the opinions, experiences, and meanings of ordinary members of the general public. This needed to happen *before* I started to explore how policy-makers and people engaged in supporting the region perceive the problem rather than beginning with policy-makers and allowing their reflections to over-determine the understanding of the general publics' perceptions of the region. Such an approach required a 'bottom up' methodology, and for this reason, I based this study on the principles of Grounded Theory (Strauss et al., 2008; Charmaz, 2006). Literally, this method 'grounds' the analysis in the reflective understandings of respondents, keeping as open mind as possible throughout the research process and using participants' meanings in order to generate further avenues for exploration, and later theoretical claims. In practical terms, this means that the research process is like a 'wheel' rather than linear (Burnham et al., 2004), representing a continually reflective method with a constant internal critique regarding the relationship between the methods, the findings, and the question. Evidently, the study has not attempted to create objective truths about the areas examined but to relate the narratives and connectivities which permeate the case study regions.

This approach to research inquiry played an important role in the selection of the two case studies. As is clear from above, understanding meanings is a very important part of this study. Therefore, it meant that from the outset, it felt important to know and understand the case study locations as well as possible. The case study of Cornwall that I use here is one such study. Located in the southwest of the United Kingdom, I have researched aspects of Cornwall, identity, and economy for many years now (Bosworth and Willett, 2011; Willett, 2013, 2016) and more recently, have started to consider it as a complex adaptive assemblage to think about how that might help us to make development more sustainable, fair, and resilient (Willett and Lang 2018; Willett 2019). Cornwall therefore was an obvious choice. Whilst this is true, knowing an area extremely well has its limitations and risks. The first of these relates to what Bergson (2004) discusses as the 'cloaking' effect of memory on perception, and the second (albeit related) question that this raises relates to path dependencies.

Although we might argue that there is such a thing as objective reality (see Merleau-Ponty, 2004), we are never able to actually know this objective reality because quite literally, the cloaking effect of perception covers all things that we observe in a layer of memories through which an object is perceived,

imagined, and interpreted. Each moment of our lives is split into two elements – the actual, and the virtual, and which correspond to pure perception
and memory. This means that we see not only what we perceive but also what
we *think* that we perceive. For example, we all know that an ordinary sheet of
plain printer paper is white. Therefore, we will describe it to others as a white
piece of paper. However, if we view it under some type of interior lighting,
our eyes will actually perceive the paper as pale yellow or as grey. Our brain
then *tells* our eyes that what we are seeing is white because virtual perception
is cloaking actual perception. At the most extreme end of this, it is perfectly
feasible to walk in to a familiar room but not notice some small changes that
have occurred such as furniture having been added or removed, because our
perception of the room is overlaid with a memory about how it should look –
or at least, how it used to look. In this example, the viewer is literally perceiv-
ing the object in the past rather than in the present. A similar thing can happen
as researchers examining something or somewhere over which we have
become extremely familiar – we can end up missing what we observe because
the things that we perceive are becoming too heavily overlaid with memories.
At the same time, however, and as we already know, familiarity can lead to an
in-depth understanding which might be missed from more cursory analyses.
To counter this problem, I decided to pursue a case study in an area that was
completely new to me, and this newness could be compounded by working in
another country entirely. To gain the desired depth of understanding, I needed
to select a rural region in an English-speaking country as my other languages
are not sufficient to be able to conduct this type of study. For this, I chose the
United States and found an area in the southwest of Virginia which is under-
explored and is struggling to adapt to the significant changes that it is seeing
in local economies. Below I will detail the characteristics of the two regions,
providing statistical information and how they are constructed in academic
knowledges.

SWVA IN STATISTICS

For the purposes of this book, SWVA overlays the VA GO (Growth and
Opportunity) Region One, although there was a little bit of a stretch beyond
this for pragmatic purposes, overlaying with the porosity of boundaries and
experience. The region is highly rural with a population dispersed between
urban centres and deep, steep sections of the stunningly beautiful southern
Appalachian mountain range. It is bisected by the I-81 highway, which offers
an easy 70 mile journey from the far southwest, to the eastern edges of the
region in Wythe county. However, travel is less easy between and amongst
the communities deeper in the mountains. For example, from Ewing in the far

southwest tip, bordering Tennessee and Kentucky, it takes 1¾ hours to travel the 81 miles to Bristol, the nearest point on the I-81. Despite some four-lane highways throughout these areas, travel between more 'sheltered' communities furthest from the interstate is still lengthy and time-consuming. Region One borders the states of Kentucky, West Virginia, North Carolina, and Tennessee and carries a population of 389,173. This is expected to decline by about 5 per cent over the next decade—0.4 per cent annually. However, the wider labour shed area contains 1.3 million people, and this number is expected to see a 1 per cent per annum increase.

In common with many rural areas, the population is ageing as younger people move outside in an attempt to seek better opportunities (Deller et al., 2019). This has the effect of skewing things like educational statistics, as more highly skilled young people tend to have more capacity to move, making it appear that local schools do not do an effective job in teaching young people (GOVA, 2019). Per capita income is $22,535 compared to $31,177 nationally, and although it has grown over the past two years (by 2.8%), this growth is below the national average of wage growth (4.4%). Average annual wages at the time of writing stand at $34,678 compared to $55,594 nationally. Poverty levels stand at 18.3 per cent compared to 14.6 nationally, but this has improved from 19.2 per cent two years previously. Despite a 0.2 per cent dip in employment growth (compared to a state-wide rise of 1.6%), unemployment stands at 3.9 per cent compared to a U.S. average of 3.7 per cent, and labour market participation is at 50.33 per cent.

There is an increasing level of educational attainment, rising since 2017 from 16.4 per cent, 25–64-year-olds having a bachelor's degree, to 17 per cent. Over the same period, the number with an associate's degree increased by 0.5 per cent to 10 per cent and the region had the biggest drop state-wide for people without a high-school diploma, declining by 1 per cent to 14.9 per cent. Although there was a 0.6 per cent increase in the number of students with a bachelor's degree, this still takes the overall average to 17 per cent, the second lowest in the Commonwealth of Virginia, which has an average of 31.81 per cent with a bachelor's degree, with a range between 16.4 per cent and 59.1 per cent. For jobs that do not require high levels of education, the most in-demand jobs by volume of employment advertisements were for retail salespeople, retail supervisors, and heavy truck drivers. This latter may reflect an emphasis on distribution. For example, the Washington County Economic Development team (2018) showcases that 40 per cent of the U.S. population lives within 1 days drive (500 miles) of the region, and there is also an easy access from many state capitals. For persons with a bachelor's degree or more, the highest numbers of job advertisements were for nurses and speech-language pathologists. In 2019, medical and health service managers also were a frequently posted professional job vacancy.

GOVA Region One has seen a dramatic shift in its economic base over recent years. Employment in the once buoyant (coal) mining industries has halved since 2001 in the Mount Rogers Planning District (MRPDC) part of GOVA1 (MRPDC, 2018) and again in the MRPDC area, manufacturing has dropped by 40.8 per cent between 1990 and 2010, leaving at that time, 14,215 jobs (MRPDC, 2013). However, advanced manufacturing is still a significant employment sector, currently employing 17,134 individuals in the whole GOVA1 region, with a well above average earned wage of $43,828 (GOVA, 2019).

Alongside food and beverage manufacturing (employing 1,413 persons), other target industries are energy and minerals (employing 4,023 persons); Coal mining (2,514) and Information Technology (2,041). Regional strengths are in small business start-ups, opportunities for higher education, a strong work ethic amongst the labour force, a significant cluster in health care and services, and low rates of taxation. The level of business start-ups is an important point, which contributes to an overall measurement for innovation, using the number of jobs created by companies that are less than 5 years old; 20 per cent of all job creation is by young companies. This outstrips U.S. averages. However, the population is also characterised by increasing poor health, drug abuse, and high levels of disability and poverty. Moreover, there has been a decline in new business formation combined with a lack of funding, grants, investment capital, and incubator space. The lack of funding is despite regional investment of $1.1 billion from the Virginia Tobacco Commission. Limited access to high-speed internet is another challenge. Again, fibre exists in the region, but this does not reach all. Finally, the report acknowledges that there is a structural need to create an entrepreneurial ecosystem which can help businesses to expand and grow. This includes understanding the examination of niche markets and funding opportunities.

The last point to mention here relates to the domination of road travel. Although freight rail utilises the area, there is currently no passenger rail service inside the SWVA GO VA Region 1 area. The nearest railhead is at Roanoke 70 miles beyond the limits of Wythe county. There is an intercity bus service between Blacksburg and Washington Union station, but Blacksburg is 45 miles outside of the area. A report by Bristol City Council (2019) found that the intercity bus service doubled its expected passenger numbers in its first full year of operation and that the new railheads at Lynchburg (2009) and Roanoke (2017) exceeded expectations. As the next biggest conurbation along the I-81 corridor, Bristol hopes to bring passenger rail back to the city to service its business and tourism base. However, at the time of writing, the rail company Amtrak is reluctant to extend its operations.

SWVA IN SCHOLARSHIP

Southwest Virginia as a stand-alone unit is heavily under-represented in the scholarship. Moreover, it not only has many economic differences from the rest of the Commonwealth of Virginia, it also has many cultural differences, too. Consequently, in this section, I include research about Appalachia more generally. Here a note of caution needs to be made as the Appalachian Regional Commission defines the mountain range as extending from the far south-west of New York State, deep into Alabama and Mississippi (Appalachian Regional Commission – ARC, 2020). Clearly, these are extremely divergent cultural areas, not even unified by the Appalachian Trail, a long-range hiking route extending from Maine to the north of Georgia. However, *culturally*, Appalachia tends to refer to the region of Virginia's Blue Ridge Mountains to Tennessee and North Carolina's Great Smoky Mountains.

In the early days of the English settlement of Virginia, the regions' abundance of trees meant that supporters of colonial expansion could claim that it was a 'wood frontier' which could ameliorate the fears of many in early modern England that there was a problem with wood scarcity (Pluymers, 2016). Despite centuries of logging and replanting, the region is still heavily forested, although with newer growth trees following the harvesting of ancient ones. Early settlers were predominantly Anglo Saxon and German, but the level to which current populations ascribe to their ancestry changes over time. Satterwhite (2005) notes that in the early 1980s, people tended to highlight their German ancestry and only 20 per cent their British forebears. In the intervening years, diasporic revivalism and differentiated codes of idealised pasts have led to people being happy to claim and foreground their Scots and Irish ancestors. These shifts in the cultural imaginary have also led to rehabilitation with the extensive Native American history, which was absorbed into place names and medicines (Thompson, 2006). Both Satterwhite (2005) and Thompson (2006) mention how these shifting allegiances have meant that some cultural groups   such as African Americans and Native Americans – have when it was possible to find ways to 'pass' as white. The irony is that many of the people from SWVA that I interacted with over the course of this book had a keen interest in Native American ancestry, although often this was lost beneath the historic weight of generational shame. Early settlers (white, and African American) brought with them a variety of musical styles, which has been enfolded into the backdrop of the everyday, and country music (together with its histories) infuses the cultural landscape of the present (Satterwhite, 2005). These histories are memorialised in the regions like Smithsonian museum in Bristol and in things like the Crooked Road heritage trail, which as a 'vernacular expression of lived authenticity' (Chaney, 2013) supports, showcases, and memorialises the importance of music to local cultural expression.

Over the past century, coal has been an important part of the socio-economic structure of the region. It is narrated as being part of what the area gives back to the nation (Fabriant and Fabricant, 2018), and as the industry became increasingly mechanised, it has shifted from burrowing into the side of the mountains, to, literally, the removal of entire mountains. Fabricant and Fabricant (2018) report that, in central and southern Appalachia, this has led to the loss of over 500 mountains covering over 1 million acres of land. The steep decline of the coal industry has led to an increasing desperation as locals who choose to stay are forced to resort to 'demeaning' 'Walmart' type service sector jobs that fail to provide the sense of dignity and pride afforded by coal. However, the environmental destruction of mountaintop removal practices has complicated the 'King Coal' narrative, creating a lived experience which has prompted some local residents to join grass-roots environmental organisations protesting King Coal practices (Bodenhamer, 2016). Moreover, mining conditions and practices unique to the area mean that 20.6 per cent of persons, who have been coal miners for over 25 years, have Pneumoconiosis. This figure is 10 per cent more than miners in similar employment in other parts of the United States (Blackley et al., 2018). Popularly called 'black lung' (Gaventa, 2019), Huttlinger et al. (2004) find that despite having an above U.S. average resident to healthcare provider ratio, residents of coal-producing parts of SWVA have poorer health outcomes and greater morbidity.

It is easy to imagine how the poor levels of health experienced by some Appalachians feeds in to popular negative stereotypes and portrayals of 'white trash' (Young, 2017), hillbilly's and rednecks (Roggenkamp, 2008; Heilman, 2004); tall, gaunt, incestuous, and moonshine-making (Foster and Hummel, 1997). Heilman (2004) notes that unlike other marginalised groups in the United States (possibly because of the isolated rural nature of the landscape), Appalachian settlers never formed any kind of collective grouping to make their issues more widely known. Heilman (2004) goes on to argue that part of the reason for this might be because historically, the vast majority of local wealth and resources was concentrated amongst a handful of elites. Settlers to these unproductive mountainous areas were often vulnerable people – involuntary migrants who had endured some level of servitude. The term 'poor white trash' is not new, but dates back to the 1860s, building on the negative characterisations of moral depravity of settlers back as far as 1737. There is also considerable scholarship about how regional stigmatisations are reproduced through local dialects. Dunstan and Jaeger (2016) discuss how young people in educational settings feel that their accents exposed them to prejudice and stereotypes, and the experience of discrimination leads many to modify their speech as they move into more professional circles (Reed, 2018). However, Satterwhite (2005) cautions that there are problems and nuances in the discourse around Appalachian victimisation, which can code to an idealised white past rather than a more cohesive story about collective economic exploitation. Furthermore, a binary opposite narrative exists which positions Appalachians as 'noble savages' (Roggenkamp, 2008), noble, stalwart, rugged and independent mountaineers, completely attuned to their environments (Williams, 2002). In an analysis of popular fiction, Satterwhite (2015) finds that regional fiction idealises the locality as rooted and static, an authentic America protected from contemporary commercialism.

The sense of local agency hinted by Satterwhite (2005) is echoed in the tale that Gaventa (2019) tells about how the grinding poverty, poor health care, and schools of the early 1980s was facilitated by the fact that 90 per cent of the land was owned by a secretive, extremely wealthy, corporate empire. For Gaventa (2019), although voter turnouts are extremely low, there is a high rate of community activism as individuals collectivise to form campaigns about a whole range of local issues. These are communities that can and do fight back against exploitation, but in their own independent ways. Whilst the quality of schools is no longer in question, rural Appalachia is still an under-represented cultural group in higher education and in high-paying job roles (Carrico et al., 2019). Part of the reason for this lies in problems of rurality, but also in the strength of family ties found throughout the region (see also Lavender-Stott et al., 2018; Salva et al., 2019), including multi-generational families living in close proximity. This strong family required help to sustain deep rural living. The region in general is still underrepresented in terms of access to health care (Salva et al., 2019) and there is a strong relationship between unemployment and substance abuse (Thornton and Deitz-Allyn, 2010). Finally, an attachment to place and nature is signalled by Trozzo et al. (2019) in their discussion about knowledges of forest food and medicine. Here, foragers with a multi-generational family connection to the locality tended to look for plants which they could sell in order to generate income. Incomers also forage the mountains, but looking for plants which they could use in the home.

CORNWALL IN STATISTICS

Cornwall is significantly smaller in size to SWVA. It is a peninsula on the far south-west of the United Kingdom. Its border with neighbouring Devon is 52 miles long, and most of it follows the River Tamar which is only 4 miles short of the north coast. In other words, Cornwall is nearly an island off of the coast of the United Kingdom. From east to west (Launceston to Lands End), it is 79

miles long, and most of the area (with the exception of the east) has a distance
of around 20 miles from the south coast to the north coast, tapering to a point
at Lands End. Its population is growing. The latest statistics (for 2018) place
it as 566,000, up from 525,000 in 2008 and 467,700 in 1990 (NOMIS, 2020).
The success of Cornwall's population growth is driven by its popularity as
a visitor destination and its place in the British imaginary as a coastal, rural,
idyll (Willett, 2016). The high cost of housing has been a significant problem
for decades. Immediately before the COVID-19 pandemic, Cornish average
wages stood at 84.5 per cent of U.K. averages, at £26,229 per annum. This
has narrowed from 76 per cent in 2008. Conversely, the gender pay gap has
widened from 83.7 per cent of U.K. average female wages in 2008, to 81 per
cent in 2019 figures (NOMIS, 2020b). Female workers earn 72 per cent of the
overall U.K. average. On the other hand, average house prices currently stand
at £237,540, over nine times average annual incomes. In the United Kingdom
as a whole, average house prices are at £230,332, 7.5 times average incomes
(Land Registry, 2020).

   In terms of jobs, 263,800 people are in employment (out of 272,500 economically active), with 19.5 per cent of these being self-employed. The rate
of self-employment among the economically active is 5 per cent higher than
in the United Kingdom as a whole. The highest category of economic inac-
tivity is for the long-term sick (30% of the economically inactive compared
to a UK 23%) and with 3 per cent more retired people, 3.3 per cent fewer
home-makers, and 11.6 per cent fewer students. By occupation, 37.9 per cent
of employees fall into the highest qualified professions, nearly 10 percentage points less than in the United Kingdom. The most significant difference
amongst the lower-skilled occupations is for skilled trades-people. Here we
find a 5 per cent increase between Cornwall and the United Kingdom, which
might go some way to reflecting the high number of self-employed people in
Cornwall. Interestingly, the level of skills in the labour market is not particularly different to in the rest of Britain; 2.7 per cent fewer have degree-level
qualifications or above (NVQ level 4), whilst 1.8 per cent fewer members of
the Cornish labour force have no qualifications at all. In common with U.K.
trends, the workforce has become increasingly skilled over time (NOMIS,
2020c).

   The highest employment sectors are wholesale and retail trade: repair
of motor vehicles and motorcycles (17.7% of all employed), accommodation and food service activities (16.3%), and human health and social work
activities (15.8%). Perhaps reflecting the buoyancy of the Cornish tourism
industry, the percentage of persons working in accommodation and food
service activities is the biggest difference between Cornwall's and the U.K.'s
employment sectors. Moreover, although strategically Cornwall is focussing
heavily on the digital tech sector, there are 60 per cent fewer Information

and Communication jobs in Cornwall currently (1.7% of the available jobs compared to the UK average 4.2%), and nearly half professional, scientific, and technical activities opportunities in Cornwall compared to the United Kingdom (4.8% to 8.7%). Cornwall's emphasis on the creative industries *is* one of its relative strengths compared to the United Kingdom as a whole, which has 25 per cent fewer arts, entertainment and recreation opportunities (3.3% of Cornish employment compared to 2.5% of the UK). Both IT and the creative sectors are growing compared to the United Kingdom, whilst the numbers of professional, scientific, and technical jobs are shrinking in real and comparative terms (NOMIS, 2020c). A total of 88.4 per cent of all businesses in Cornwall have between 0 and 9 employees (21,435). Whilst this figure sounds high, it places Cornwall in the lower third of the U.K. Local Authority Areas to have this number of small businesses. A total of 10.1 per cent of all businesses have 10–49 employees (2,455), and only 70 Cornish businesses have over 250 employees.

Despite having general parity with the United Kingdom in terms of workforce skills, Cornwall's economy is significantly less productive. In 2017, the Gross Value Added (GVA) per head of population was 67.7 per cent of the U.K. average, and per job at 69.2 per cent of U.K. averages. Consequently, regardless of the buoyancy of other statistics, addressing the productivity challenge is one of Cornwall's immediate questions. This productivity gap is something that strategic planners have tried to address over the past two decades during which, because of its low GDP compared to EU averages, Cornwall received £1billion from European Union Structural Funding investment between 1999 and 2018. Part of this investment was used to provide high-speed broadband throughout the region, helping to combat the region's rural peripherality by being better digitally connected. The excellent nature of telecommunications in the area has led to a strategic emphasis on Cornwall's digital economy. For several decades, remote-working or 'communicating' to work from 'electronic tele-cottages' has been a part of the policy arsenal (Perry, 1993: 59), but this has become increasingly possible over the past decade. According to Tech Nation's 2018 report, Cornwall's digital tech sector is showing 'impressive growth' with no signs of slowing down (Software Cornwall, 2020). The Cornwall and Isles of Scilly Local Enterprise Partnership strategic document *Vision 2030* (Cornwall and Isles of Scilly Local Enterprise Partnership, 2017) seeks to harness innovation and creativity in order to deliver a more productive economy. It promises to invest in research and development in high priority clusters: targeting support for the underemployed or on low pay to be able to access skills and training, linking education providers and businesses in areas of deprivation, and improving local transportation. They also promise to capitalise on Cornwall's world-class cultural environment and invest in natural capital leading to environmental growth. The 'Vision' sees key economic clusters in aerospace, digital innovation, creative and cultural sectors, education, advanced engineering, marine energy, food and livestock.

CORNWALL IN SCHOLARSHIP

To say that Cornwall does not enjoy adequate scholarly attention would be paranoid. Its strong local/national identity has meant that it has had a university-led Institute of Cornish Studies since the early 1970s. However, it *has* been rather under-represented in U.K.-wide scholarly discourse (see also Payton, 2002). Consequently, when Michael Hechter (1975) was writing about the Celtic peripheries, he found a neat way of excluding Cornwall from his story, arguing that Wales and Scotland were 'internal colonies' of England. Equally, in the early 2000s when the British New Labour government was pushing a policy agenda for regional assemblies, the scholarship about the regionalism agenda also found a way of not including Cornwall in the discussion (Elcock, 2008; Fenwick et al., 2009). The argument was that it did not have *enough* sense of identity, and what it did, was conflicted. The irony being that as one of the U.K.'s Celtic Nations, Cornwall launched a very well-supported campaign for devolution to the area believing that it too warranted a decision-making forum on a par with the new Assembly in Wales (Willett and Giovannini, 2014).

The strength and quality of Cornwall's distinctiveness and uniqueness have underpinned much academic research about the area. The mythology begins with the argument that in the deep past, Cornwall (like much of what is now considered England) was an independent kingdom. Using one of Smith's (1991) markers of nationhood, it has its own regional myth of descent distinct to that of Britain's Brutus myth (Stoyle, 2002) and a patron saint (St Piran) who is said to have discovered tin, the mining of which would form the backbone of the Cornish economy for centuries. However, from around the tenth century, English 'encroachment' began to 'colonise' and Anglicise the area (Angarrack, 1999). Over the course of the centuries, the processes of Anglicanisation all but wiped out the region's language, which clung on by threads, through place names, snatches of dialect, and in particular closed occupations, such as on fishing boats (Mackinnon, 2002). This historic sense of difference to its geographical neighbour has persisted through time. Tregidga (2000) argues that the dominance of Methodism in the religious landscape and the historic support of the Liberal Party (and later the Liberal Democrats) signal the continuation of Cornish 'oppositionalism' and positioning of difference. Whilst scholarship used to be concerned that Cornish distinctive cultural identities would become diluted – particularly due to the heavy level of inward migration mentioned above (Williams, 2003) – in practice the opposite has happened. Instead, symbols of Cornish identities have grown and amplified. For example, it is difficult to spend any time in the area and not encounter the flag, and language, which is visible at many local events and is even employed by local businesses as a marketing tool.

The increasing pride in Cornish cultural identities has its roots in the 1990s as a campaign tool to counter the dire state of the economy at the time. In order to achieve the statistical visibility required to receive the EU structural funding monies that it would be eligible for, campaigners found that the uniqueness of Cornwall's identity played very well with EU officials (Willett, 2013). This was also a campaign that the populace could get behind, as citizens were reeling from a series of bad economic recessions in the 1980s and early 1990s, a struggling tourism industry, and far worse in terms of identities and place in the world, the closure of the last of the Cornish tin mines. The mining of Cornwall's rich mineral deposits had been a part of the Cornish economic identity for millennia. There is even a contested narrative that Cornish merchants traded tin with the Phoenicians (Champion, 2001). The innovations that accompanied the booming industry enabled the Cornish inventors to file for more patents in the late 1700s than anywhere outside of London (Nuvolari, 2004). The only reason that this changed in the early 1800s was because innovators found it better to share information than compete. However, as metals mining began to decline toward the end of the 1800s, the new industry of leisure tourism started to emerge as a means of providing additional support when the traditional industries of mining, farming, and fishing had difficult years. More recently, tourism has come to dominate the economic landscape. Although mining remains in the form of a reduced China Clay extraction, there are tentative excavations for Lithium, a current emphasis on the aerospace industry, and an extremely unpopular detour into trying to attract manufacturing 'branch plants' (Spooner, 1972); it is through tourism that people know the region.

In terms of providing jobs, tourism has been important. However, it has brought its own significant issues. The seasonal, low-skilled nature of its employment opportunities has entrenched a low-wage and precarious economy. Moreover, it has become a very particular lens through which the region and its inhabitants are perceived. The visitor imaginary of place has had various changes in narrative emphasis, from the wild and untamed Celtic rusticity, the bucket and spade beach holiday, and the latter-day Kool Kernow incarnation as a coastal rural region with an active, outdoorsy lifestyle punctuated with top-class food (Willett, 2016). As a direct result of the way that the visitor lens overlays (or cloaks) how they understand the region, it can be very difficult for people to accept that it is an area which experiences high levels of deprivation. Cornwall's visitor appeal has also led to its popularity with persons wishing to purchase a second home, relocate, or run a house as a (lucrative) holiday let. As a consequence, persons earning Cornish wages need to compete with the increased buying power of individuals from wealthier parts of the United Kingdom. This situation has led to a lot of disquiet amongst people with less choice over locational decisions, who can also experience levels of rural stigmatisation not dissimilar to that of the southern Appalachian region, whereby the 'slower pace of life' so attractive to tourists and immigrants becomes translated to the capacity of an imagined 'backward' populace. Scholars such as Dickinson (2008) go so far as to describe this as a form of internal colonialism. Finally, research shows the grinding nature of rural poverty and reminds us that there are many people that live in Cornwall who for various reasons surrounding poverty and deprivation are unable to access the very environmental amenities which are so attractive to visitors (Szabova et al., 2020). This may go some way to explain why Cornwall has higher rates of suicide than the average for England and Wales (Hill et al., 2005).

RESEARCH PRACTICE

In order to explore each region as a complex adaptive assemblage, my starting point was to begin by talking to ordinary members of the public to explore how they experienced life in the regions within which they lived, what kind of relationships they had with the place, and also what kind of skills or knowledges people held. The object of this was to be able to draw the region as an assemblage. By way of questioning, I asked the people that I formally interviewed how they experienced living in the area, what kinds of things felt important to them in their area, how they pass the time, and what kinds of things would they like to see in the future. I also asked questions about the types of jobs that were available or which they felt were accessible and tried to get some understanding of how people routinely engaged in the labour market.

I was very conscious of wanting to hold 'conversations' rather than 'interviews'. In part, this was because I was very aware of how people can come to 'perform' themselves in particular situations (i.e. Goffman, 1959) which can impact heavily on what kinds of information that people feel that the researcher wants or needs to know and can also make people feel quite self-conscious. In order to address this – and also to encourage more discussion about the local environment – I originally decided to follow the principles of embodied research (Spatz, 2017; Thanem and Knights, 2019; Vachelli, 2018). The idea behind this is to engage in some form of physical or tactile activity which helps to provide the space and opportunity to reflect on a topic in depth, in conversation, whilst undertaking a form of activity which might itself could act as an affective resonator to generate further discussion. The rapport that people can generate in such a group environment can also be helpful for the discussion (Macpherson, 2016). I was also very excited about the prospect for more place-specific discussions of conversations held whilst walking (Evans and Jones, 2010) and had imagined that this might be a fascinating way to be introduced to how participants imagined the area. Later, and considering the performative norms around walking (Macpherson, 2016) which can impact on the types of discussions held, and thinking deeply about the embodied aspects of the process, I expanded this out to invite people to undertake an activity with me. I began by envisaging this part of the research as a series of walks – or activities made with two or three people, around a place which they felt was important. Later on in the research process, I also wanted to interview people who might be considered as 'regional elites' in some way. This might be because of their roles in an aspect of social and economic development or because of their activities within the business community.

I began with the southwest of Virginia, and following a scoping trip in February 2018, I lived in the city of Bristol – which straddles the border between southwest Virginia and east Tennessee – for a period of 10 weeks from May to July 2019. I was very lucky to stay in a house where the owner was extremely happy to talk to me lots about the area, and to introduce me to a range of different people that she knew, and to reflect at length about the thoughts that emerged from all aspects of the research process. I voraciously read books about the region, and historical and contemporary novels set throughout the locality. Sampling began on an opportunity basis, and from there grew using snowball sampling, as people were recommended to me, trust was built, and my own understanding about the region grew and deepened. From the outset, people were extraordinarily welcoming. From putting in place the things that were needed to stay in a place for a length of time, to suggesting people, places, and organisations that I might like to talk to as part of the study. People were interested in what I was doing, curious about the project, and were happy to be of assistance. My sense too is that this is an under-researched area and that people were extremely keen to contribute on this basis.

My primary mode of transportation was usually a bicycle, and the locality does not have a functioning public transportation system. Therefore, the majority of my fieldwork occurred around Bristol area, where I was living. When I obtained a car for a three-week period, I was able to move to the outer reaches of the locality, extending along the I-89 into Floyd county. The car facilitated an enthusiastic exploration of the area much further afield than my 30-mile cycling radius, which ensured that I was able to take up opportunities to both interview people and to participate in a range of invited activities. It is fair to say that I was embraced by the wider community, which led my involvement in a wide range of activities. From Bluegrass to hiking, farming to 4th of July parties, to guided tours of places of meaning to my companion. This helped me to develop the interpretative framework required in order to be able to fully understand and appreciate the meanings of the phenomenon that interviewees told me. It was also interesting how much additional information I picked up towards the end up my stay, when re-reading transcripts of conversations held at the beginning. I interviewed a total of 32 people – 26 members of the public (from a wide range of ages and backgrounds) and 6 persons who held some form of post involved in regional governance and economy.

In terms of embodied research, whilst the idea of engaging in a recorded discussion during some form of practical activity captured people's imagination, with one notable exception where we ended up doing an art-based activity, this did not come to fruition in the SWVA interviews. Perhaps I imagined a reluctance on people's behalf and was unwilling to outstay my interviewees' generosity, perhaps it was more complicated to arrange a practical activity, or perhaps participants felt more comfortable in a more guarded interview/conversational setting than when they might otherwise have been a little distracted by the activity.

Embodied research also worked less well in the Cornwall example too (with two notable exceptions) but also for different reasons. Generally, joining a pre-existing group on their scheduled activity or having the activity organised by a charismatic local figure tended to make people more willing to agree to this style of interview. The Cornwall interviews occurred between October 2019 and April 2020. In the latter stages in particular, fieldwork had to be limited to Skype/Zoom conversations because of the COVID-19 Pandemic. Some earlier conversations also happened over Skype for work commitment kinds of reasons. Unlike in SWVA, I incorporated a select couple of interviews with governance/development employees early on. This was for opportunity reasons. Early inquiries through my networks generated a buzz of interest that I was reluctant to allow to dampen. Moreover, the insights that these participants offered allowed for a much richer understanding of the first few interviews in this series. Where embodied principles worked brilliantly was as a well-planned and organised event. I obtained a small amount of funding to work with a local artist and a community activist to invite people to a one-day event including refreshments. The morning involved a walk around the area with the community activist providing some historical input. (With permission) I recorded conversations with participants throughout the walk, over lunch, and in the afternoon when guided by the artist, we created a painting which represented life in the locality. The community activist was a key ingredient towards bringing together the diverse range of experiences amongst participants.

I have lived in Cornwall for most of my adult life which meant that I have a rich understanding of the area but with the limitations of the Bergsonian cloaking effect of memory. Nevertheless, my life as an academic has meant that my experience of the region is very different from that of most people. The depth and breadth of my own networks meant that it was easier for me to know who to ask, when I had specific questions, or realised that there were specific groups of people that research showed *needed* to have a voice, but didn't. On a personal level, I found it fascinating and dismaying that many of the issues that I experienced, in my adolescence, were still a factor in the present.

Completing and writing up the SWVA fieldwork before the Cornwall research was also extremely beneficial for viewing the region through fresh eyes. The people, perceptions, and institutions that I had encountered helped to make things in Cornwall visible to me, and my experience of voraciously reading SWVA, Appalachian, and southern fiction rekindled my old interest in Cornish or Cornwall-based novels and novelists, and histories, all of which contributed to my own interpretive framework.

Chapter 5

Southwest Virginia

So what is the southwest of Virginia like for people that live there? What does its regional assemblage look like, and what does this mean for how people in the region adapt their present in order to find their future? This chapter uses the concepts developed in chapters 2 and 3 in order to draw out the SWVA's region assemblage. In the latter part, I then examine what this means for the region moving forward.

In developing the intertwined, interactive, complex, nested network of people, concepts, structures, and institutions which make up the assemblage, Deleuze and Guattari (2004) speak to challenges about linearity. In chapter 4, I considered the question of linear versus emergent time, exploring a regional economics that is based instead on evolutionary rather than mechanical principles. In their book *A Thousand Plateaus*, Deleuze and Guattari (2004) take the questioning of linearity a step further, calling their publication a 'rhizome book' rather than a 'root book'. By this, they mean that the book has no *actual* beginning and no *actual* middle and ending. Instead, they imagine it as an assemblage, constructed only of middle. For the reader, this means that although (Western) convention requires a reader to begin at the introduction and work ones way through to the conclusion, Deleuze and Guattari want to free their readers to start at any place that they wish. They might begin at some point in the middle and skip chapters forwards or backwards as they please, and the book will still make sense.

In many respects, this challenge to the linear narrative overlays the way that many of us imagine a story in our minds. We might be immediately clear about the key narrative moments, the threads that hold it all together, and have an idea where the story begins and ends. But then we might find that in order to make that beginning sensible, we first have to explain something else, and that is neither as punchy a beginning, or really a good place to start. And so the problems of ironing out an assemblage into a neat, linear story begins. This is my problem here, articulated by 'Stephen', an IT worker from a town in the northern part of SWVA. He apologised for the length of the interview that we had and for the many apparent digressions and tangents that he took as he sought to explain how he perceived the region and narrated his view about how people approach these problems. He stated, 'you pull on these different things and when you yank on one, you're not just affecting that one. There are threads going that way and threads going this way. And when you pull on one, there are others'. This is the dilemma at the start of this chapter. Which thread of the region assemblage do I tease out first? For what feels like quite an arbitrary decision, I have decided to let myself be guided by the analytical theme which generated the greatest number of codes. For the SWVA material, this theme was '**money**'. The other themes that emerged from the interview data are represented below in bold type.

MAKING A LIVING

Perhaps it shouldn't be surprising that aspects surrounding money figured heavily in a piece of research largely focussed on economic development. However, although people knew about what my research entailed, I was asking questions about the kinds of things that people felt were important within their community, how they like to spend their time, and what they wanted to see in the future. In its various forms, economic activity arose in many different ways. From people talking about how they or their families earned (or used to earn) a living, the kinds of jobs that were or are available, why they wound up in the area, the cost of living, the problems in the contemporary local and global economy, and the particular characteristics of people in the region that supports what they do.

When people discussed work and working lives, one of the things that leapt out is the rapidity of change. Nonagenarian member of the Woods family, Great Aunt Anna talked about the subsistence farming that she had grown up with and how she had helped to tend the (vegetable) garden and work in the tobacco fields. They raised crops such as corn, beans, and sweet potatoes, growing everything that they ate with the exception of staples like flour, coffee, and sugar. Food grown over the summer and fall needed to be preserved or canned in order to last through the harsh winter and spring months when there was little food available. Millennial public sector worker Clara relates that her octogenarian grandfather *grew up (in) a two-roomed shack right by the side of the road, and he and seven of his brothers and sisters lived there, and it had a dirt floor, and he would talk about how he could look up at night*

and the stars were there through the cracks in the home. And they had to walk
15 miles to work, and if they had a horse they would ride there.

This began to change from the 1930s and 1940s when improved transportation made the ten miles or so into the towns suddenly seem accessible,
although it should be noted that this happened at a different pace in different
parts of the region. It is hard to imagine what a rapid change that the arrival
of rail links between the towns and the hollers (hollows, or valleys) deep in
the mountains must have made, and the arrival of the motor car – and the
vastly improved graded and paved roads that supported driving – must have
had on communities. In their book about early country music stars, the Carter
Family (Zwoniter and Hirschberg, 2004) relate how AP had to walk for a day
over Clinch Mountain to get from his valley, to the next, in order to court
Sara, who would become his wife. Just a few years later in 1927, the money
brought in by his job as a rail worker allowed AP's brother to purchase a car,
which (despite the dire state of the roads) allowed the family to attend the
historic Bristol Session which launched country music as a recorded phenomenon and the Carter Family into stardom.

The car de-territorialises previously fixed communities living deep in
the southern Appalachian mountains. Many of these communities could
trace their histories back to settlers arriving in the late 1700s, having been
granted tracts of land as a reward for their efforts in the American War of
Independence, 1775–1783. These settlers must have been tough, independent, enterprising, creative, and determined in order to manage making a life
in a low mountainous area, thick with ancient forest. It would also have been
an isolated existence, with one's few near neighbours often some distance
away. College-educated cultural entrepreneur and public sector worker in her
late 20s, Dana tells that *Appalachia is formed from the German Scotch Irish*
and the English who came, and the Germans built barns, the English built
churches, and the Scotch Irish built stills. And upon that, society was built.
When you look around you're like, man that makes a lot of sense. If you com-
bine agriculture and religion and booze, you're going to get this authentic
culture and all these things. Throughout the region, people will still proudly
tell you that they are Irish, or Scottish, Scots Irish, German, or part Native
American. They may never have set foot in any of these European countries
but are referring to their genealogical background and a heritage which permeates the music and socio-cultural background which emerged here. This is
one of those instances where the echoes of past histories ripple into the present in a visible reverberation throughout time. Dana reminds us here that the
early origins of the settlements was as a cultural melting pot, which has ended
up creating a unique culture all of its own. The families that grew up here
became deeply embedded, and over 200 years later, it is not uncommon to be
told (as by the Woods family) that the holler in which they live is populated

predominantly by descendants of the original settlers, and that these descendants often still own the old home-place. College-educated Marsha claimed that *Everyone in the area with the same surname can be traced back to the same pair of brothers that arrived . . . hundreds of years ago. It's also a really localised name – it's not at all common a few miles up the road.*

These newly settled communities evolved into something where the people were both extraordinarily self-reliant, and also extraordinarily resilient. As Dana reminds us, *the mountains dictate the way that people have been since they settled here.* In the early days in which the land was settled, an individual or family would have needed to be able to clear land and fell trees, make the resultant lumber into a house, farm the land, make tools or be able to make trades in order to purchase other tools, and farm the land. They would then need to be able to cook, preserve, or trade crops, whilst taking care of the animals used for food or labour. This is a multiple skill-set that belies any attempt at an industrial division of labour. Rashid sees these characteristics still present in the rural dwellers of contemporary southern Appalachia. Rashid is a well-educated millennial man from the northern United States, with a non-Western migrant family background. One of the things that drew him to the rural parts of southwest Virginia was the way that people's working lives are not limited by the repetition of a reasonably narrow number of activities. He notes that *there is more people around us that can do five different trades than anywhere I've ever been, its amazing. People can build an entire house here by themselves.* Again, these are settler characteristics and traits but which have been culturally retained, because they are still useful. Dana explains the importance of usefulness to cultural retention, stating that *we obviously don't use outhouses. Bathrooms work better. They're in our house. There are certain things that you don't need to keep with.* Part of the point of this is that this independence of spirit, need for personal freedom, and Jack-of-all-trades ability and practice has stayed useful within the rural culture of the southern Appalachians in Virginia.

Partly, this might be explained by the on-going importance of agriculture as a way of life, and partly to the approach to time and temporality which exists in this area. Nevertheless, these were not communities comprised of atomised individuals. On the contrary, they are deeply interconnected and interdependent. This too is a necessary set of characteristics brought through from settler times. Dana relates that *if it's broke you fix it, you don't call someone to fix it. You might not be able to do that on your own, but you have three friends that can, so it's like an understood thing that you reach out to those people for that, and they reach out to you for something else. It's part of what makes this place what it is, that reliance on other people, but also that everything comes full circle.* Culturally, the tight internal networks of this part of the region assemblage are designed in order to be able to collaboratively solve problems and share skills and strengths. The church becomes a locus for this kind of bridging social capital, bringing otherwise disparate people together, developing relations of interiority through a set of shared beliefs and ideas. Once introduced, deeper connections can be forged over a period of extended interactions that helps to fulfil the need for practical support and company in an area of rural isolation. People also spoke of how the community had historically supported each other through difficult times. Loretta recalls this too. *If somebody in the community died and we'd put a big box out and everybody that come in and traded, we would put something in the box. And they would be real full. It would be lots and lots of food. That was one thing, they helped each other.* The practice of the community bringing food to help persons who were experiencing difficult times is a trope which re-occurs throughout novels set in the locality, such as the books (one of which made into a film) by Adriana Trigiani, set in the coal field town of Big Stone Gap.

So geography and farming as a predominant means of supporting oneself acted as territorialising factors, which helped to create fixed and stable communities. Whilst parts of the forest had to be cleared if crops were to be grown, wood could be used for heat, construction, or sold for lumber. To supplement these efforts, there was edible vegetation to forage and animal life to hunt. This does not mean at all that the region was a closed system. On the contrary, some people would have left, either temporarily or permanently, to settle or trade elsewhere. However, travel would have been long, arduous, and dangerous. Whilst some of the coal mining regions deeper in the mountains towards the borders of Kentucky and west Virginia would have seen the arrival of the railroad in the latter 1800s, the more agricultural locations had to wait until the 1920s before they were more readily able to connect with neighbouring towns and the outside world. This revolutionised the kinds of lives that people were able to lead and the possibilities open to them and disrupts entirely the old, largely closed system within which they had lived for over a century. As a consequence, younger people such as Aunt Anna found that jobs became available in the towns. Beth Macy relates in *Factory Man* (2015) that this opened up new possibilities and new worlds (or new lines of flight). An additional effect was that the next generation along were able to offer their children a college education if they so desired, improving social capital and life chances amongst the broader community. Consequently, in a downward causal effect, the injection of the new to the lives of one generation was to amplify and ripple outwards in later generations.

The new mobilities and fluidities of the early to mid-twentieth century also fuelled a new movement in the local economies. Enterprising people were better able to staff factories, which grew readily utilising local strengths and the environment. For example, the dominance of the furniture manufacturing industry in the area throughout the twentieth century is directly related to a combination of the availability of lumber and the business acumen of certain local characters (Macy, 2015). The cut-and-sew clothing manufacturers that Aunt Anna worked for would have made garments for the local area, including the tough, hard-wearing work-wear that Bristol's LC King (the last cut-and-sew factory remaining in the area). But they would also have sold their manufactured goods further afield in the United States. Aunt Anna was able to use the skill as a machinist that she would have picked up throughout her childhood, where, like in many similar American households of the time, most clothes were made by hand at home. This kind of acculturation would also have created a broader affective environment whereby individuals and families sought out opportunities to make a bit more money, and in her time as a machinist, Aunt Anna sold her colleagues pretty little sun bonnets that she made at home to raise a little extra cash. Like the furniture factory workers that Macy interviews, the Woods family relate how the chance to be part of the cash economy also created new opportunities whereby people didn't *have* to be confined to the holler of their birth, because they didn't have the money to relocate, as they may have had to in previous eras. However, many chose to stay because of the *pull* of the mountains.

Something additional that illustrates the enormity of this social shift almost creates a rupture between the past and the present, relates to the strong temporal resonance of the phenomenon of bartering. On the one hand, this is a practice of past communities, whereby you went to the store not to shop, but to *trade*. Indeed, when Loretta discusses her parents' occupation as storekeepers, she talks about how *everybody would come in to trade*. In a place and time where money was scarce, if you needed a particular thing, you would have to work out how and who you could swap things that you owned, had made, or grown with in order to get the item that you wanted. Legendarily, the U.S. renowned Barter Theatre in the small farming town of Abingdon, about 17 miles from the Virginia/Tennessee border, got its name from this practice, and theatre-goers might trade chickens or other goods with performers in exchange for a ticket. This made going to the theatre accessible for the many people who lived on the outside or on the fringes of the cash economy. This practice is immortalised in the name of the regions' most well-known theatre. However, bartering still lives on in the lives of some who live in the hill communities. Kath, a retired environmental activist, relates, *I don't know if you know about the history of Appalachia, but it's very isolated. People came here and there was nothing, and if you needed something, you grew it or you made it, or you bartered for it, and being poor makes you creative. If you need a broom, you made it. If you wanted something, you bartered for it. And that continues to this day. I had 9 loads of firewood this year, and I paid for it by the barter system, this favour, that favour.*

For Kath, trading or bartering is as much a part of how she manages her every day on a retirement income, as is the other point that she raises and which we have already touched upon: the creativity that was necessary for survival in rural America. Like for many American rural, farming communities of the time, resources were precious and scarce. At the Carter Family Fold, where country music legends AP and Sara Carters' old home-place is recreated, curtaining material was re-purposed but made beautiful out of hessian sacking. The Woods family spoke of how as children some of their clothing had been made out of the finer cotton of old flour sacks. In recognition of the fact that so many people re-used the sacking in this way, flour manufacturers printed patterned floral or gingham designs, and the person purchasing the flour might select a sack on the basis of the patterns' utility in domestic garment creation. Stories of the transition from subsistence farming to the cash economy are extremely common in the area, as is strong visual evidence of the tools and materials that were necessary to survive in past times, and which are displayed for sale in the numerous antique stores. As with the Woods family, people young and old still frequently tell stories about the lives and practices that used to be commonplace, and which are distant not just temporally but also culturally, from contemporary, Western modernity. But this distance is a complicated one. Clara's story about her grandfather being raised in a house with a dirty floor is a recent one, which is still very present within the cultural memories and stories that form part of the fabric of the assemblage of SWVA in general. This recalls Bergson's philosophical question about whether the past actually passes or whether it remains active in the present. These pasts related in this study might be distant and alien to how anybody lives in the present, but people still remember the time when many people were literally dirt poor and existing in ways that are more commonly associated with communities in the global South.

THE U.S.-WIDE COUNTRY ASSEMBLAGE

In the world that Kath describes, materials were precious and needed to be re-fashioned in order to make necessary tools. Things literally could be broken down as far as their particular molecular assemblages. Fabric could be made and re-made into several different garments or furnishings. Rather than disposing of cloth that had become worn or had otherwise been cut into smaller pieces, it was re-used as quilts or rugs. Although there is a high level of disposability and little or no recycling in much of contemporary SWVA (indeed, because of a lack of a market in recyclable materials, there is no longer doorstep municipal recycling in the city of Bristol), the echoes of previous practices remain. Octogenarian Loretta proudly displayed the numerous quilts that she made in her spare time, discussing the intricacies of some of their designs and talking fondly of some of the women that she quilted with. These were no longer constructed from old, re-purposed fabric but the material is purchased to order. Quilts might not always be made for their utility but for decoration or for an available and sociable pastime whereby people can come together in stitching sessions to share news, thoughts, and skills. They continue to occupy an enduring role in cultural memory and practices. Equally with canning, which persists across the generations, although the fruits and vegetables preserved might have been purchased in the supermarket rather than grown in the garden. In these spaces, the past folds into the present, offering available possibilities as means to pass the time, decorate the home and community buildings (as in the case of quilts), or to provide homemade alternatives or supplements to a strong availability of ready-prepared meals. Additionally, these activities are also associated with companionable pursuits, providing opportunities for (usually women) to come together to talk, catch up with the news, and share gossip.

Again, these are practices that far from being unique to the mountains of southern Appalachia are shared across the assembled histories and performances of rural communities throughout the United States. This shared experience connects even the most isolated communities or in the much nicer phraseology of one participant who discussed his old town, deep in the hills as *sheltered*. As a consequence, even the *most* sheltered holler is also just a part of a much bigger cultural movement which rippled and amplified throughout the nation. This deep connectedness between the cultural experience of people in the region assemblage of SWVA, and rural assemblages throughout the United States, is reflected in the unexpectedly explosive effect that the recording of country, or 'hillbilly' music, had on the recorded music industry.

According to Zwonitrer and Hirschberg (2004), it was quite a surprise to budding industry mogul Ralph Peer that from his speculative Bristol Sessions, country music hit a collective nation-wide affective nerve and resonated and reverberated so strongly with the music consuming public of the late 1920s and early 1930s. Not unlike later technologies such as radio, TV, and the internet, the nascent phonograph industry brought recorded sound from distant communities into people's homes, both territorialising and deterritorialising cultural experience by easily sharing different musical cultures whilst at the same time reaffirming one's own musical cultural symbolisms. With regard to country music, for the first time an aspect of U.S. popular culture reflected back the lives and experiences of people working in the mountains and plains beyond the city. Consequently, a number of musicians – such as AP, Sara, and Maybelle Carter – became huge stars across the country. In this respect, these sheltered and remote communities many days or weeks of travel apart were actually so deeply inter-connected with other parts of the United States that they were a part of the same or similar set of shared affective experiences. This was about geographical seclusion whilst culturally being central to assembled narratives, symbolisms, and meanings about what it means to be an American. But these assemblages were beginning to deterritorialise in places, around the advent of industrialised towns and cities as the epochal assemblage within which the United States and SW Virginia sat, had begun to formulate an entirely new, industrialised way of being that disrupted previously agrarian codes, norms, and structures. From this temporal rupture, new modes of becoming began to emerge, bringing with it new ways of being that could not have been previously predicted.

For the southwest of Virginia, this process happened a little differently to some others. Retired pharmaceutical worker Jan tells a story of her own grandparents in Texas whose farm *probably had 50 or 100 acres at the most*, which would not have been as viable in the newly emerging industrialised early twentieth century. She relates of her grandparents that *And all of their children went to the cities, and my granddad became a mechanic for the county roads back when they were cutting county roads out of the forest with mule teams. My grandmother, she came off of the farm and she worked building aircraft in an aircraft factory in Dallas, so they had a totally different life than they grew up with. And those little family farms are just gone. They're gone.* Here, Jan is talking about how the rupture in time brought about by the destabilising and deterritorialising lines of flight that were rapidly emerging into new cultural assemblages of their own, happened at a different time and pace in some parts of the United States, to others. In SWVA, there was not a complete abandonment of the countryside for the work in the towns. Instead, despite widespread changes to farming and economic opportunities, people, where possible, have stayed in their rural lives or hybridised it with supplemented work in towns. The reasons why are a mystery to Jan. *These people still have farms that they've had for how many years. So it's different. I don't know why. There's no more life in these little towns up here than there were in small towns where my grandparents people came from. But I don't know what the difference is. Texas grew, and these people stay. I don't know.*

One clue lies in the importance of family. Project worker Louise told me that *You'll find a lot of people, even if they leave, a lot will come back. Sometimes to tend for family and sometimes because they realise that the big city wasn't for them.* Often people that moved away discuss how they had been compelled to return either because close family members needed their support or because they missed their family. On the one hand, this acts as a deeply territorialising example of bonding social capital and rigid relations of interiority, creating a kind of closed system policed by what is sometimes interpreted as a *clannish* mind-set. The boundaries of this are sometimes narrated as being rooted in the family obligations to older generations who provide accommodation and other forms of support for younger family members. College-educated Marsha tells *that the family is, you know, they live in the holler and where my grandparents live, I have an aunt who lives there, my uncle lives there, my cousins stay there. Just kind of that's the family. They call it the compound. And that's just where they live, and my mom and dad bought a house like half a mile away from there, just to be close. And that's what it's like. They have their little holler, and have kids, and their kids bring their families there, and they all kind of stay there.* As the land becomes used up, *that's where trailers come in! Like really! My grandparents have – the original house was called the house down the holler, now it's like fallen in and everything. But they moved to a house a little further up. And as they got older they moved to the house at the front, like where you first drive into the holler. And then my aunt and uncles moved in there, and they had a house on a hill. And my other aunt and uncle moved in and put in a trailer over here. Then my dad moved in and put in a trailer here. And then somebody put in a trailer over here. And literally, however many acres it is, they just pop trailers in.* Here, the large tracts of land associated with SW Virginia farmland are helpful in enabling multiple generations to have the security of a place to live.

A further reason why people stay or return is that the landscape acts as an important territorialising aspect. Specifically, the mountains or the hills. An IT worker who had relocated from one side of the area to the other, Richard echoed what I came to realise was a frequently made distinction between the sharp, craggy, brutal newness of new mountains and the gentler, heavily forested, more rolling topography of old mountains that have been eroded over millennia of time. Other participants, such as younger millennial municipal workers Hope and Ben, spoke of these mountains as beautiful, providing shelter from some of the worst weather in the area. Here the mountains literally protect the communities that inhabit them, providing an imagery of assembled humans, what is reputed to be amongst the richest biodiversity in the United States, and the flora and fauna that this is comprised of, as being literally held in the hands of the valleys and hollers of the long mountain ranges. This echoes Tom's assertion that his old, remote community deep in the mountains is *sheltered*.

Moreover, the mountains provide spaces for recreation and play. According to Marsha, *even when you're a little kid, there is always plenty to do here . . . hiking, fishing, going to waterfalls. One of the best things about living here is that it's so pretty and there's always something to do outside.* Indeed, hiking and spending time in nature is a surprisingly popular pastime. Taken together – including the kinds of individuals that would have been attracted to and remained in the Southern Appalachian mountains in SWVA – this means that the environmental characteristics of the region shapes and has shaped the kinds of people that it attracts and retains. Richard talks about how although he finds the landscape deeply attractive, it is actually the *ways of living* that people in old mountain areas practice that have such a draw. This includes the small-town nature of population distribution, the climate, biological environment, and the types of people that also choose to live in such a space. It means that if people want to live off the grid, deep in the countryside, they can. Also, if people want to live in towns with a good level of local amenities, this is also possible. Part of the reason that people stay is not just because their families are comfortably safe and familiar, but also because they appreciate the cultural backdrop that has emerged to create these safe and familiar people worlds.

THE ASSEMBLED NATURAL AND HUMAN ENVIRONMENTS

Here we can see that the natural environment is quite literally folded in to the human environment. The kinds of cultures that we see have been and continue to be affected by the physical geography of the area, just as the activities of people have affected the immediate environment. In one of my early weeks in the region, Georgia and I got talking about how densely wooded I experienced the area, and how bizarre it was to get to the top of a hill and only be able to see glimpses of view because of the trees. Georgia asked me what size of trees I was seeing, pointing out that most of the ones that are commonly seen are relatively young and certainly less than 50 or 60 years old. Michael also remarked on this, on a hike in a national park not too far away in East Tennessee. Logging decimated the ancient forests and would have affected the other creatures living amongst the trees, even though it made living in the area more fruitful and easier for human inhabitants. It also made it easier to farm, which further decreases the available space for wildlife to make a home. As Peter Crow recounts in his book *Do, Die, or Get Along* (2007) about two coal mining communities nearly 35 miles away from what is now the I-81 interstate highway, mining also has dramatically altered the landscape – and continues to do so even though the industry has shrunk dramatically. In the early twentieth century, heavy pollution from mining run-off was common, which impacted on air quality and water toxicity and therefore its capacity to support the rich biodiversity that is part of the fabric of the region assemblage. This would have affected the health and wellbeing of all biological organisms within the locality. In turn, the availability of wild animals to hunt, fish to catch, and edible plants to forage helped the early settlers and later inhabitants to be able to support themselves, especially in times of hardship. This intimate and survivalist relationship with the landscape, organisms, and geology that formed part of the region assemblage echoes in affective temporal resonances up to the present day, manifesting itself in the satisfaction that people even now take in hunting food and in U.S.-wide debates about gun control. Now, available technologies have radicalised humans' ability to alter the natural environment, as we see starkly with the 'mountain-top removal' style of mining that has replaced tunnelling into hills. Quite literally, after burrowing in to the mountain in the centuries-old fashion, strip mining maximises yield and minimises the amount of physical labour (and therefore cost) that is required in order to turn a profit in the coal-mining environment. First, the trees and other wildlife are removed from the mountain. Then the geological infrastructure is also removed as a millennia-old mountain is reduced to flat-land. This sounds like a drastic and shocking thing, but Crow (2007) tells of a perspective which claims that the resulting flat land in a remote location with previously only steep mountain sides is a gift full of potentiality for nearby towns, offering finally some flat develop-ment space. More than this, one train of thought imagines this as a potential saviour for ailing communities, decimated by the loss of coal to the area.

This is an argument which holds that the environmental part of the region assemblage is there for humans to exploit in whichever way best fits. But this is a complicated set of threads to pull. As former industry employee (Steve) relates, coal has held a really important function in generating the energy to facilitate many things which are central to cultural and economic assemblages far beyond the locality. In some regards, it acts as a kind of connector, linking the Appalachian coalfields tangentially to the rest of the United States. This raises many tensions that are echoed in other mining parts of Southern Appalachia – particularly in the State of West Virginia but also in Kentucky, too. These are articulated in the film (*Coal River Mountain*, 2017), which describes how some members of the community are devastated at the environmental destruction that accompanies new mining methods. The literal loss of a mountain from the visual landscape, the loss of farms and old home-places to which families are deeply attached, and the high levels of pol-lution which accompany the extraction and processing of the coal have led to many local people (as well as environmental campaigners from further afield) to campaign vigorously against what they see happening. This is combined with fears of atmospheric pollution that is credited for making local residents very ill. On the other hand, many people who owe their livelihoods directly or indirectly to the excavation of coal have a different perspective rooted in the fear not only of losing their jobs but also of seismic changes and personal tragedies that accompany such a dramatic change (more on this below). For these people, mining is not simply a matter of the sensitivity with which people treat the planet, it is about the loss of a whole way of life and specific cultural norms and patterns of behaviour through which they have become accustomed to navigating their lives. The natural environment, and the things in it have literally created and shaped the human cultures which have come to dwell in and amongst it, creating constellations of symbolic meaning through which individuals and communities make sense of their worlds.

At times, it is an easy shorthand to create a binary between those that are motivated by concern for the environment and those who follow what Evans et al. (2002) call a more productivist version of rurality. This is then often overlaid with the binaries between political left and the political right, between progressives and conservatives, and between people who care about the environment and people who are motivated primarily by dollar signs. But this is a grotesque over-simplification. For example, Clara states that *my grandfather for instance was a coal miner. He worked in the coal mines for 25 years. And he's like yeah coal. Some of the folks that say they're tearing up the landscape, they're not from here. So they didn't have family that worked in the mines.* Clara goes on to talk about the way that the coal industry has contributed to the community and helped to keep it alive and vibrant. Here, the loss of coal isn't simply about the jobs that it provides but about the communities that it supports. Environmental activist Kath includes coal in her list of the things that her region has contributed to the national story and assemblage of the United States, although she tempers this with her belief that the industry has bought off political leaders to the detriment of the local-ity. Furthermore, Craig also talks about how environmental campaigning has brought together the community, split between people who tend to be more conservative, and a newer post-hippy population. She says that *some of the places where those two fractured aspects of [deleted] come together are in protecting the natural environment of [deleted]. We've had problems with the oil pipeline, the Mountain Valley Pipeline. And everyone in [deleted] had a fightback.*

Craig's statement is interesting. It is not news to point out that the elec-tion of President Trump to the Whitehouse in November 2016 reflected and crystallised a narrative of deep divides within the American body politic. At times, this has led commentators to reflect that we are currently observing two very different Americas, operating in two distinct assemblages, with very few points of contact or congruence (Russell Hoschschild, 2016). I was expecting to find this quite sharply in a location which returned a Republican vote of over 80 per cent in some counties, with most counties polling well in excess of 70 per cent (Politico, 2019). Even Montgomery county, which includes university town Blacksberg only just passed a Democrat vote (46.9% Clinton/ 45.6 Trump). Part of me was also expecting to experience some awkward-ness between my position as a liberal and an anticipated very right-wing local political culture. However, what I found was that I was not only wel-comed, but befriended by many people with very different political views and backgrounds to myself. In addition, many of the people that I spoke to talked about the places in which people that were a part of very different political assemblages intersect. Often this was expressed as a circle where the polar ends of the political spectrum meet and join together. For example, Annie spoke of the intersection between libertarian Republicans who want to live their lives free from any interference and the back-to-nature anarchist libertarians amongst whom she associates. Annie joins this intersection as being part of a specifically Appalachian assemblage. She says that *Appalachians historically don't like authority. That's why they came here to begin with. So just don't tell me what to do.* For both ends of the left/right spectrum, this spills over into a mistrust in the government and the political class, who both sides feel are too heavily indebted to powerful interests and undoubtedly fuses with the assemblages of self-reliance and independence in which the culture of the region assemblage is infused.

TEMPORALITY AND CHANGE

Earlier, we learnt how the close supportive relationships of tightly interwoven kinship groups help to keep people in the region in closely bounded relations of interiority. However, this kind of familial closeness also has a potential down side – that residing so close to the family with such tightly bonded social capital means that there is more pressure and obligation to fall in line with family expectations. In turn, non-conformity carries a greater individual and social cost. Being cast out of a group which literally comprises one's entire world (the family as well as wider support network) is significantly more costly than losing contact with a group which matters less to an individual's life. Moreover, a society where relationships and groups are heavily kinship based are going to have less space for non-kinship support groupings to emerge, and therefore alternative supportive relationship structures to be put in place.

   That said, there is some scope for openness even within what can easily be imagined as a very closed system. For example Melissa, a high-school graduate in her early 20s' talks about how people are having to confront a cultural homophobia through family members being unwilling to hide their sexuality any longer. Melissa says, *There's a lot of people here my age that still have an older person's mentality because that's who raised them. And in the same way,* (her boyfriend) *is much more traditional in his beliefs than I am. But even he, his brother is gay. But even he is much more open.* This recalls something that Abraham Verghese (2016) writes about in his book about his time as a health professional dealing with HIV and AIDS in the early 1980s in Johnsson City, half an hours' drive to the south of the SWVA border, in

East Tennessee. Verghese talks about how the AIDS victims that had to leave the area in order to be themselves (returning to be with their families during their illness), and those that stayed, literally forced their families to see non-heterosexual relationships with far greater empathy. Rather than being 'easy to other' outsiders, members of the LGBTQ community began to become the familiar figures of loved family members. Maintaining a homophobic position in this instance would not only cause significant pain to the family, but the unknown and unfamiliar were no longer unknowable. Of course, Verghese is relating an extreme example and discussing it with regard to the AIDS epidemic of the early 1980s, but what he does demonstrate is that there are spaces through which the unfamiliar (and therefore potentially dangerous) are able to be made familiar (and therefore safe). In true evolutionary fashion, change to deeply held beliefs and attitudes is possible if and when people feel that they *need* to adapt to a new world order. In this instance, the depth and strength of family feeling acts as an impetus, driving some degree of adaptation, allowing new ideas in.

Similarly, Dana discusses how she and her husband approach a kind of 'safe exposure' of her neighbours to different cultures. She talks here of a food project, combining Appalachian food with a non-Western food type. She explains that they *don't serve anything that is like 100 per cent either. They are all a mixture of both. That in and of itself makes a point. It combines the unknown element and means that they probably like it more, but they would never have tried it without the comforting element.* Even if they might not self-ascribe in this way, the food project is an example of cultural activism, trying to create cultural changes within their locality. This is discussed as an important task because *there are things that make this area look very ugly. And there are things that make it in the minds of outsiders very unwelcoming. And those things do exist. I'm not going to sit here and say that they don't, because they do. But the overwhelming thing is that it's not the majority. That's a common misconception that those small groups of people that do have every single stereotype that SWVA offers, that's a very small group of people. Do not view the whole area through that.* Dana acknowledges that there are some challenging aspects of the culture that need to be addressed. However, she believes that this is in no way reflective of all, or even most people within the cultural assemblage. She also carries a faith that people actually want to learn new things and new ideas or want to be part of a more open rather than closed system. In such an analysis, this calls for collective discussions about the unfamiliar which are gentle, comforting, mutually respectful, and loving. Furthermore, that even though it might appear on the outside that tight relations of interiority risk overly strong territorialising factors which preclude potentially deterritorialising new ideas, we see that the security that can be drawn from strong relations of interiority can also actively *facilitate* change. The other thing that Dana (and several others) raise is about the negative stereotypes that many people hold about the 'hillbilly' dwellers of the Appalachian Mountains, and we will return to this later. The point here is that even within what we will later discuss as the temporality of the SWVA region assemblage, there is an enormous capacity for adaptation to a changing world.

But change and perceptions of change are complicated in SWVA. It is not as if one can draw a neat line between the past and present and say 'this is the change that we see'. Instead the various assemblages that construct the wider region assemblage have their own, differing temporalities. We have seen some aspects of cultural change, and we have traced the enormity of some of the socio-economic changes that have occurred throughout the past century. On the other hand, we have seen a temporal slowness whereby Hetty can claim that *there's been a few new houses built, but out where I live there's hardly anything changed from what I see now from when I was a girl growing up there. It's the same families lived. It's just the continuity of it that gives you . . . it's just comforting in some way.* Hetty finds comfort in the lack of change that she observes in the pastoral nature of the holler in which she grew up and now lives in again once more. In these mountainous valleys, it is easy to feel that not much has changed for centuries – which is a little deceiving because at one time the fields would have been forest, and later still, the fields would have been full of very different crops. The tobacco barns would no longer be in a state of disrepair, the local store would return to its position as a vibrant hub of the holler rather than a dilapidated building on a trajectory towards unmediated entropy, and the paved roads that facilitate regular movement in and out of the area in the greatly expanded horizons of twenty-first-century mobility would not exist. But the important thing is that Hetty *perceives* the locality as not having changed very much. This also provides a bit of a commentary about the *imagined* timelessness of the pastoral scene, whereby settled farmland can be perceived as a window on a bygone age.

Nevertheless, it is also understandable why Hetty sees the area in this way. Melissa encapsulates this beautifully when she says that *we're out here in these hills, and time moves differently here.* She goes on to qualify this by saying that *we're not exposed to a great amount of culture that you are in a bigger place.* It is interesting that Melissa makes the affective connection between the speed of time encapsulated in temporality and exposure to new things and ideas. Frequently, this was affectively attached to the things which connect the region assemblage to other parts of the state, nation, and world physically (such as in terms of roads, air transport, or rail) and culturally through the media, film, music, and the internet. These are the relations of exteriority whereby the region assemblage becomes attached to other assemblages, well beyond its borders. But these relations of exteriority are unevenly distributed around the region. For example, there is a good interstate road that connects SWVA easily with Washington and beyond to the north and south through Tennessee. A further interstate connects the area with north Carolina and beyond. It is also possible to see why the Washington County Economic Development team makes the claim that they occupy a *'strong strategic location between the northern and southern US and have access to 40 per cent of the US population within a day's drive'* (Washington County, 2019). However, for communities that are further from the interstate, life feels very different. Development worker Clara asks us to remember *those folks who live a long way out in the country – which is what I would say. It may take 45 minutes or an hour if you're going to buy what they need in order to be able to do the things that they want to do.* And the places where *you can't bring in anything else because the roads aren't wide enough for the trucks to come in and out.* In other words, although *some* parts of the region have easier access to the outside world, this is by no means applicable to other parts of the area. The towns and communities that are situated some distance from the interstate, deep in the mountains, are far less accessible and far less connected, and therefore struggle significantly more to be able to adapt to changes in the social, political, and economic landscape.

That's not to say that more struggling towns can be solely attributed to distance from the interstate or a 4-lane highway. For example, Peter Crow in his 2007 study of the old coal towns of Dante and St Paul suggests that despite their location far from the interstate (and relatively close to each other), St Paul was able to adapt, whereas Dante has struggled significantly because of its history as a company town. By this, he means that (in common with other communities in the coal region in particular) the business providing the core of jobs (and in the case of coal, also owning the land) also controlled the decisions over local governance. In this example and unlike St Paul which had a different ownership structure, Dante did not become an incorporated town, with its own governance structures independent of those of the primary local industry. As a consequence, decisions were made on the basis of what was best for the company rather than what was in the best interests of the local population and small businesses operating in that locality. Frequently, whilst the operations part of the company was based in the place where the resource is extracted, the companies themselves have been owned by interests in Pennsylvania or elsewhere rather than being founded and run by local business and capital. Consequently, companies are only invested in place for as long as its operations are profitable for the company itself. The interests and needs of the immediate community or the broader region assemblage are irrelevant to distant corporate bodies. One previous coal industry employee described this as an over-emphasis on what he calls *the bottom line*. Despite being broadly favourable towards an industry that had provided an income and way of life for himself, his parents, and grandparents; he states that *I just think you've got bean counters, accountants, all they know is that they are putting numbers together and they don't care about anything else.*

Local governance structures had an impact on the ability of communities to navigate the post-coal environment. According to Crow (2007), Dante was limited to having to follow the needs and wants of the distant company that ran its structures and services. St Paul, on the other hand, was better able to adapt as a community to the social and economic changes that it was to face with the widespread decline of the end of mining because residents could make their own decisions about what were necessary courses of action. An important part of the reason for this is that as an incorporated town, it had to have a local council, which ensured that decisions about the town were made by people who were directly invested in how local industry developed and grew. Their emphasis was on the town and wider community rather than productivity and profit for a remote enterprise. This should not be taken to read that St Paul has emerged unscathed. It also has had to find a way to cope with the loss of the industry which dominated it and formed the bedrock of its culture assemblage. We know that being forced to abandon old and familiar path dependencies and structures is deeply painful and disorientating (See Bergson, 2004; Connolly, 2002).

We also recall Durkheim's concept of Anomie whereby rapid social, economic, and/or political change which breaks down the norms around culturally available patterns of behaviour, often leads to a period of 'normlessness' or social problems as people struggle to find new norms which can help them to adapt. Anomie makes the link between this period of normlessness and behaviours that might be considered as 'deviant'. Although this is another element connecting the region assemblage of SWVA with that of the much wider assemblage which encompasses the United States more generally, the effects of the opioid crisis on the abandoned coal mining regions (including West Virginia, and Kentucky) are well documented. In her (2018) book *Dopesick,* Beth Macy reveals some of the societal struggles that the town and other neighbouring communities have faced in the early twenty-first century. However, these issues not-withstanding, a contributory factor in why the town has been able to maintain a sense of vibrancy, despite their troubles, is that its history has enabled the development of structures which facilitate a ready flow of a diversity of knowledges. This has enhanced its capacity to adapt due to more laterally defined power structures rather than vertically hierarchical, which facilitates the ready flow of information (see also Boschma and Frenken, 2011; Martin and Sunley, 2006; Boschma, 2015; Dawley et al., 2010). This also illustrates the importance of historical affective feedback loops for how spaces are able to adapt to contextual and environmental changes, which the actants within an assemblage encounter.

Nevertheless, there is a risk of sliding in to a situation where one 'blames' a town assemblage or locality for its misfortune. For example, 'this' town is at fault for not having been able to put in place adequate structures and for having been too tightly caught up in path dependencies derived from specific histories. Or even collective grief at the loss of specific industries. Whilst it is true that actants within an assemblage have agency to act, interact, and plot their paths for future activity, they are also heavily constrained by the wider environment within which the assemblage sits and in the spaces of possibility that they provide. For example, it is not the residents of Dante's fault that they were raised in or followed a job to a town with a hierarchical power structure which would compromise its survival going forward into a post-coal environment. To understand this better within the southwest Virginia context, it is useful to look deeper into an analysis of communication, which can alert us to some potentially serious inequalities that arise within the region assemblage, on the basis of landscape, infrastructure, and development.

We know that southern Appalachia is frequently characterised as being slower and remote. Less generous representations of place imagine it as backward and ascribe people and place with many unpleasant characterisations and characteristics (Roberts and Townsend, 2015; Satterwhite, 2015). As with all stereotypes, these are founded on grains of truth that become magnified and amplified to include *all* members of a particular group. Several participants talked about the ways that people from the area are perceived by outsiders and how this has affected them. Tom relates his time working in the coal industry, discussing how sometimes it meant that he worked in other parts of the United States. From his experience and in the way that he narrates it, people from the north of the United States often made fun of his accent. He states that *I guess we're just funny*. But this is not limited to America's north/ south divide. Two female college graduates who studied on or just beyond the outer edge of SWVA relate how other students responded to the way that they spoke. For Marsha, her accent became a totemic badge of difference, which marked her out as a *country bumpkin* with all of the negative affective symbolisms and meanings that this connotes. So she changed the way that she spoke, to be more like those in the city in which she studied. However, this impacted on how her family came to perceive her. She says that and *they would be like 'oh, you don't talk like you're from here anymore. You talk like everyone in [deleted] talks. And yeah, it's like they disown you because you left for 5 minutes. So that's kind of weird.* Dana also, spoke with anger as she related how although her college was just two hours away from her home, *when I went to college people would have me repeat things because of my accent. Obviously it's there, it's always been there, it's gotten a lot better since I went to college, but how is that possible.* Dana clearly located being treated *like a parrot* within a hostile and painful affective repertoire. She did not experience it as a sympathetic or fond marker of difference but as a belittling and unkind act that reinforced her sense of being 'other'.

These characterisations are affectively linked to a perception that people from the region occupy a conservative lack of progressiveness. But there is another story, which once more connects this region with rural America, in general, and southern Appalachia, in particular. What we find is that because of the ways that contemporary culture is accessed, SWVA is *bound* to occupy a 'different' temporal scale to mainstream America. In previous times, the country store provided a vital space for members of the community to meet and share news and information pertaining to the lives of local people. The Sears catalogue and later, Radio and TV, helped to keep up with what was happening in popular culture. Nowadays, in all but the busiest communities, these stores have closed, people have less time to sit and gossip, and popular culture has moved from the more didactic imparting of information, to a more interactive one via various internet platforms. In short, old ways of sharing knowledges have died out, and new ways have not yet adequately been put in their place. Not unlike Melissa's earlier comment about how *time moves differently in these hills*, Dana talks of how popular culture has tended to lag somewhat behind what is going on in mainstream America. But this also connects to vital pieces of connectivity infrastructure. For example, she relates that *I had a cell phone in high school, but I couldn't use it until I was coming back from college, so that would be 2008 or 2009. It wouldn't work. Service wasn't available.* Factory worker from the east of the region, Otis brings this up to date. He states of the holler in which he lives that *you have to get satellite, and there's just not close enough satellite to get good reception. A cellphone will hardly work here. You get the right spot, and you can make a phone call. You can send a text easier. But something strong like making a picture. That's real difficult. It takes more oomph I guess. And that's a complaint in a lot of rural areas. There's just not enough people living within a small area to justify them getting a tower to supply those people.* At this point, it is important to make clear that access to the internet and mobile phone are not luxuries in twenty-first-century Western culture but represent a vital space for how people are able to navigate lives, share practical and cultural information, and make a living. Failure to have these things represents an inability to function in ways that are considered not only normal, but essential in contemporary life.

Access to the internet and cell phone coverage was a strong reoccurring theme across many of the participants' stories in more rural parts of the region assemblage. Richard relates how a previous Congressman Rick Boucher *was a huge advocate for trying to, for getting lots of fibre. Internet fibre, the 58 corridor.* A strong central broadband fibre infrastructure has now been put in place, funded by Tobacco Commission support. But the problem has been in bringing it to communities and more isolated households, and money has not yet become available in order to ensure that this happens. Some smaller communities with high levels of social capital have been able to organise to provide the service to local residents. So Julie, a writer from the east of the region tells that *Part of the reason that they have this is because there is a co-op run by citizens that puts down the fibre. They're not motivated by financial considerations, but they're willing to do what's best for their community rather than what's best for their pocket books all the time for the short term. It's about what the community is going to need in the long term. So there is good internet here, so there are a lot of people that work from home. I work from home.* However, her neighbour, who works for a global agribusiness firm, does not yet have home access to the internet because the roll-out process hasn't got to him yet.

Dana talks about how difficult this can be for running a business. She said that *we do all of this with no internet connection at our house. And that's a technicality based off of zoning or something. But there is no internet in this house . . . when the leaves grow on the trees the signal isn't high enough to get the internet. So in fall we get internet. In summer we do not.* Otis talks about the fact that internet providers don't bring the service the final mile, or 5 miles to people's homes as a kind of *rural discrimination.* Local activist Annie concurs. She states that

> *for people to be able to fully participate on an even footing in a twenty-first-century internet world, having access to high speed internet really does level the playing field in that rural people used to have to go to urban places for work or whatever . . . in the state that we signed there were a lot of folks working on the fight for rural broadband . . . I live in a cabin that has never had a phone line out to it. And a lot of people have that . . . A lot of electrics were wired in the 1950s or the 1960s, but a lot of folks never had a phone line in to their place, and there's not even the physical infrastructure to have high speed internet.*

Annie's point outlines two issues. First, she is stating the fact that some people in the region still live lives that make do without things that in the twenty-first-century Western world, we consider to be essential. Second, this has a significant impact on the ability of such people to fully participate in things that are considered to be normal in contemporary life. She tells that *a lot of people I know that live rurally have cell-phones, but they use them for when they go out and about running errands . . . There are known spots where you'll see someone sitting in their car where someone has driven out to get to the spot where they can get cell service . . . So I think it's a really big deal because it's hard to do things, it's hard to participate in a social networked kind of way without being able to.* This recalls Dana's earlier point about the difficulties in running a business when not only do you not have broadband internet at home, but when you also cannot access a cell phone service that will get you connected online.

Rashid moved to the locality because he fell in love with the area and saw it as a place that an ambitious, young, ethnic minority person like himself could thrive. He still values much about the life in the region but contrasts the connectivity that he experienced as a teenager compared to SWVA. At the time that people in SWVA could only ever access the internet via dial-up, he *could talk to people from New Jersey across the world with no lag whatever, and if I wanted to I could use my smart phone to access knowledge.* The broader, long-term implications of this are that not only do local businesses find it more difficult to thrive than their non-rural counterparts in other parts of the United States, it reinforces the affective constellation of symbolic markers that reaffirms the 'apartness', 'otherness', and 'backwardness' through which rural America, in general, and the Southern Appalachians in particular, are characterised.

In many respects, this kind of characterisation has multiple impacts. First, it renders a 'truth' to unkind representations of the 'backwardness' of the whole of the region assemblage. Second, these kinds of stereotypes perpetuate a myth of truth which impacts on how others see the area and the degree of sympathy or empathy which outsiders hold towards local struggles. This affects both the resources that are available and the willingness of others to redirect necessary resources. Third, it means that knowledges within the region-assemblage and between the region assemblage and other assemblages that it is connected to do not flow as freely or flows much more unequally. People that live in larger communities and towns are more readily able to connect and be connected, becoming 'plugged in' to knowledge flows. This reinforces the already existing strong urban/rural divides within the region, but also means that adaptation across the region assemblage more generally is slower than for other, better connected places. In turn, this risks the region lagging further behind economic cores, becoming more and more peripheralised (see Willett and Lang, 2018; Willett, 2018). Fourth, it means that individuals and communities that are struggling to cope with the enormous changes in their economic base over the past few decades are at an immediate disadvantage because it is even harder than it needs to be to find out the kinds of knowledges that they need in order to navigate every day (see Strover et al., 2020). For example, it means that people are less likely to know about the changes to the local economy that are happening, and which they might be able to get involved with. Finally, it reinforces a sense of remoteness, isolation, and 'apartness' which, whilst this may motivate some, is more difficult for those reliant on a vibrant local economy.

On the other hand, one of the positives about the slower pace of change in the area is that it provides the time for people to get used to new ideas. First and as we have seen above, the economy has changed quite significantly over the past few decades since the 1990s. Again, this is a story which links together the experience of people in SWVA to the broader American story, demonstrating how the region is not simply *connected* to the wider assemblage of the United States but is an intrinsic part of it. One factory owner relates this from a personal angle. He says that *if you're living in this town or this area, somebody in your family had somebody that worked here. Prior to NAFTA there were 130 operators that worked in here. But after NAFTA. Well really China, WTO was worse for* (his industry). *We're down to 33 people and that's fine. That's manageable.* The acknowledgement of this story worked well for President Trump in his campaign for election to the White House. It is also attached to an affective repertoire which resonates strongly with the precariarity of experiences related by many participants in this study. Soon-to-be-retired educator Michael explains that it has become much more difficult for people with low levels of skills to get a job. He talks about helping adults obtain their General Education Diploma (GED) and that *15–20 years ago they could get a job with that. You know brick mason. Or [name of a local factory] they made batteries. But these jobs are gone.* He observes that the difficulties in finding secure employment for the low-skilled or persons from more challenging backgrounds fuel the rise in crime and drug addiction in his home town. This then becomes a vicious cycle as it becomes harder for people with a criminal conviction to get back into the job market on leaving prison.

Often (particularly older) participants would discuss employment as having once been something that had been stable and secure. Indeed, the local employment market seems to have been buoyant enough for it to be quite common to hear how a participant or close friend/relative *followed a job* to the locality. Now, however, this has all changed. Waitress Melissa feels that getting a good job is something that has become particularly difficult in post-crash United States, Richard discussed the long-term impact of his fathers' job being bought out in the 1990s, and Georgia tells a heart-breaking story about the death of her baby son because of her lack of health insurance. Tom was made redundant from his coal job, Jan experienced the loss of her home following the failed relocation of her job, and Kath told how on retirement her government job cancelled her health insurance when she was diagnosed with cancer. Fortunately, her political representative was able to get this reinstated, but she endured some terrifying weeks when she was unsure that she would be able to access necessary and life-saving treatment. Not all of these stories of precariarity are strictly job related. But they all feed in to an affective assemblage which acknowledges an extreme vulnerability, through which the future becomes a risky and therefore worrying place. Hard times are something that you have to prepare for, and this helps to create a culture of fear as life problems and difficulties are always things that you have to fix yourself. Neither were stories of precariousness sought out. They were offered during a general recorded discussion about life in southwest Virginia. It also means that the fearfulness, through which many people in the area have come to approach their lives, makes people feel averse to further changes which make interpreting the present and selecting the most appropriate course of action even more difficult. It also means that it can be more difficult for people to let go of old interpretive narratives which have served them well for a long time, but which no longer are a good foundation for understanding the present. Change is a risk, and in order for that risk to be made, it should be a necessary step.

To illustrate, Clara uses her grandfather as an example of a popular set of perspectives in the western part of the region. *So he grew up, and the furniture industry was big in the county, and he doesn't understand that that's long gone, and a lot of it has gone overseas now, and there's not really a hope of us getting that back anytime soon. So he's like, we need to bring the furniture industry back. But he needs to understand that there are new ways of doing things.* Clara's grandfather has lived through enormous changes to the way that people and society operate. But the change of familiar industrial base is just one step too many, and people find it challenging to be able to incorporate the way that the local economy has developed when other changes to the stability of the region assemblage are also still in flux and have not yet settled into a regularised landscape. Clara refers to the process of helping local people come to these kinds of realisations about the ways that the economy is changing as a period of *hand holding*. Project worker Tammy works to try to connect the gap between the requirements of local industry and the knowledges that local people have about job opportunities in the area. She talks of how there are a lot of highly skilled manufacturing openings, which clashes with how the region has come to be narrated. Tammy tells of success stories and initiatives whereby people are supported to find their way into the good local jobs that are available. She also challenges and explains the apparent contradiction between a *belief* that there are not good jobs in the locality with the fact that she claims that there *are* good jobs by referring to the traumas experienced by the loss of some very old factories. In this story, young people are being told by their parents not to train for or take up factory jobs, because from their experience, they have seen that factories contribute to precariarity in as much as that they close, and employees find themselves out of work and seeking further employment. Being out of work carries implications of having to navigate the psychological stigma of unemployment in the United States with the physical difficulties of managing on the minimal income provided by welfare payments, whilst a new job is found.

For other people, the issue is not unemployment but about *under*employment. It was not uncommon to learn – either as part of the interview process or through regular conversations – that the person that you were talking to was overqualified for the role that they took. Sometimes, they were significantly overqualified. Partly, this seems to have been that there were not the higher-level jobs available and partly that there was not the money about in order to make these kinds of investments. Marsha relates that *people say any job is a good job, and there are jobs here, but not every job is a good job. A lot of people are underemployed. We don't have a high unemployment rate, but we have a high underemployment rate.* She also notes that *there are high paying jobs here, but I don't know how to get them. They're not open to me.* This indicates that there are blockages to key information about how to access some types of employment in the locality. In other words, knowledges and information do not accessibly flow around the region assemblage in such a way as to connect up all parts which might be interested in particular ideas and developments. As a consequence, significant talent is left under-utilised – not necessarily because the opportunities are not there, but because *they don't know how to access them.*

Unemployment rates in SWVA in March 2019 stood at 3.9 per cent. This is only slightly higher than in the United States as a whole (Go Virginia, 2019). However, despite this and the fact that average wages are increasing, the region is experiencing a projected population decline of 0.4 per cent annually. Here, we see the importance of narrative for setting the story about how people inside, as well as people outside, perceive the locality. For example, Clara claims that *a lot of people focus on the negative rather than the positive, or even the reality. So here's a good example. Yes, we've lost industry and recently we've just had a company close in Chilhowie that employed just a little over 100 people. So yes, that was a loss to our community absolutely. So they focus on the job loss. However, we have* [name of company] *which is our largest manufacturer here in the county hiring 100 people. So it's not that there's not jobs available, it's that perception that we're losing jobs, which is kind of true in a sense, but there are other companies that are looking to expand and do better.* Clara is making the argument that the most interesting or sensational stories to share and talk about are the ones which relay on-going decline. They are the ones which attach themselves to strong and powerful emotions, eliciting a bigger response, and so validating the story-teller. In many respects, these tales resonate with the feelings of depression, loss, and confusion as old industries and ways of life have disappeared and guiding patterns of behaviour and path dependencies have become obsolete. The pain through which the communities have experienced changes then means that stories about pain and loss have a stronger affective resonance, and therefore are more easily shared than ones that emphasise positive characteristics and attributes. This in turn supports the decision of many to leave, albeit with a heavy heart. What we can see from here is that an important part of the problem is that communities have not always been provided with tools that they can best utilise in order to navigate change. This can be for a number of reasons, but all have the longer-term impact on how people in places narrate the assemblages of which they are a part of. But there is a strong *counter* narrative to the one about a downhill trajectory.

HIDDEN GEMS

Like assemblages, stories are multi-faceted, containing only an illusion of linearity. Alongside narratives of depression and loss are other narratives of astonishing people and organisations that have an energy and drive that not only counters decline, but actively takes it forward to a higher level. These are the people and organisations that have what Bergson calls the *elan vital*, the life force or vital impetus that can drive the group forward, creating new lines of flight – new knowledges around which matter, objects, individuals, institutions, and organisations can grow and develop. In turn, this vital impetus also creates spaces of possibility. Openings through which new and previously unpredicted possibilities can start to emerge, but which helps the region-organism to be able to adapt to the changes in the environment in which it now finds itself. It is these people and organisations that I will talk about in this section. Much of this will be centred around the immediate Bristol area. Partly this will be for reasons of resources during the fieldwork phase.

The first of these stories lies in the revitalisation of town centres in many communities throughout the region. Many towns are part of the Main Street programme, which is designed to bring once-dying Main Street's back to life. It is a community-led initiative, relying on the vision, drive, energy, and commitment of local people. The goal is for these spaces to become vibrant and attractive community, shopping and leisure hubs. This is something that is being successfully managed despite a historic shift towards out-of-town shopping, and the more recent threat of online shopping. Rita spoke about how this happened in Bristol. *Downtown was just tumbleweeds a mere 15 years ago. Actually about 20 to 15 years as far as the things that I mentioned before nationwide. . . . in the late 1970s we had a really bad flood that wiped out nearly half of our downtown. Those businesses that were wiped out some didn't open up at all. Those that did reopen afterwards opened up in the mall* (some distance from State Street, its main street). *So we lost a huge chunk of our businesses.* From having been a town centre that was nearly wiped out by the natural environment within which it is geographically situated, Bristol has now become a lively and artsy hub with an excellent and very active library, some fantastic art venues, friendly stores, nice places to eat and hang out, and regular community music events. From a tumbleweed town, it has even managed to establish a Smithsonian museum in the State Street area, based around the fact that through the Bristol Sessions (discussed above) it is the 'Birthplace of Country Music'. This ensures that it earns a lasting place in the Assemblage of U.S. history, far beyond this small corner of SWVA, on the border of East Tennessee. Annie echoed a regularly articulated awareness about how much the region had contributed to the national story. Coal is a part of this, but also the young men who fought in the Revolutionary War, which defeated the English at the Battle of Kings Mountain. However, just because a community plays an important role in a national cultural event, it does not necessarily follow that the nations' most important series of museums will automatically establish an outlet in the locality. The community itself needs to have the vision, energy, and adaptive capacity to keep the event alive not just in the minds of the town or region assemblage but also in the national consciousness. That the Birthplace of Country Music Museum exists is a testament to that *elan vital* – the vital life force which seizes opportunities and creates new things. As is of course the inspirational Carter family, introduced above, who went on to play a key role in the historical development of country music.

This kind of success is not an isolated incident. Local novelist Adriana Trigliani from Big Stone Gap wrote a popular trilogy of books based on life in the area. The first of this series was entitled 'Big Stone Gap' after the coalfield town in which she lived, and where her novels were situated. In 2014, it was made into a film that is now showing on Netflix. Prolific international author Barbara Kingsolver, winner of the 2010 Orange Prize for Fiction, also lives in the area and infuses many of her books with both her environmentalism, but also her sensitivity to the issues and lives experienced by many in the southern Appalachian Mountains. Critically acclaimed local photographer Ben Wallis has regularly exhibited his images in both the Smithsonian and Britain's Natural History Museum and continues to have his gallery in Bristol, on the Virginia side of State Street. Globally celebrated country music star Dolly Parton wrote the foreword for his 2016 book. Similarly, LC King's denim manufacturer on the East Tennessee side of State Street has a significant hipster following. According to Rashid, *I think they're awesome. And so does every musician within the Nashville scene. They go and buy things from LC king, there is something about that. It's like in Harry Potter where they go to that one wand place because why would you go for wands anywhere else. It's an expression of how authentic you believe yourself to be when you go and buy things from LC King.*

In an era when local newspapers on both sides of the Atlantic are increasingly struggling to survive, the local newspaper covering southwest Virginia and northeast Tennessee combines news with investigative journalism. The Bristol Herald Courier won the highly prestigious Pulitzer Prize in 2017 for a series of articles about the gas industry in the locality. Georgia describes the topic of the series. She says that *the articles are about how natural gas companies took advantage of people in the present. The money system, forced pooling and how it works, they just took it. Natural gas companies came in and they just took natural gas right out from underneath people's property. They didn't buy the rights they just took the gas from them. I think at some point in time the courts ruled you got to pay these people back, so they paid essentially they scammed a way not to pay anything.* This recalls the community between Abingdon and Lebanon which fought off efforts to dam the river and flood the valley or the tree-sitters and their helpers trying to stop the construction of the Mountain Valley (gas) Pipeline. The self-reliance, independence of spirit, mistrust of the powerful, and willingness to do something about what they believe in combines to impel some people to do things which are really special, spilling over into the national assemblage far beyond merely the region. In these respects, this is not actually about the things that separate and connect, deterritorialise and territorialise the relationship between the SWVA region-assemblage and that of the whole United States. Instead it is about the ways in which SWVA asserts itself as an intrinsic part of the U.S. story, and therefore the U.S. assemblage, to which it adds territorialising elements.

But an important part of this story is the enormous commitment to place that we discussed in part above and which asserts its own vital impetus and life force, as is articulated by this exchange between Millennial municipal workers Chrissy and Noah. Chrissy states that *I always wanted to move out of Bristol when I got older, but then I got older and I was like, I like it here. I mean I went other places, and I was like ewwww. (*Noah*) Where's all the Mountains.* Despite the fact that the region is still experiencing net population decline, many people are not just located within the region assemblage, they are *of* it, just as they are *of* the United States. This means that many people care deeply about the people that they live amongst, the natural and geological environment that they are a part of, and how their region finds their way into the future. To illustrate, the drive to support his local community got local educator Ben Talley into the National Teacher Hall of Fame and, as a part of this honour, got to meet the then President Obama. He has also written books about the work that he does helping the school children that he works with to feel part of the natural environment that they are situated in and the communities that they live amongst. He has extended this to working for many years with offenders in the community gaol, helping them to obtain their GED (General Education Development certificate), the equivalent of a high-school diploma. Like the furniture manufacturer from near Galax John Bassett III, in Beth Macy's book *Factory Man*, Talley saw something that he felt needed to be changed and worked dedicatedly to be a part of making that change happen.

The point here recalls that of the different fates of Dante and St Paul (above) and is echoed in this statement from Rita. *The problem with that is we've seen industry take down our community. We've had coal was huge, and now it's not. And we had all of the people like you say who are so qualified and have worked all of their lives and are so close to retirement, that we don't have anywhere. And my big fear is that if we were to have another big industry to put all of our eggs in that basket as well. So I think that it needs to be a multilayer thing.* Rita is arguing that the strength of the region and its best adaptive potential lies in the many people and small businesses that do amazing things. She points out that single businesses and large industries might have provided employment, but that this has not always translated into commitment. As we have seen, this has had a number of detrimental effects when such industries collapse. Rita's solution is to grow economies from the ground up, focussing on small businesses, which she claims make up 70 per cent of the workforce. For Marsha, this needs to follow a slower, more adaptive process. *I think it would be wiser to focus on smaller business and focus on the businesses that want to succeed and grow, but that's not where the big money is. Everybody wants big money fast.* Marsha feels that too much focus has gone on providing *big wins*. Instead, she is urging an emphasis on the cumulative effect of *small victories*, and on the *elan vital* of small industries that are trying to succeed and flourish, in an environment of which they are a committed part. Of course, this is not to argue against encouraging and supporting large industries and businesses that are working within the region assemblage. Far from it. However, to emphasise, this overlooks the underutilised and under-celebrated potential of regular people in the locality.

What are the re-occurring themes that we can take from this chapter? The first is about the ability of individuals, communities, and regions to be able to process and adapt to the changes that happen in their immediate physical, natural, and socio-cultural environments and to the broader national and global environments within which their assemblages are situated. Change is a part of life, but it is also a part of life which needs to be managed. It is essential that inequalities in access to communications infrastructure are tackled. People need to be supported in being able to access and make best use of the resources that are available to them and that they are able to use them to create the kinds of information flows that they feel are necessary in order for their communities and their region organism to flourish. This might be by going the 'final mile' (or five) to improve internet connectivity, by making it easier to understand what kinds of employment sectors match ones with high-level skills, by bringing passenger rail back into the heart of the region, or by something else hitherto unexplored which could link people to the things they require in order to flourish. As we have seen, there is a significant amount of energy and dynamism within the locality, with lots of people doing really interesting things. The task now is to be able to utilise this energy – that we have called *Elan Vital* or the life force. This is a role for planners, policy, and local communities in order to consider what kinds of (infra)structures are necessary to enable this kind of flourishing.

This contributes to the second point of this chapter. Another thread that runs strongly throughout the stories of participants, and the region in general, is that of independence and self-reliance, founded in the historical legacy of early settlers and reinforced by the grit and determination required to make a living in a place where life can be difficult. Whilst the factories of the early to late twentieth century provided a cash income and an improvement to precarious lives, they also represented a rupture in time whereby people went from being able to choose how to spend their own time in their own employment to being *em*ployed within a large-scale factory system. Whilst the number of factories and industries that are making a success of their time in SW Virginia is still strong (even if the industry base has changed), there is a lot of scope for growing and supporting small businesses. Frequently, the regional development literature discusses this as being about supporting the creative sector (see Bell and Jayne, 2010; Herslund, 2012; Nathan, 2005; Stam et al., 2008; Lee et al., 2005; Willett, 2016). Although there is undeniably a high degree of creativity in the region, this is not what is intended. However, small businesses do need to be supported to flourish. Currently, there is some provision for this such as at Virginia Highlands in Abingdon. However, it needs to be extended and made more accessible. More work needs to be done to both reach the kinds of people who are interested in developing a small business and to be able to utilise languages which can also connect with the needs of ordinary people in the ways that they imagine their worlds.

Chapter 6

Cornwall

By definition, spatial assemblages are complex, rich, multi-layered, and deep. Incorporating multiple pasts and presents, subjectivities and objectivities, remembered and forgotten, and with a spatial reach far beyond the place in which they are situated. They incorporate well-populated lines of flight which excite and delight some segments of the community, generating new assemblages to fit within and outside of the territory. Other lines of flight from previous times lie forgotten, buried in the dusty corners of the museum or library. Some phenomena within contributory spatial assemblages territorialise the region and some also deterritorialise it. Sometimes objects, symbols, and/or ideas, which act as territorialisng factors in some parts of the assemblage, operate as *de*territorialising factors in others. Or fail to resonate in some spaces, whilst chiming loudly in others.

The assemblages which constitute (and are constituted by) Cornwall epitomise these processes. Participants in this part of the study brought a multiplicity of perceptions, perspectives, and experiences. Sometimes these resonated with each other, at other times factors that one person took for endearing, another saw with sadness or anger. Ideas both territorialise, binding people and other ideas together, *and* deterritorialise, spilling the assemblage beyond its tentative imagined boundaries. Perhaps dissipating, but perhaps expanding 'Cornwall' outwards, beyond its territorial limits. Complex adaptive assemblages also have complex relationships with temporality and the interaction between the past (or many pasts) and the present. The cultural meanings, memories, and practices which spill out of this set of affective feedback loops quite literally fold the past into the present, providing the present with interpretive meaning and using the past as a framework for navigating the uncertainties that lie before us. Sometimes the pasts that surface also territorialise cultural assemblages and bind them together, and at other times they de-stabilise and deterritorialise.

As one of the nations that make up the United Kingdom of Great Britain, Cornwall's past is rich, complex, and deep. Covered by the Framework Convention for the Protection of National Minorities from the Council of Europe, Cornishness carries different meanings for different people. One set of narratives was highlighted by the participant who took pride in translating local place names from their original Cornish through to their Anglicised variant and using that as a way of telling stories about local histories. Matt greeted us using the ancient tongue, which although not in common usage is still spoken and learned and permeates the landscape in dialect, pronunciation, and social and economic culture. He spoke with pride about community efforts throughout the ages to preserve local buildings and objects of significance, maintaining a living heritage that bound the past and the present as part of the textured fabric of the oral and visual landscape. Some commonplace, lived practices, which were part of people's every-day, now are performed as sport, or recreation. The popularity of (pilot) gig rowing is one such example, where gig rowers display their prowess at regattas throughout Cornwall, the Isles of Scilly, and beyond rather than use their strength and speed to win the opportunity to guide ships into harbour. At the quieter side of this narrative sit people like Mandy, who whilst discussing questions of rural isolation was also at pains to make clear the importance of Cornishness, culture, and heritage, which affectively fused with her concern for more vulnerable members of the community. Some people take pride in their Cornishness but adopt a version of it which makes other people feel uncomfortable. Perhaps through statements, which border on a form of xenophobia, or maybe because they see no discrepancy between being both 'Cornish' and 'English'. At another part of the assemblage are the people who moved in, or whose families raised them in the Duchy (never a county). This incorporates people like Amy, whose life has been intimately shaped by her experiences growing up and living her adulthood in the region but who baulks at calling herself 'Cornish', preferring to describe herself as from the town in which she was raised and still lives.

Immigrants and the children of immigrants can have a complex relationship with Cornishness. Some police the boundaries of what counts as 'Cornish', excluding themselves as not fitting the category of having had three generations of their family born and raised in the place. This statement might be repeated even in a social situation where people who clearly and comfortably identify their Cornishness make much more inclusive comments about how it is an identification rather than an accident of birth. Others embrace the differences of Cornishness and throw themselves into cultural and heritage organisations, institutions, and events, in many cases helping to keep these alive and contributing to the vibrancy of their communities. A further position is dismissive of any differences at all between England and Cornwall and is unwilling to engage with the area on any other terms than that for them; it is a nice place to live. All of these are factors which are objectively true and yet open for dispute, debate, and discussion, now, in the past, and in the future. They both bind people together in a shared sense of space and construct fracture lines and divisions about deeply held feelings.

Territorialisation and deterritorialisation also occur through the practical movement of people in quite complex ways. Although (as in SWVA) the economy and jobs loomed large in many different forms throughout the interviews, the thread that I am going to begin this chapter with relates to the fluidities and mobilities of people into and out of the region. Although this was not the biggest theme that wove its way throughout this phase of the research, these mobilities and fluidities underpinned much of how Cornwall is experienced by research participants and intersected with economic questions in many different ways. As a consequence, it had a significant presence throughout much of the conversations that we had.

To start this discussion off, I am going to begin with Rosa, a student. Rosa exists in an interesting double space where she is very deeply an insider – a Cornish woman by virtue of a proudly Cornish parent, with a large and close extended family that live nearby, and of which she is a part. But she was raised and spent most of her schooling in a deeply rural part of the United States and so at the same time is located in the community, and people who she has never previously met are able to place her into a community context. She is also an outsider, examining the space in which she has lived and come to love over the past few years with eyes that are less affected by the path-dependent or popular narratives encountered through the process of growing up in a place. Rosa says of her new home: *I've never lived somewhere that people wanted to come, and like get souvenirs from Cornwall, things like that – I love going around souvenir shops.*

Rosa is alluding here to the fact that Cornwall isn't just an isolated rural peninsular with a stunning and dramatic coastline, but it is a rural peninsular which, through its visitor economy (which is an enormous part of the fabric of Cornwall) has a role in the wider popular imagination of the United Kingdom. Traditionally, one would add 'love it, or loathe it' to this kind of statement, as it typifies an idea and institution which at the same time territorialises *and* deterritorialises. This works on a spectrum that includes feelings and beliefs that as it dominates Cornwall's economy it is something that needs to be not only endured but also capitalised on. Others start from the lens that fails to see what rural places are able to offer the contemporary economy beyond the amenity value of the environment, and so believe that if Cornwall did not base the economy on tourism, it has nothing else to offer. Some people are ambivalent to the activity, accepting that this is part of the experience of being in Cornwall and that summer queues on the roads, at beaches and other attractions, and in Accident and Emergency hospital waiting rooms are just part of summertime life in the region. It is typified by the sign held over the main artery road at the July 2020 post-COVID-19 opening of the region to visitors, asking drivers to stay away (Daily Mail, 2020). It also represents a significant part of Cornwall's economy as evidenced by the intense pain and business closures caused by the rapid reduction of visitors over the course of the pandemic. Other people point out that as an industry it offers predominantly low-paid, low-skill seasonal work. This does not provide an income which is enough to live on as an individual or as a family in a housing market that is inflated by the relative cheapness of real estate compared to the wealthy southeast of England and the desirability of Cornwall as a lifestyle choice. In the words of Amy, a parent and community activist in her mid-40s, the price of these people 'living their best life' is *that I'm living a shit life, so you can live a good one.* Amy refers here to the wide differential between the cost of rent or housing to buy, compared with local earned incomes (of which we will speak in more depth later). It includes the broader effect that this has on the lives of people that live in Cornwall not because they chose to relocate, but because this is where they are from and grew up.

But the point raised by Rosa is about how wonderful it is to be living in a place that people find so attractive to be in – either to visit, or to move to. For Rosa, this perspective is informed by spending her formative years in a place with all of the (perceived or real) disadvantages of rural areas, such as isolation and being imagined as 'backwards', with the added psychological and practical impact of this place not being somewhere that anyone chose to go to. In the United Kingdom, residents of the nation's capital and metropolitan areas readily visit Cornwall for a staycation, and Cornwall has had over a century of highly successfully adapting its visitor industry through changing visitor expectations. For Cornwall, this means that it has a very different rural experience to what perhaps might be considered as the 'norm'. It means too, that territorialisation and deterritorialisation happen not only in terms of the flows of ideas in and out of the space but also in terms of the flows of people on both a short term for a few days or weeks or longer term as immigrant residents. As a consequence, the new ideas and the fresh energy which are important if the region assemblage is to adapt and evolve to contemporary challenges and opportunities are (potentially) constantly flowing inside and outside of the locality. Speaking of her home town, Amy recognises that this has potential positives because it *means that it doesn't, you know, it doesn't become sort of entirely stagnant.* In practical terms, whilst many rural regions experience population decline (Argent, 2016), Cornwall has experienced a population increase from 424,500 in

1981, to 566,000 to in 2018 (Nomis, 2020). This has undoubtedly brought with it change and disrupted old, traditional patterns – whilst at the same time preserving or conserving other aspects of patterns and structures. Migration to Cornwall and the outward migration of large numbers of young people are both at the same time territorialising and deteritorialising factors.

In an uncritical analysis, drawing heavily on evolution, one might assume that the changes brought about by an interchange of people will better facilitate adaptation to the contemporary global economic environment. But a closer look highlights that change is value-free rather than necessarily always an objective good. Indeed, the impacts can have broader effects on how individuals and communities are able to mediate their lives. This is illustrated in the flip side of Rosa's observation, by Ruth, a sciences professional, working with young people, who relocated to Cornwall several decades ago. Ruth says that *when I moved to* [deleted] *it had – it was like a little fishing village, and it had a butcher's, and it had a grocery store, and a SPAR shop. Now it's just got White stuff, and FatFace and tourist shops. So I think there's been a big commoditisation, if that's the word, of those pretty places, so they don't feel so much like villages any more.* [although the] *Food's got better. Seriously though, you can go out to a lot more places now and have really nice food.* Ruth describes here the way that the tourist industry has come to dominate communities that have managed to capitalise on it. The visitor – especially the upscale visitor catered for by this particular town – provides a more lucrative income for shop owners albeit for a few months of the year than the resident community who need the shops for groceries and other necessaries which they have not got into the habit of purchasing in the supermarket or online. Whilst this has undoubtedly affected the liveability of this particular place, it also has brought with it some exciting cultural changes and possibilities if individuals have the resources to access them. In this example, it has helped to create a new and potentially exciting line of flight around good quality food.

In practical terms, it also means that some coastal communities slide towards becoming resort towns that as the spectrum outlined above show-cases meets with approval or acceptance in some quarters, ranging to frustration and opposition in others. As highlighted in the BAFTA award-winning film *Bait*, this creates a friction between the coastal resort and deeply embedded and intertwined local communities trying to make a living. As a film, *Bait* shows how the activity of commercial fishing at the same time provides aesthetic detail to the resort backdrop, whilst also clashing with the visitor experience in complex ways, ranging from loud and noisy early morning starts of fishers to competition with visitors over accommodation. It also articulates how as a set of ideas and an economic activity, the visitor economy ripples and reverberates throughout the complex adaptive assemblage of Cornwall, dividing and uniting, territorialising and deterritorialising.

But one of the things that the visitor economy also does is expand the reach of Cornwall well beyond the boundary of the river Tamar, which forms most of the border between Cornwall and its neighbours. It means that this place is known about in the present day, as its strong maritime trading heritage and mining expertise meant that it was known about worldwide over the centuries. The affective reach of the visitor economy, however, works in particular kinds of ways and creates certain types of knowledges about the area. Erin, a PhD student in her 20s was able to draw on her background in project work in her observation that *(Cornwall) almost suffers from being such a lovely place to be, because there's one tourism aspect that – seems to be that there's also quite a few people who move down because they are trying to get away from things, and they see Cornwall as that haven where they can come, certainly when I was working at* [deleted], *there are quite a lot of people who moved because they had health issues or they had mental health issues, or they had possibly domestic abuse up country or had difficulties and then moved down to because that was a place they could be.* The visitor experiences a particular performance of place, designed to make for a restful and peaceful holiday. A female participant from a coastal community concurs. She says that *it's where they come on holiday to get away from everything. That's my interpretation, so when . . . when people come on holiday to Cornwall, they tend, in my experience . . . to go for rural communities, their peace and tranquillity of space away from whatever urban environment they live in, you know, that's what I get from people. So they assume that when you live down here, you don't see anybody for a week, because you all live in a little farm cottage somewhere, you know, you don't live in St Dennis* (a large, industrial village).

The success of the quiet, sleepy, visitor experience fuses with the rural idyll (Lowe et al., 2012) to become an affective performance through which holidaymakers come to know the area. As visitors disperse to their homes in the United Kingdom and the rest of the world, they take with them their acquired knowledges or truths gleaned from their experience of the visitor performance. In some respects, this recalls the Experience Economy of Pine and Gilmore (2019) who argue that the contemporary economy has shifted from an emphasis on the kind of service that enterprises can provide, onto a focus on the type of experience that consumers are able to have. With regard to tourism, the visitor in Pine and Gilmore's example of Disneyland is fully aware that they are participating in a fantasy world. No one actually lives in Disneyland, and it is constructed purely for the pleasure of the paying consumer. Both visitor and experience provider know that behind the Micky Mouse costume is an underpaid teenager rather than the actual cartoon character. Over the duration of their stay, the visitor colludes with the attraction operator in the fiction that the performed fantasy is a reality. No one believes that they are participating in any kind of lived reality. Tourism in areas where people *actually* live operates in a very different way. The visitor is invited to 'know' the place they stay in and is encouraged to believe that the performed reality is a truth to take away. Therefore, regular life in Cornwall really *is* about living in an isolated old cottage, spending one's time walking the cliffs, surfing on the beach, and eating artisan food at great restaurants.

These knowledges also extend to the kinds of economies that the tourist region is engaged in. The visitor is directed towards assemblages which cohere with the kinds of experiences that they want to have. Poverty porn is not a part of the expected Cornish tourist experience, and so consequently tourists are not directed towards the areas which challenge the rural idyll. Equally, few people intend to spend their long weekend or two weeks summer vacation examining local industrial estates. As a consequence, the economic activities which the holiday maker encounters as they are corralled through their carefully orchestrated and signposted experiential assemblages are connected with the hospitality industry – providing entertainments, edibles, or souvenirs. Resultantly, these visitor assemblages, which are about Cornwall but extend well beyond Cornwall, means that tourists take away and remember only (or predominantly) symbolic markers associated with leisure and pleasure. As they come to 'know' the region, they also know that its economic activities are predominantly visitor-related and the more that associated imagery resonates. Ideas, objects, and symbols presenting a different version, or an economy that contains twenty-first-century innovation and dynamism, fail to gain purchase, in a self-replicating feedback loop.

These visitor experiential knowledges, and those from marketing to potential new visitors, create their own set of assemblages which are both separate to the complex adaptive region assemblage of Cornwall, as well as being a part of it. It constructs a regional imaginary that is *both* of Cornwall and not of it. It countermands the tough realities that people such as Amy have to navigate. She states that [deleted]'s *beautiful and all of that, but my god is it tough. I mean, you know, we're coming to the end of winter, and everyone's feeling a little bit gnarly. You know, I mean, we've been wrapping up, and it's been a tough winter. It's cold, it's windy, it's lonely. If you're in a boat, you know, if you're in a caravan, you'll be shaken by it. Yeah, you can call it romantic, and if you're making a choice and you know you have options, then you can live it like it's romantic. If you don't have choices, if you're there because you have to be there because you can't find anything that you would feel more secure in, then, you know, the romance has kind of gone. Living with the mud, not being able to access anything is desperate and depressing and no way for people to be living.* Amy's reality jars against the visitor assemblage, contradicting and resisting it. She highlights that rural poverty and deprivation mean that the lived reality of many is very different from the visitor experience and notes that when viewed through the lenses of visitor assemblages, practices of deep poverty become reinterpreted as 'romantic'– failing or unable to see the pain in them. But Anna operates inside of Cornwall, involved in local activism. Trying to be a voice for others disenfranchised by what she experiences as a lack of opportunities and basic quality of life. Whilst fed by a (hopefully) pleasant few weeks at the beach or enjoying the natural environment, the visitor assemblage gains its energy from elsewhere, beyond, in the stories and pictures shared by friends and in the written and visual representations of the area in popular culture, market-ing, and travelogues. Whilst being tethered to Cornwall, it operates (far) out-side of it and so is harder for campaigners such as Amy to engage with. In this respect, the visitor economy both territorialises and deterritorialises. It gath-ers together symbolisms surrounding Cornwall and Cornishness, taking them into the broader world, whilst at the same time over-writing other realities in a tension between authenticity and commodification. Whilst many people liv-ing in Cornwall might be aware that the visitor space is a performed fiction, it still has come to dominate how the area is imagined. This distant, dispersed, and amorphous assemblage is hard for local campaigners to engage with. Even if she were able to reach them, would past or future visitors want to think deeply about Amy's reality, during their precious holiday time? These different assembled meanings, symbols, ideas, and practices have a linguistic repertoire with few points of resonance.

Amongst many residents of Cornwall, this visitor assemblage echoes and reverberates through communities, intersecting with and fuelling other nar-ratives. One of the ways that this happens is around the narrative of decline. This is quite a complex process, which I will describe below. Decline fea-tured heavily in both of the large group discussions that formed the basis of the research for this chapter. Even when individual participants sounded comfortable with their communities, their lives, and where they lived, decline slipped in to the conversation in the forms of nostalgia and sorrow for what had gone and what was felt to be lost. At one point, it was so strong that I had to question whether there were any compensations to living in Cornwall at all. People spoke of their (once thriving) local towns and the confidence loss as old, traditional businesses had gone or altered fundamentally. In mid-Cornwall, several people mourned the changes that had occurred in the China Clay industry in recent decades, which had once been a major employer. For example, Graham, a retired tinkerer, who 'lives his life in his garage' as a hobbyist engineer recalls that once *you knew that your bosses started off as a tea boy at 14, and he had to do every job on his way up until he qualified to be a captain or a manager. They knew how to respect the men, they did respect the men. But at* [deleted] *. . . it was shit, they really do not care.* One female participant, now an education professional, recalls the patriarchal sense of being cared for by the company. *So when they had a good year, they would give all their employees a share of some of the profits, a small pay-out. So obviously* [deleted] *then, everybody would go into town and spend their PPS. They could be very good pay-outs, I remember our last pay-out . . . *laughter* it was a substantial amount of money, so that I could buy a combination microwave and a washer-dryer. So you can imagine, if every household had that sort of money in addition to their own salary, that then boosted the economy in the area because they could all then go around and spend it in the local shops.* Moreover, the way that the industry was structured meant that people in nearby communities remembered a significant amount of personal security. *It used to be when you left school, boys would always get an apprenticeship to go and work in the pits, and it was a job for life. And there was always the less able people, you know, poor boy that wasn't quite with us, but he was always the tea boy, and sweeping up the [inaudible] and all that, . . . he would be there because he was so and so's boy, and we'll look after him. But obviously, as things get more competitive and then they have to become more business-like, over the years they've changed, you know.*

What is really being discussed here is the shift to a more neo-liberal version of the economy. The global economic assemblages within which the complex adaptive region is situated have morphed fundamentally, creating a very different contextual environment for local businesses. Participants are remembering how in past times, the dominant local (clay mining) industry provided assurance and protection alongside jobs. People recalled that they had had an expectation of a secure job in a company which took community responsibility seriously and which had important spill-over effects on other businesses in the area. Neighbouring towns were able to thrive, people had money in their pockets, and associated industries in sectors such as haulage and engineering were also flourishing. This confidence rippled out into the broader regional economy. In echoes of Beth Macey's observations in SWVA, or SWVA participants discussion of 'the bottom line', once dominant industries which looked after their workforce are sacrificed to rational efficiency and global economic changes. Unlike Macey's furniture factories, or the loss of demand for coal, these changes have not necessarily been about offshoring or changing demand but about increased mechanisation. As a highly versatile material used in products as diverse as paper, pharmaceuticals, and aerospace, the market for clay is expanding. However, *it's just that you don't need nearly so many people involved as the machinery is so much bigger and better than it was, so you need far fewer people to do the same job.* Other industries have been vulnerable to the same global changes described by Beth Macey. For example, engineer and garage tinkerer Jonathan describes what happened a few years ago in his job, which he had moved to Cornwall in order to take up. *Most of the people I used to know were engineers, down here, because I always worked as an engineer, most of the people I knew were from that background. Now they've pretty much all moved away. I used to work in a company up the road and we had . . . it was all laser cutting technology, and we used to do mobile phone things . . . So we used to do millions of pieces. Exactly the same, that were all inspected by computers and sort of really high tech stuff. We had a sister company in America and a sister company in China, sister company in China closed down, everybody left, walked up the road, opened their own company and took all the business off us, shut the company down. So that was 150 people were made redundant. That was it. So it's like in the end, you sort of go and everybody is sort of all looking at the same jobs in engineering companies, you go to interviews and you see people that you've worked – 'hmm, strange'. But even they, you know, they'd sort of just shut down one by one, just different companies disappeared. So not quite sure what their people in Cornwall do nowadays.*

Jonathan articulates the disorientation of rapid changes in work. It was not only his company, but many others throughout Cornwall who found themselves vulnerable to changes in the global economic system, and which resulted in large-scale layoffs. This meant that getting additional work in the same sector was not possible. As a consequence, individuals have had to navigate a rapidly changing labour market, examining how their particular skill-set can be made applicable to the opportunities and openings available at the time. We will examine this in greater detail later, but first I want to explore the affective relationship between shocking and rapid change, and how contemporary Cornish economies are narrated. This is important because it provides some information about how change is managed and navigated by the population. We already know that rapid change can be a challenge for individuals and communities, because it can take a while for people to catch up. New knowledges are not always readily shared around the region organism, skill-sets become newly redundant, and it is not always obvious or evident what new skill-sets are required within the new evolutionary trajectory of the region organism, how these skills might be acquired, or even where to find out this kind of information. Moreover, at the same time that the economy switched, we have also experienced a rapid transformation in how we access information, moving from object- and place-based information gathering and sharing (via, for example, noticeboards, posters, or leaflets) to one that is largely online. Ben muses that *it is horses for courses, the internet is great because you can reach everyone without anyone having to get up. But how do you know if they see it or not? And if they see it, how do they remember that information, whereas if they got a leaflet at least they've got something which they can hang on to, but a little local club.* In other words, sharing information around the complex adaptive region relies on using the platforms that the wider public is also using. People need information about how information is going to be shared – and of course the equipment in order to be able to do this.

As Bergson (2004) tells us, we rely on our memories in order to be able to know and understand how to navigate the things that we encounter in the present. But rapid change means that the regularised pathways between the past and the present no longer have the interpretive guidance that they did have. Consequently, the individual, community, or assemblage is left uncertain over how to act. Perhaps alternative memories can act as pathways to navigate the change, but this cannot be taken for granted. As an example, for most of my decades as a car driver, starting the ignition involved taking a key, inserting into the lock on the steering rack, and turning. Imagine my discombobulation when presented with a car with a credit-card-sized shape that, once in position, allowed for the activation of the ignition on depressing a start/stop button – if the clutch pedal was also engaged. Most of the memories that I was able to access about how to start a car were no longer helpful. Instead, several additional layers of process were required which were not readily able to work out with the level of knowledge (or memories) which I had at that current time. Without additional information, even when in possession of all of the tools required to complete the function, I was unable to start the car. Transferring this across to rapid changes in local economies, it is really important that people are supported in knowing how to adapt their skills to the changing environment, and for that, new memories or additional information is required.

Navigating this kind of transformation in the region assemblage is complicated in Cornwall by the affective action of various narratives. A sense of loss or sadness about Cornish identities is noted by Patrick Laviolette (2003), musing about how the outward migration of young people to the better prospects elsewhere throughout the past few centuries has threaded a sense of loss through Cornish culture. This fused with the confusion and pain involved in rapid economic transformation, such as the collapse of metals mining, which began its long goodbye in the 1890s. The articles in the Cornish Magazine (Quiller-Couch, 1898/99) depict a community trying to pick through an economic landscape where the centuries-dominant mining industry was no longer in the ascendancy. It relates the conversations whereby investors settled on tourism as an opportunity on which to rest future prosperity, thus becoming an early pioneer in post industrial tourist economies. The sadness underpinning these losses is picked up in the code of 'decline', which reverberated through the words of many participants. Even whilst at the same time discussing how much they love their communities, and what a wonderful place they feel Cornwall to be, participants spoke of how hard it is to be there and how isolated in can be. Sometimes this was infused with a nostalgia for the past, but mostly it was about shops and businesses that had closed or were at risk of closing. A local haulage firm that had given way to a national chain. A town centre that was not coping well with the onslaught of online shopping. And how Amazon had opened a distribution centre (further threatening local shops but improving the service to local online shoppers).

The affective symbolic repertoire around sadness, loss, difficulty, and decline creates its own amplificatory and self-replicatory feedback loops which gain fuel from the dominant visitor economy perception of place. Familiar and visible economies have disappeared or shrunk with alarming rapidity. Others have morphed in ways that are hard for people to keep track of. For example, the very real question raised in one of the discussion groups, about whether farming is now predominantly part of the tourism sector. The familiar economy which has remained large is that of tourism. This familiarity provides an affective hook to attach itself and enables it to become amplified itself out of proportion. As a consequence, when asked about the local economy, participants automatically reached for tourism. As a second-order response, offered after a little reflection, participants might talk about trades such as plumbers, builders, and electricians. It is only when pressed that people are willing or able to recall newer and exciting aspects of the Cornish economy. For example, *J and I attended a thing at* [deleted] *Business Park, didn't we, about wind farming and solar energy. And Cornwall generates an enormous amount of that solar energy, of which apparently only about 60 per cent can get up to the grid because of the available technology. We generate more than is able to be used.* Here, the participant is discussing how Cornwall has been an early adopter of green technology, with the first windfarms being erected in the early 1990s. They are aware of some of the sectors where Cornwall has significant strength; however, this is not the first set of thoughts that they encounter as they reach into their minds and memories in order to present the local economy. Similarly, Ben and Jonathan have a little exchange which demonstrates a deep awareness of the growing digital tech sector. Ben: *And there are actually computer game manufacturers and computer games programmers who work from Falmouth. There's quite a prestigious company working there, but you wouldn't know it to look at it, you know, you wouldn't find them I don't think.* Jonathan: *The King's College Hospital's got a place in* [delete] *– a little satellite place, it looks after all it's, sort of IT issues – it's very remote for King's College, but there you go.* This exchange came as a kind of third-order response, once discussion about tourism and trades had been exhausted. Participants *knew* of other opportunities in the local economy, but they were not easily accessible knowledges. They had to think hard in order to be able to access them.

The self-perpetuating feedback loops of the visitor experience, which affirms and reaffirms that Cornwall has little to offer outside of the visitor

industry, fuses with the confusion and loss as familiar industries have disappeared or morphed out of recognition. Tourism is a recognisable memory
pathway in an uncertain landscape. It dominates life in Cornwall every summer, and its affective markers resonate through visual representations in the
media, in film and on TV. It is reinforced through job searches, where despite
publicised skills shortages in key sectors, such as in digital technologies, the
jobs that are easiest to find tend to be in activities associated with holiday-
ing. For example, Sophie discussed how despite being a graduate in her 30s,
the majority of the jobs that she has encountered have been in care work and
summer seasonal jobs. In fact, she found that hospitality and retail tended to
form the backbone of the available work offered. Shortly after their move
to Cornwall, both Sophie and her husband had to work several part-time
jobs just to make ends meet. *And between us, there have been points where,
certainly where* [her husband] *has ended up with three or four part-time hospitality jobs all going on at the same time in order to be able to get a decent
full time wage, and certainly when I was doing the project work, I was also
then doing like, the project, and then part-time balancing it, or topping it up
with something else in the retail or in hospitality . . . I got a project work,
and again, like, short-term temporary contract, and there seems to be a lot
of short-term temporary contracts that are around, and I think partly that is
because Cornwall just is so seasonal. Cornwall just is such a seasonal place,
and as a business you have to make the most of that, so you taken on when
you need to and don't commit any further than the end of that season . . . and
I think it was very much the kind of, I don't know, the MO is that you want
lots of bums on seats rather than a few solid people, you want all the flexibility to have as many people as you need or want in a short space of time
and then no commitment to keep them. Because you can't do it all year.* She
describes a precarious existence of short-term contracts and low pay, where
she has had to be extremely adaptable and emphasise her transferable skills
in order to be able to get work at all and has often found herself to be very
overqualified for the roles that she has taken. She now considers herself to be
extremely lucky because both her husband and herself have permanent jobs,
in non-tourism-related sectors.

For participants in one of the focus groups, tourism jobs are the kinds of
employment that you have if you need a stop-gap. They described an employment culture steeped in zero-hour contracts, where to retain the flexibility that
Sophie discusses, you can get a call on the day if you are needed and you
don't know if you have work from one day to the next. This means that you
then cannot register with a temp agency, and it is a practice which includes
some high-profile local employers in the visitor economy. Such activities
were not imagined as sustainable jobs long-term, although they recognised
that for many, this was their reality. Instead tourism work was perceived

as a right of passage for young people still in education, who want a bit of extra cash. One parent worries about her son, with a first-class postgraduate degree. *So, he's come back. Can't drive, so he's working seasonal jobs for a time – short, time limited period at the moment, but that's all zero hour contracts, they ring him up, you know, so actually that's probably not going to be his career path going forward, but it does worry me that that could be for a number of people, the career path that they're basically not going to be able to afford even rented accommodation in the village, are they?* This parent articulates a much bigger problem affecting the Cornish labour force and cohering with Sophie's contributions above. We are starting to observe how highly skilled young people, with much to offer the local economy, are being heavily under-utilised.

We have discussed at length in previous chapters on how important it is for the complex adaptive regional assemblage to have fluidity and mobility inside, as well as outside of its borders. In the previous chapter on SWVA, we considered these mobilities and flows of information particularly with regard to high-speed internet. But we can apply and extend this to geographical movement too, and this is where we raise the most dominant code from the analysis of the interviews from Cornwall: transport. The parent above is discussing life in a village for her extremely well-educated adult son, who is unable to drive. As a consequence, he is unable even to take a job in the largest big labour market less than 10 miles from their rural home. *If you can't drive, then it's very limited bus connections. Probably, if you're doing like, a 9–5, you may struggle to get to somewhere like Truro if you're relying on public transport, that's fair isn't it. You might make it by lunch time if you're lucky!* In its report about the maritime industry in Cornwall, Pye and Alexander (2018) make the claim that one of the barriers to growth of this sector is the fact that many businesses struggle to recruit and retain staff because their enterprises are often located in more remote parts of the countryside, remembering, too, that Cornwall is characterised by a highly dispersed settlement pattern.

Sophie's experiences illustrate some of the difficulties involved. She was living in a North Cornwall village and took a job in a small tourist-focussed town 18 miles away. The route did not have a bus, so she had to drive to work. In the peak summer season, her journey time increased significantly from 30-40 minutes each way, up to as much as an hour-and-a-half because of the increased pressure on a transport infrastructure characterised by country roads and small lanes. Once arrived at her destination, she then had to *do quite a lot of manoeuvring to try and find some free parking to go to work, and then if you can't find free parking, you then have to pay tourist price for parking, for going to work.* Not only are low-paid employees having to pay high travel costs to go long distances to go to work (and the cost of petrol and diesel are high in the UK), but they are also having to pay parking charges which may be set at steep visitor rates. Later, Sophie moved to a more highly connected community in terms of public transportation and to a job in a town (15 miles away) with a bus route between the two. However, she still needs to use her car. She relates one experience where she was unable to drive to work and was fortunate that there was one bus available to get her to work on time, before 9am. However, *I think I got the bus at seven, and arrived at work a couple of minutes before nine.* Her 30-minute journey took nearly 2 hours by taking the early morning bus because, in order to make the service more viable, it called at many different communities around the area in a circuitous route to town. Consequently, whilst the journey functioned in an emergency situation, it was not viable for day-to-day transport.

Sophie is lucky. She has a driving license and a car. This provides her with some personal mobility. Younger people are particularly vulnerable. Above, we noted the difficulties of a highly educated young person struggling to find work for which he was trained for because he was unable to drive and lived in a community without a functioning bus route to get him to work adequately. However, even when public transport is available, it is not necessarily accessible. Ruth describes how this affects some young people that she knows. *So if you're an apprentice, getting minimum apprenticeship wage, which is £3.90 or something an hour, you're getting £117 a week. So you're spending £9.20 a day on the bus; that's nearly 40 per cent of your wages on transport. So then you're going to be disinclined to get out of your bed and go to an apprenticeship, when nearly half the money's gone. So a lot of these things are kind of – you might start with an enthusiastic young person, but then all these barriers come into play that actually reduce their choices, down and down and down.* The journey that she discusses in this example is less than 7.5 miles. There is a regular bus route between two busy towns, but the young person has had to get an apprenticeship in a town in which they don't live. The cost of the regular bus is so expensive that it takes up most of their meagre wages. The effect of this constricted mobility within the spatial complex adaptive region assemblage is that the energy and enthusiasm of the young person become ground down, dissipates, and leads to disillusionment. Ruth goes on to describe how this affects someone in her community. *So there's a there's a young lad who lives in my village. So he doesn't drive. He sits at home all day long. What I'm seeing with him is his confidence is really starting to dip. Because his friends have obviously gone to college and gone to university, and now he's left behind.* For whatever reason, this person had made the decision not to go to college with his contemporaries. But the effects of isolation and lack of opportunity for young people not in education, employment, or training are a debilitating and self-perpetuating feedback loop of loss of confidence, hope, and possibility. The resultant disenfranchisement – together with the increased difficulty of accessing education and training once over the age of 19 – makes it harder for young people to climb out of the depression that they get themselves into. This is not about a poverty of aspiration. If anything, high aspirations in this sense of hopelessness are too painful as they cannot be realised. But it *is* about a poverty of available opportunity.

Rosa has a slightly different issue. She lives in a place that is served in terms of both busses *and* trains. However, she is a wheel-chair user, and the location of the train stations that she would need to use are up steep hills. As a consequence, *I'm on buses all the time. That's a bit of a pain. Because from my house driving it's about half an hour, but on a bus it's more like two and a half hours. And that's both ways. And it's a bit painful sometimes.* Like Sophie, Rosa is lucky that she is able to take a bus to her daily commitments. However, at a 5 hour round trip this is the available option of the desperate. It reflects the determination, commitment, and drive required in order to be able to function as a vulnerable person, and still be able to access opportunities which are much more readily available to others. It starts to suggest that in order to be able to 'make it' as a person with some level of vulnerability in Cornwall, you have to be exceptional. This and the experiences of some of the people introduced above starts to indicate that many talented people are unable to play a full role in Cornwall's complex, adaptive assemblage, flourish as individuals, or contribute their talents to their communities.

Some young people find alternative but risky work-arounds to their transport issues. Ruth talks here about friends of her children. *Some young people will ask an adult, you know, ask the parent, can you give me a lift here, there, everywhere, that puts a strain on the relationship sometimes. Some people don't have a network that drive. So two things happen. So they Facebook Messenger all the people that they know, or WhatsApp, and say 'are you in* [local town]*?' – I regularly get messages from young people saying 'are you in* [local town] *today? Can you take me to* [town 7.5 miles away]*?', y'know, and I don't even know these young people that well, so they are desperate, they're reaching out for whatever kind of transport from A to B they can get that's not expensive or is free.* Even where parents are able to accommodate their teenage child's need for lifts, it can put a strain on family relationships. Particularly when families are having to factor in scarce economic or time resources. The way around that (and to have cheap/free travel) is for young people to ask their networks if they can car-share on journeys that the adult is undertaking anyway. This is a risky option because sometimes they are asking people that they scarcely know in an attempt to do the things that they feel that they need to. It also introduces the extreme importance of strong networks in order to be able to function in this kind of rural area – even with public bus services and generally pretty good broadband connectivity.

Using the example of a small town a few miles over the Tamar river into Devon, project worker Dan discusses the importance of excellent networks in more detail. The first quote sets the scene. *But also there's a mind-set there . . . that they just won't countenance moving out of* [deleted] *and even though they could do and there are some links and they could get into* [deleted] *or whatever. But they just won't consider that, and therefore they're going to be working in the cafe or Waitrose or I think there's a local – there's a factory that makes something . . . . But it's quite limited if you're just going to stay in the local area. And getting to college is fine because there is a bus that they put on. And I think the feedback I was getting around public transport is quite often it doesn't coincide with start and finish time to work. You're either gonna get late or have to stay late to then get the bus, you know – those things don't tally.* People in the town tend to look for jobs only in the town, even if these jobs do not match their skill-set or the talents that they have to offer. From an outside glance, this could have been interpreted as evidence of a particular kind of insularity and unwillingness to travel. On further examination though, Dan found that the problem lay in an available public transport system which didn't enable these young people to take advantage of the opportunities available elsewhere. This inability to travel and lack of geographical mobility severely limits a person's ability to flourish and contribute fully to the regional complex adaptive assemblage. Dan continues, *I was at a careers fair talking about apprenticeships, and within five miles there are only two apprenticeships, and I mean, it does change day to day. But on that day there were only two within five miles. I think within 20 miles, there were about 38. So it raises that question about, you know, if that young person can't travel 20 miles because they haven't got a moped or a driving licence, can't afford a car, whatever, then actually they're limited to looking at two apprenticeships or probably just getting a job in the local factory or whatever.* As the focus group participant above discovered regarding her postgraduate son, having severe limitations to one's ability to move around the geographical space of the region assemblage means that young people have to take what is available rather than where they can really help the complex adaptive region assemblage to adapt and thrive in the contemporary world. When we use words and phrases like 'overqualified' or 'under-employed', we are not only discussing the fact that people might not be earning as much money as they are capable of doing. What we are really discussing is the fact that the considerable capabilities, talents, potential, or enthusiasms that many have are being wasted or squandered. For rural economies, this is a considerable issue because fewer people in the locality means that there is less capacity available to absorb potential that is being wasted in this way. To draw a metaphor to illustrate this, it's a bit like being gifted £1000 which you have to spend by the end of the week. However, you are only able to spend £500 because you don't have the requisite infrastructure. Therefore, next week you have to go searching about to find the extra £500.

Erin drew on her experience in project working to argue that funding to tackle rural poverty needed to be able to pay for driving lessons, because being able to drive is a necessity and basic skill in places like Cornwall where a car is essential for functional travel. Dan discusses the 'wheels to work' scheme, which goes some way to helping unemployed people gain mobility by paying £40 per week to fund a moped and licence. However, this is still a sizeable part of a young apprentice's income that is not available to people aged 16 or 17. Ruth also mentions that the local authority would soon draw down a sizeable investment from central government to make improvements to local busses, and as I write, although there has been little change in terms of fares, the quality of busses has increased dramatically.

For many though, the key to being able to flourish and contribute lies in having strong family networks. Dan discusses this with regard to a young person that he had worked with. *There was a lad who lived in* [deleted], *and finding work from there is just a big ask – but he's got family that live in* [deleted], *so he was able to move to* [deleted] *and live with them. It's not like – it's not going to open up a massive kind of number of opportunities, but a hell of a lot more than you would find in* [deleted]. *And it just struck me that that kind of is about the resources that you have. So the resources within your family, because if you can move to get somewhere where there are more opportunities, and then you're at an advantage over someone who doesn't have that. His granddad bought him a moped; again, that's family resources.* Once more, we start to see the vital role of strong networks in order to be able to successfully navigate the rural assemblage. For some, kinship groups – family becomes the space that can help more vulnerable members of the community to do stuff. This might be in terms of sharing information (about jobs and opportunities), facilitating relocation, or about sharing physical resources in ways that open up further opportunities. Networks are a kind of ideational fluidity, helping to ensure that possibilities flow in mobilities which are accessible to a wider section of the community. In Dan's recent example, the gift of a moped had a value far beyond the few hundred that the machine and license would have cost. It enabled a geographical mobility that in turn facilitated a job, and so, potentially, a future. This also is about much more than simply a figure in the unemployment statistics, or part of the GDP metrics. It is also about much more than reminding us that we are discussing here a young person's life. Instead, it takes us into the perspective on power opened up by the Complex Adaptive Regional Assemblage. Power works differently from the mechanical power of Newtonian force, and instead it can ripple and amplify around the assemblage, extending the affective impact of a thing beyond all kinds of proportionality. Unemployment and hopelessness is one such phenomenon.

Amy discusses the long-term impacts that being poor has had on her. *It's a reflection of my ability to take part in society because I'm poor. That's what that is. It's not a lack of awareness. It's a lack of ability to take part, and that's economic. So, I know that, you know, there's this sort of geothermal hub. There are opportunities around Cornwall for people to get into high tech careers and all of those things. I don't know realistically how many . . . I don't know, I feel a bit lost with it, really, I sort of hear about these things but it doesn't feel like they're targeted at me. In the same way as, you know, I would see an advert for this hotel, you know, as you close the toilet door: £29 per person. That ain't for me, you know. Going down to the festivals they have in* [deleted] *which are wonderful and draw people in, but are generally not for me because, maybe it's not my cup of tea, but also, the things that are attached to it to take part in it tend to be pretty expensive, you know, a night time thing during Falmouth Week would be twenty quid a ticket.* This is a very complex set of points in this interview extract. Amy points out that she *does* know about a lot of the interesting and exciting developments that have happened in Cornwall's economy. She also knows that there are some opportunities for people to get into economic sectors that are a long way outside of the traditional perceptions of place as predominantly 'cloaked' by a tourist perspective, and she lists here some renewable energy initiatives. The problem is that her inability to engage with the area in cultural terms negatively impinges on how well she feels able to engage in high-skilled economic sectors.

With echoes of Durkheim's (2002) concept of Anomie, she finds that being able to participate in 'normal' life in her community costs more than her precarious financial situation will allow. Whilst £20 for a ticket to an evening festival event might feel negligible to many, for her, it is too large a sum from an overstretched budget. The idea of spending £29 per person on a meal out is completely outside of the realms of the possibility for her. This builds an affective system whereby Amy feels economically excluded from most of the cultural activities in her town, which then spills out into how she is able to engage in economic potentialities. The cultural backdrop of her town is inaccessible. Even things arranged as 'free' events but which borrow symbolic markers and affective resonances from the events from which she is excluded, also feel inaccessible because by now, the economic inaccessibility caused by low income has spilled over into a cultural exclusion. Dan notices this with regard to poor families that he works with who live near the sea but never go to the beach, because it is *not their family culture*. Over time, the individual comes to feel like this free thing, and a signature of Cornish symbolism, is not for people like them. In terms of jobs and economic activity, this means that the highly skilled works are activities undertaken by people like 'them'. Amy has few shared cultural reference points with 'them' beyond her excellent education and the place that she lives. This is not about the fact that Amy lacks confidence, and so can be given the target of growing her aspirations and sense of self-perception. Instead this is a societal issue associated with entrenched inequalities of wealth. Amy *knows* that she is worth more than the societal value placed in her. She is fully aware that she has more to contribute, and this is reflected in her voluntary work. However, this knowledge is not reflected in the economic sectors which feel accessible after decades of being ground down by trying to raise a family amidst housing precarity and extreme low income. Fully recognising that her talents are being wasted, Amy can only see a future of low-paid jobs ahead of her, and this makes her angry.

It is with Amy in mind that the experiences of the youngster with strong family networks and resources, that Dan relates, become so important. This teen has been offered the chance to side-step the spiral in confidence and exclusion created by (particularly early) experiences of un/under-employment. The gift of the moped has the potentiality to amplify the extent to which this young person is able to flourish as an individual, and play as full a role as possible in the socio-economic environment of which they are a part of. It also illustrates Putnam's (2000) point that good societal networks constitute 'social capital' which better enable (a more efficient) societal flourishing.

Better public transport connectivity is not only about ensuring economic productivity but has impacts and effects on other parts of the community too. Mandy, a health practitioner, relates the experiences of some people that she has worked with in the past. *So, two areas, one lady was in* [deleted] *and trying to get to* [her nearest town, 9 miles away], *and she was actually struck off from being seen because she missed her appointments because the bus couldn't make it, and this was an 89 year old woman living alone relying on a bus service. It's absolutely awful, so in terms of people accessing services who are already fragile, it's really tricky. Another lady who was from* [a hamlet], *which is in the middle of nowhere, also really wanted to come, but she just had her car taken off of her because she reached a certain age, and her eyes were failing, and she really couldn't get to anything, and nobody was able to offer her support. Nobody was even prepared to go to her because you are limited within what you're allowed to do within certain services.* We already know that being able to drive is crucial for being able to navigate both Cornwall and SWVA. But not being able to drive anymore both indicates that you are already vulnerable and increases your vulnerability significantly. As people get older, they become less able to drive safely. In rural areas in particular when a person has built a life in a community where a car is essential for 'normal functioning', this loss quickly slides into isolation and loneliness.

Although retired people do have important support like free bus passes in the United Kingdom, rural policy professional George reminds us that this is only of value if there is a bus service locally to use.

Moving to a better-connected location is not necessarily the solution, because although the person might be more *infrastructurally* connected, they might find themselves even more atomised in terms of other networks on which they rely. Mandy continues, *then people are forced to move into towns and cities where they're not from, just so they can access services, but then they are still isolated because they don't know anybody, you know, they haven't got those people that they grew up with around them.* This contributes to a high rate of suicide amongst older people, in particular, reflecting their loneliness and isolation. Mandy also notes a difference between older people who have moved to Cornwall to retire, and so are often involved in lots of local activities as they seek to build their networks in the communities that they have come to, and more established, Cornish people, who remain in the (more isolated) family home and whose networks might have dissipated through the outward migration of their own families. Community activist Matt looks at how his community has spent considerable time and effort trying to maintain the services that those with less geographical mobility rely on. He is bruised by a (successful) battle to retain a doctor's surgery in his village rather than for locals to have to travel 2.6 miles to a neighbouring village. *So I really agree with the Parish Nurse, but it almost feels like because – we're almost trying to do our own NHS (National Health Service). We're trying to run our own – we do our own toilets. We thought we're going to have to do our own surgery. We run all our village halls, we run our own community bus, but everyone's taxes are still the same. And it just seems it's a prime example of where rural areas are discriminated against.* In this example, maintaining services for all is imagined as an important part of maintaining a living community. But there is a tension between the amount of self-help and local energy required in order to be able to do this in the face of increasing agglomeration of services. Matt's community feels that they have to fight for access to services which are a basic provision in places with higher population densities. He even goes so far as to describe this as a form of 'discrimination'.

This community is lucky in as much as that it has found a way to mobilise a cross-section of its residents, getting and keeping them involved in activities which build a mutually supportive local network of good friends, alongside strong local services. For it, the magic bullet was to bring people together around a local club which spilled over from a shared activity, to a social group (facilitated by the local pub) and from there to an extended group of friends, ready and willing to become involved in activities which supported the community. To borrow from Putnam (2000), this village exemplified the fact that local clubs and associations can become a nodal point about which information and support can flow, and people can become mobilised. This then slips into local governance, as socially engaged persons become more politically involved, and, when working well, can help local councils to become more demographically representative and work more closely with local people. It also ensures that local political representatives more fully understand the needs and requirements of the communities in which they seek to make changes. This is vital work if community assemblages are going to be able to adapt, survive, and thrive. As a collection of buildings, institutions, and practices which have existed for a long time – especially in a place like Cornwall – where part of the assembled built environment very visibly is centuries old, it is easy to imagine a timeless quality to towns, villages, and cities. We implicitly think of them as always having been and that they will always exist into the future. We might narrate that this or that place is in decline or this or that place is in the ascendency. By which we mean that some places are adapting more successfully to contemporary social, environmental, and economic conditions than others. But the idea that this cluster of ancient cottages, or that town which supported the building of grand buildings in which to conduct its business and administer the locality might not exist in perpetuity feels strange, unreal, and inaccurate. However, a glance around Cornwall's infrastructure of back lanes takes the casual explorer through hamlets and past Methodist chapels (probably converted to residences) and centuries-old Anglican churches, seemingly in the middle of nowhere. These large and grand structures are both a testament to the vibrant communities which were once numerous and wealthy enough to build such constructions and a memorial to changing local economies and settlement patterns whereby residents, unable to continue to support themselves, have moved elsewhere. They bear stark witness to the value-free nature of fortuna, which brings change, but communities don't necessarily get rewarded for 'effort', or how much they 'deserve' to succeed. Instead, the communities which we see today are the ones which have found ways, through the decades and centuries, to successfully adapt to the new ways that the world has become. We discussed above how failure to adapt haunted members of one community who participated in this study. Even whilst they maintained a vigour and vibrancy which indicated that they would continue to persist for some time, the threat of decline echoed around their community assemblage, made present by relatively recent memories where the community had started to feel that the deterritorialising factors pulling at it, bringing change, and was starting to rip it apart at the seams.

As alluded to above, sometimes the (apparent) success that some communities have had in the visitor industry has brought with it its own set of challenges. As communities become considered to be more attractive (and again, as depicted in *BAIT*), more people start to view the local housing stock as investment potential or as a retreat from their busy city lives. This movement predates Airbnb by decades, as holiday homes and second homes have come to dominate many of Cornwall's more attractive spaces. A male participant from one of the focus groups states that *it's spreading, the second homes, it's not just the heart of the village anymore, it's bungalows, and I just know we won't have a youth club, we won't have a school, we won't have a pub open still, and that's already beginning to happen. BAIT* constructs the world whereby old character cottages in picturesque locations have long been attractive as non-residential buildings. However, whereas traditionally, it is the older housing stock that has been prime investment material, recent years have seen this extended to newer build houses. The effect of this – and the thing that haunts this particular community – is that whilst second homes and holiday lets might support the visitor industry-oriented businesses in the summer, it reduces demand for the services that make these communities liveable. Ben states that's *because of its* (Cornwall's) *little community, so it only takes half a dozen houses to be empty to make the whole village seem completely unwanted . . . and it is really nice, you come down on holiday and you see the villages, like 'ooh it's nice in here, very pretty', and there are all these people who are enjoying themselves, but if you come back out of season you're like 'hmm, there's no one here', there's that bloke who lives in his house, and other than that the village is completely empty – it is a disastrous situation.* The nature of Cornwall's small, rural communities means that not many houses need to be taken out of commission before the impacts are felt on communities. With too few residents in the winter, local services which make the locality liveable become impossible to maintain. As we observed above through Ruth's reminiscence about the visitor success of her local town over the years, it is more lucrative to provide businesses which service the visitor market than the needs of local residents.

The next question relates to why the popularity of some communities should necessarily lead to the loss of the full-time resident population. This occurs for a number of reasons. First, and most dominantly, it means that popular demand for housing extends well beyond people who live in the locality but includes those who have made their lives (and their incomes) elsewhere. Because of the widespread income differentials throughout the United Kingdom, it means that people who have made their money in wealthier parts of Britain have a much greater purchasing power than those who rely on local wages (which are some of the lowest in Britain [NOMIS, 2020b]). This increased demand and higher purchasing power moves house prices outside of the reach of local incomes, as articulated by this female focus group participant. *It means that I can't live here. I had to go into* [delete]. *And I'm on a very good wage for the area, but it just pushes the prices way out of possibility, and it means that the young people in the village who, yep,* [name deleted], *he can't live here, because we can't afford it.* Despite having a good income in comparison with the wider area, this participant has had to move out of her local community in which she has her networks and into a cheaper part of Cornwall, over 10 miles away.

Tom also talks about the difficulties that he has had. He lives in a community that has not been able to adapt well. As a consequence, it has seen local services and facilities dissipate, to the point where even the local shop has closed, and it has become a kind of dormitory space. His job takes him to another community some distance away, and this village is a vibrant and lively one amongst which he has developed a strong friendship group. However, as a place that is attractive to visitors and to wealthier inmigrants from outside of Cornwall, local housing is unaffordable on his income. An obvious way around this would be to build more housing stock that is affordable to local incomes. However, this is easier in theory than in practice. Matt explains why: *lots of people are in favour of affordable housing until there's actually a site . . . and actually there's the opportunity to be built, and all of a sudden, people come out of the woodwork deciding that that's the wrong site, and it shouldn't be close to their house, and it should be somewhere else.* This is an issue encountered by assemblages of development that extends far beyond Cornwall and is possibly even nearly a universal experience. So much so that it has its own acronym: NIMBY, or Not In My Back Yard. But there is an additional problem with building affordable housing locally. Matt continues: *Even the places . . . there is a site over here that's got planning permission and was supported by the Parish Council, but you can't then get the developers to build because they're not gonna make enough money out of it, and what they're interested in is sites in* [nearby town] *where they can build 300 houses and make so much more profit.* In a profit-driven environment, small developments of cheaper housing are not as lucrative an investment of time to the developer. Communities have had to come up with some highly innovative self-help solutions with the limited resources that they have, such as community land trusts, whereby the locality takes buildings or renovates housing to provide some affordable to own or rent properties for local people.

On the one hand, it could appear that in the value-free change environment of the complex adaptive assemblage, it does not matter that people find themselves priced out of the areas that they are embedded or located in. Or that some communities slide into becoming resorts or visitor spaces rather than lived in towns and villages with the services required to look after local residents – including vulnerable residents. However, if we look at this through the lens of Putnam's social capital and networks, we can see that it means that the vibrant networks – which are vital conduits of information, ideas, and support to enable the complex adaptive assemblage of the town, village, or city to evolve – break down in these environments. This isn't about the rights of people, like Tom and others, to live where they choose, amongst their friends. Instead, it is about ensuring that the complex adaptive regional assemblage of Cornwall is connected and interconnected. That knowledge and information have easy routes to pass around the region, so it can better understand the environment within which it is situated, what talents and skills it has to offer, and what is needed in order to utilise these. Family and friendship networks are both part of the glue that binds Cornwall together in territorialising effects, the conduits through which vital knowledges and information are shared, and the means through which support for those who find themselves temporarily or permanently vulnerable can be accessed. However, there are other processes which problematise the ability of networks to stay together and operate in the ways that they can. Maintaining liveable spaces helps to ensure that there are enough people living in a community to make a regular bus service more viable, helping to ensure that people are able to contribute their talents and skills rather than rot. It is this spectre of the beautiful, but sterile, lifeless, unliveable space which hangs over some participants and their narratives of decline.

Affordable housing has other impacts too on the capacity of the region assemblage to adapt. Amy talks about the precarity involved in renting a home to live in. *I was renting a house, me and my family, for £750. This is a three bedroomed, ex local authority house and £750 a month, and it was bought and sold and bought and sold while we were living in it, which is as it is, you know, really unpleasant but as a tenant, you have to tolerate the whims of people who own the property.* This was the second time in a year that she personally had experienced her home being sold by her landlord and subsequent notice to leave by the purchaser. In the latter case, the new landlord decided to switch the property from a family home to a house of multiple occupancy, more than doubling the rental income. She continues, *I moved into this house. This was the sixth home, the sixth year that we've moved, and my son was six. It was his sixth house.* Amy tells a story about how moving annually had been such a feature of her son's life that he was expecting to move again a year after. Over this time, they had been overcrowded into cheap(er) homes, tried to move a little further away to where properties were more affordable (but outside of important family and education networks), had to move because of changes in family size, and had their home sold. Because their combined incomes, whilst at Cornwall averages, were too low for even cheaper rental properties, they needed to be subsidised by Housing Benefit from the local Council. Consequently, effectively, their landlord's investments were being subsidised by the tax-payer. Amy notices that not only has this level of precariarity affected her life and the possibilities that she feels are open to her, but this has impacted on her children too.

Their life has been ruined, stunted? Certainly been badly affected by growing up in austere times. Their expectations are pretty low. And even if they want to aim high, because they're certainly capable of doing it, they're aware of being saddled with debt, you know, and they don't want it. Amy does not feel that her children are able to fulfil their potential and contribute in the way that they could because of the experiences that they have had growing up in poverty. This goes on to mean that they are unable to participate as fully in flourishing networks in their localities, contributing their talents. The difficulties that people experience in their day-to-day lives are not only an individual problem, but it inhibits the way that people can share and receive information, blocking the conduits and flows that are necessary for good adaptation. Long term, it negatively impacts on the ways that our communities are able to evolve and flourish.

For Cornwall and many other rural regions, it contributes to another set of processes which destabilise the complex adaptive, regional assemblage: outward migration. Tom feels that the combination of low pay and high costs of housing means that *the likes of me, and the likes of my friends, that are actually Cornish, that want to stay in Cornwall, but it seems to me are actually being pushed out – they have to go upcountry or abroad just to try and earn money, and try and live, have a better life.* The problem here is not only about a lack of opportunity, but that even if an individual can make a personal accommodation with living on a reduced income, they may still be unable to afford to live in the communities within which they are networked and connected. One woman observed that *It's interesting to look at the demographic of even this room, how many are Cornish, and how many are not. And that has changed our village enormously – not saying it's for the good or for the bad. But it has changed it. So there's very few Cornish people that are around now.* For others, leaving Cornwall is almost a rite of passage, which, after the individual has spread their wings and explored the world a little, they are then able to return when they choose to settle down. For example, *for me, this is always home, and I've come home loads – and then it's like, you mess around in your 20s, and you live in Oxford and you live in Dorset, and you have various relationships, okay one relationship, but various relationships. And then you're like, actually, okay, now I'm grown up and I want to settle, I want to actually settle down. And for me, there was no choice about where you settled down, it was always going to be here.* Pete talked about how *when you're young, you do want to go away a bit, and spread your wings, find out what it's like, because it is quite quiet here, and then go away, and then realise, it's quite nice, and I liked it – with the kids, I remember when we moved back here walking* [deleted] *up to school, saying to him, walking through the fields to get to school. You're not gonna appreciate it when you get older. He wants to get away – but when he's older, he might do exactly the same, he might want to come back.* Rosa discusses that even though she feels at home and happy here that her contemporaries and fellow students are 'down' on Cornwall, often looking forward to the time when they are able to leave.

The assemblage clustered around outmigration is also a complex one. It incorporates a desire for flight and exploring other opportunities, but it is also fused with a feeling that opportunities elsewhere are better than those found locally or that there is something 'inferior' or possibly even 'backward' that young people want to dissociate themselves from. Whereas in previous times the Cornish diaspora referred to overseas migration, now it incorporates those who have moved elsewhere in the United Kingdom. As with tourism, it expands the assemblage of Cornwall well beyond territorial borders, with certain sectors of the diaspora organising self-consciously to promote Cornish business and culture. The tongue-in-cheek 'Cornish Embassy' is one such body, collecting together Cornish expats and asking them to be 'ambassadors' for Cornwall and the Isles of Scilly (Cornish Embassy, 2020). This also illustrates how there is nothing straightforward about territorialisation and deterritorialisation. Whilst outmigration clearly deterritorialises, it also presents opportunities for extending complex adaptive regional assemblages into other assemblages, building networks and acting as conduits of knowledge, ideas, and information. Literally, they have the potential to act as deep connectors between region assemblages and other places and peoples. Many out-migrants find that as they get older, the draws of 'home' are significant, and that their attachments to people and place matter more than they had expected them to do. If they can, they return. This doesn't always work, and some returnees feel unable to find a job locally that can cover the high cost of living, especially if they are unable to leverage a more expensive property in the South East against Cornish house prices. Others, like Pete, are able to work from home, using the networks and skills gained whilst away, combined with the Duchy's excellent broadband to connect themselves to U.K.-wide and global workplaces.

This aspect of inmigrants or returnees being able to bring their real or perceived advantages is an important one to reflect on. The phenomenon of the digital nomad who does not have to be tied to an office so can live anywhere is a well-travelled one. It was observed in the early 1990s when fax opened possibilities of tele-commuting (Perry, 1993), and underpinned the strategic shift to the digital economy, which has gained force from the early 2000s until the present day. It has been fuelled by EU structural funds, which determined that rural areas should not be disadvantaged in terms of digital infrastructure compared to the economies of scale of their urban counterparts (Raisanen and Tuovinen, 2020). One of the things that we don't know though is the extent to which people already living in rural areas are able to access digital nomad kinds of employment opportunities. Anecdotally, the person who was able to make their relocation/return to Cornwall possible by reducing the necessity to spend time in the office was raised regularly by many different participants. Jeff, a local business leader, discussed a slightly different phenomenon. He talked about how many people are able to bring their contacts and networks from their city life with them when they relocate, and so have an automatic client list when they move or start their small business in the region. On the one hand, and echoing the neo-endogenous growth literature (Bosworth and Bat Finke, 2019), we start to observe how inward migration might be extremely effective at injecting new skills, knowledges, and networks into the region assemblage. However, Jeff also notes that for the most part, such businesses tend to be content to remain as sole traders, or as very small businesses, not keen to take on the additional work required to grow their enterprises, and use these networks to make something bigger. Sophie also discusses how even home-grown, U.K.-wide enterprises can pay their Cornwall-based employees significantly less than those based in other parts of the United Kingdom. This is a shame because it risks fuelling internal inequalities. It means that not only do some inmigrants (and returnees) have a significant structural advantage over persons raised in Cornwall by virtue of their comparative wealth and social capital, but that these advantages risk becoming hoarded, rather than shared, exacerbating inequalities. Some of these can become very visible as we can see below.

We already know from NOMIS statistics (NOMIS, 2020c) that Cornwall has a well-educated workforce when compared with the rest of Britain. Statistics do not keep data on where workers come from, but a popular narrative claims that as a general rule of thumb, professional level or more highly qualified jobs tend to be filled by people from outside of the area. Ben, himself an immigrant, observes this of one of his working environments. *All of the office staff, probably – well, I would say 95 per cent of the office staff came from out of Cornwall and 90 per cent of the shop floor workers were Cornish. It was a real definite line you could see you know, you just – you could see where the skills difference was. It was quite interesting, really.* Ben observes a further structural inequality which is also cloaked in the ways that rural areas are perceived compared to urban or metropolitan spaces. As we discussed above, rural (and/or peripheral) regions are often characterised through the lens of the metropolitan = good, rural = bad dichotomy (Deller et al., 2019). This extends to people who live in or are from these spaces. The narrative which Ben refers to is one whereby local people either are imagined as less capable to fill particular roles or be nurtured through career progression, or where path dependencies developed and transmitted over decades means that they are less able to understand what skill-sets to invest in, the routes to professional roles, and how to present their resumes. Sophie discusses the complexity involved in getting a professional job in Cornwall.

She has a postgraduate degree but had to change her career. On relocation, she had to be very creative in her assessment of her transferrable skills, which took her on a journey a long way from her original job as a teacher. These structural advantages and disadvantages indicate blockages in the mobility and fluidity that exists within the complex adaptive region assemblage. This further problematises the ability for an inclusive socio-economy.

Sophie's journey provides us with another insight into what could be regarded as a key strength of the Cornish economy. *I've had to upskill and put into practise all of my teaching skills, plus all of my management skills that I've picked from somewhere else, and all the tech skills, and all of the training and development skills, so I've upskilled massively.* In order to survive in the local job market, Sophie has become infinitely more differently skilled than she would have been if she had remained in her previous career and previous location. Whereas before, she would have learned a lot around a relatively small topic area, in Cornwall she has had to diversify her talents which have given her an extraordinary breadth to her abilities. On a personal level, this means that she is much more resilient and adaptable in what she is able to do, with positive implications for her employability. For Cornwall as a complex adaptive assemblage, if Sophie is representative of the wider labour force, this would indicate an extraordinary amount of potentiality and a lot of possibilities for the future. In echoes of this and speaking as the COVID-19 lockdown started to come into force, Jeff acknowledged the trauma to be experienced by the regions' tourism businesses, but was positive in other ways. He felt that the nature of Cornwall's economy and its dominance of small businesses meant that they are much more agile and able to adapt to change, and he pointed to a local gin company which switched production almost overnight to making hand sanitizer. Other radical shifts include a food truck that transformed into a locally grown veg box scheme.

It is, however, important not to make it sound as if resilience and adaptability are all a region-assemblage needs. As we know from our material about complex adaptive systems, organisms require fuel and resources in order to be able to operationalise the creativity that they have, and it is clear from the interviews above that contributors do not feel that this is something that is happening adequately. Senior professional George, who works in rural advocacy, notes that this has been a long-term issue in rural areas which are consistently underfunded compared to their urban counterparts. Over successive decades, where there have been boosts to funding for rural economies and services, the urban has been increased even more so which has merely increased inequalities. Part of the problem is that metrics and mechanisms designed for the distribution of resources tend to be urban-centric, so render rural issues and challenges less visible. Reduced investment reproduces low incomes and relative poverty. Sophie alludes to this as she ended her statement quoted above, making the observation that *my wages are down here compared to what I was on before.* Despite having a diverse range of skills, and having demonstrated the capacity to adapt and transfer her skill-set, she is still paid less than she was years ago as a newly qualified teacher. Resourcing and adequately remunerating the local labour force is a long way off what it needs to be.

The final thing for us to note here in this chapter is with regard to identities and locatedness. Decades ago in the 1980s and 1990s, there were very real fears that the inward migration, which led to a 50 per cent population increase in just a few decades (Perry, 1993), would lead to an erosion of Cornishness. What has become apparent in the intervening years is that there is something about Cornwall which connects people at a really deep level. Cornwall *makes* people Cornish. In common with participants in the SWVA interviews, there was something about the place and the kinds of lives that people were able to live there, which meant something to locals and drew people back when they could. Whether it was Mandy talking about the importance of local culture, heritage, and traditions, especially for combatting isolation; or Matt, who was so deeply embedded in the histories and lived presents of his place that it was difficult to separate out the boundaries between him and his community; or Graham, who wasn't sure why he would want to spend time anywhere else. Whether participants had their eyes full of the idyllic notions of knowing a place and being known in it, or whether they struggled to live there but were committed to trying to do something about it. Or whether, like Sophie, they had moved in and found that a cultural environment which encouraged creativity, non-conformity made them feel more at home than the places that they had moved from. This love of, and commitment to, the place is also a kind of energy, a life force which helps to impel the complex adaptive regional assemblage forwards, into the future.

Chapter 7

What Do We See?

Spaces of Possibility in Southwest Virginia and Cornwall

Both regions have emerged from very different backgrounds, with very different histories, experiences, and cultures. But even so, there are some regularities and similar stories which can be found between the two. Both have seen their economies change quite significantly over recent decades; both have witnessed the collapse of employment in the extractive industries and the way that factory work has changed and shifted. Both have a resilient, practical, self-reliant population that is used to having to approach life through creative solutions. Both have significant (but different) problems with mobilities and fluidities of knowledge and people around the region, as old ways of sharing information or of transportation have changed, but people have not yet found ways of navigating those changes. And both have experienced how the car has brought opportunities and services closer and made them more accessible. At the same time, made them more remote and consequently, to the car-less, *in*-accessible. We have also seen the precarity and vulnerability of working people as even before the devastation of COVID-19, they navigate an increasingly changeable and unfamiliar social and economic landscape.

We could, of course, say that these are all practices and processes which are to be found in late capitalism and that much of the problems that we discuss are directly impacted by the social and economic relationships fostered by neoliberal economic systems. In particular, this relates to factors which look on workers as economic units in a drive to *the bottom line*, where the purpose is to make the business a profit rather than to support the lives of the people and communities that staff the business. We might also point out that the movement of such businesses to places overseas with cheaper production, or their closure due to being unable to compete with such a ruthless business model, is emblematic of structures that cause the precariarities and vulnerabilities which lead people to struggle so much.

But the purpose of this book is not to critique the economic system, but to look for what Deleuze and Guattari (2004) call the 'spaces of possibility' that can help places to adapt and evolve. Such structures, as objects, change continuously (see Latour, 2004), so such an analysis would be quickly out-dated, particularly in the light of the Global COVID-19 Pandemic that has changed so much, and is likely to continue to instigate unknown and unpredictable developments over the next few years at least. Moreover, to look only at the structures in which people are situated and the exclusions and problems with them can be terrifying and overwhelming as to change an oppressive structure is an enormous undertaking. As a consequence, it can remove any sense of agency that individuals and communities have any capacity to make the changes that are necessary in order to move forward to a future where they are able to flourish. Instead, this chapter is looking for the spaces in which individuals, communities, and regions have agency in the on-going processes of shaping their regions.

Perhaps a starting point might be to ask what the complex adaptive region assemblage makes visible within the region. The short answer, and which I have tried to show over the preceding chapters, would be life force or energy, connectivities of knowledge and things, and power. What Bergson (2004) would have called the *Elan Vital*, or the vital, life force, which impels people to keep moving forward, was very visible in the SWVA research, in particular, as well as being present in the Cornwall case study. Sometimes, it impelled people to do extraordinary things. It is this *Elan Vital*, this energy that like a little flame needs to be nurtured and fed if it is to grow into a roaring fire in front of which we can keep warm. More than anything, we need to ensure that the emerging flames are protected from the wind and the rain while they try to develop, that they are able to keep and grow their energy rather than see it dissipate because of unfavourable environmental conditions. The old adage that 'what doesn't kill you makes you stronger' is only partially true. Sometimes 'death' comes from a thousand small cuts until suddenly the flame isn't there anymore.

This brings us to another important factor to draw attention to. In this book, whilst we have talked a little about economies, and the ways that economies are measured, this is meant only as a proxy for making visible *some* regional difficulties. This book in general, and this chapter in particular, is interested in improving the *lives* of the people who live in the places that we observe. The fact that by improving lives we may see an improvement to economic metrics is incidental. But this needs to be the focus rather than on improving the metrics and expecting that this will improve lives. This is a lesson that Cornwall teaches us. We have seen how over the past few decades the pay gap between Cornwall and the rest of the United Kingdom has begun to close (Nomis, 2020b), as has the disparity between Cornwall and the rest of the United Kingdom in terms of productivity (as measured by Gross Value Added) (Nomis c). However, we have also heard from research participants how difficult many people's lives still are, and indeed, how decades-long issues have not been fixed, and one of the things that was striking about this series of interviews was about the depth of the narrative of decline. Whilst some metrics have shown an improvement over time, this has not necessarily been experienced or felt by many. The lesson to take from this is that any discussion about the way forward needs to dispense with traditional measurements of regional inequality for a while and focus on the things that are really required by people in the locality that we are looking at. Inquiry needs to focus on the lived experience of people in places.

Over the remainder of this chapter, we are going to begin with *Elan Vital* in both of the case study regions, incorporating too the flip-side, of an amplification of hopelessness. I consider how the talents that people have might be nurtured and fed and how that latent potentiality might be provided with a map for how to navigate change. Next, I explore how people can engage with new knowledges and practices – the themes of connectivities and power threads through this chapter. It is hard to separate the life force and energy from the things that keeps that energy alive, and this is one of the functions of connectivity. Power, in this context, represents the latent power and agency of individuals and communities, and the need for this power and agency to be unlocked if the region is to be able to flourish. To misquote Marsha, this approach relies on a multiplicity of 'small victories' as opposed to big wins but which help to create a more resilient complex, adaptive, regional assemblage.

ELAN VITAL

Panaigua (2013) found that the commitment and attachment to place that rural dwellers had, combined with a sense of permanence and rootedness, was an asset that helps to drive resilience and adaptation. This is echoed throughout both case study regions. People *cared* about the places that they lived in. Of course, some young people want to spread their wings and spend time in other places. But many also want to return, if the opportunities are available to them. This was often articulated in terms of the 'pull' of familiar landscapes or of the family/friendship networks that individuals were a part of and wanted to be close to. It is about a sense of locatedness, commitment, and desire to be in a place, which drives the individual to find ways of being in it. This fuels the *elan vital* in the case studies. For the most part, participants were living in places where they wanted to be and were trying to find a way to be able to stay. We even see that in persons like

Sophie, who moved to Cornwall a few years ago but who have embraced the place and have made a home there, despite the challenges that she and her husband faced.

But perversely, what this can also mean is that the fact that living in a place is seen as desirable, results in talent being almost taken for granted and wasted. This desire to be in place also means that people are willing to accept jobs that they are very overqualified for. Again in both places, we hear about individuals with postgraduate qualifications, doing jobs which do not require an undergraduate degree. This represents quite a significant under-utilisation of available resources. Where people are quite well-qualified but are unable to use their skills because they can't find, or don't know how to find, jobs where their talents could be most heavily used. The under-utilisation of talent was a bit of an emerging theme, and improvement to connections arose as the most important way of tackling this. Connections are both the physical connectivity of being practically able to move about a geographical space and ideational connectivity, enabling the sharing of information.

This is exemplified in the conversation with Dan, where he told how young people were having to take up jobs that were available in the locality. These might be in cafes and supermarkets rather than in sectors where their talents were best suited or where they could get training that would help them to have a career rather than just a job. Dan told how the inability to travel outside a narrow geographical space meant that people were consigned to jobs where they could survive, but not flourish. Clearly, this is an individual problem, but it also is a much bigger problem for *elan vital* in the complex adaptive regional assemblage. It means that the energy, or impulsion, the drive or the flame that could help the region to flourish, is allowed to dissipate right from the start. Even more than this, Ruth tells the story about further wastage, where persons literally rot in isolated communities because they are unable to access opportunities which exist, but they are not able to physically get to. A job in a town 10 miles away remains hypothetical if the individual has no possible way of getting from their home to the job. Melissa observes that over a period of time, entry-level jobs have become all that is available for many people even at a job stage where technically people should have moved well beyond such roles. Again, this is a personal tragedy in terms of job satisfaction, personal flourishing, and incomes, but as Michael explains in a response which recalls Durkheim's (2002 [1897]) anomie, lack of secure employment risks a wide range of social problems which again have a negative affect on *elan vital*. In fact, rather than amplify *positive* affective responses, it can have the opposite affect, amplifying hopelessness throughout the region. We see this happen in both regions, as nostalgia for the past, and a sense of loss at familiar certainties passing without seeming to add anything new, dissipates the vital force and threatens to cast a fog of depression.

We also see people in both regions who exist towards the margins of traditional economies, who are intelligent and aware of the worlds in which they exist, but who do not find ways to 'fit' well into the ways that the contemporary economy has changed. Perhaps they are young people that have a particular, deep interest, but who have not found a way of connecting in to networks that would show them how to use that interest as the basis and foundation for a paid job and career. Perhaps in previous times, they might have found a way to monetise their hobbyist skills as makers, amateur inventors, engineers, or digital tech genius' but are uncertain of the roles that might be available to them, the routes towards these roles, and whether such positions once found might be 'for people like them'. Instead, they practice their talents and creativity outside or on the margins of the regular economy rather than being able to find a place to flourish creatively, but also financially.

This question of fit is an important one which Amy demonstrates. Sometimes, in the process of trying to survive, an individual's *elan vital* becomes so ground down that they don't feel that they are able to operate on the level that they *could* and so end up under-selling themselves and their capabilities. People sometimes feel that they need to accept lower-skilled jobs where they feel comfortable, even if they can contribute more, because they have come to feel that they are not actually worth more.

These are human problems underlying regional metrics. For example, although we know that Cornwall has a general parity with the rest of the United Kingdom in terms of workforce skills (Nomis, 2020c), we are learning that it is not enough for these skills to be latent within the workforce. In other words, skills need to be *activated* and operationalised, and for that people need to know how they might use those skills in the locality, and they need to be able to physically or virtually get to the places where they can use those skills. So *how* can this vital force of *elan vital* be put into action? And how might the sites of potentiality and possibility be used to actually make beneficial changes?

MOBILISING CONNECTIVITIES

We learned in chapters 3 and 4 that for the complex adaptive regional assemblage to be able to work well, it needs to move. Assemblages are mobile, always changing, and fluid. In fact, stasis implies a kind of death. Deleuze and Guattari (2004) describe a world of maps, connections, and flows. Importantly, movement doesn't always imply expansion, such as, for example, economic growth (although it might be). Instead it can also mean change. Change in the flows between assemblages and change between the objects, processes, ideas, and institutions collected together within, between, and around assemblage phenomena. This section is entitled 'mobilising connectivities' as a way of signalling this. Merely having a connecting link between two assembled phenomena does not mean that there is going to be a flow between both or that connection is going to be able to be used. There are many reasons for this. For example, of an unusable connection, we might first point out the importance of physically being able to move around the geographical space. Cars are expensive, and so for SWVA we might want to recommend some form of bus transport to help to enable people to get around the region. As a solution, this would make a lot of sense from a British perspective. Despite several decades of heavy reliance on car use, and despite the severe dent that COVID-19 has made on the use of public transport, people still use busses. In Cornwall for example, one might expect that towns will have some form of bus service between them. It might not be adequate for daily travel to work use or for accessing services from remoter areas, but it will exist as a mechanism of getting around the region if you have a lot of time on your hands. But this would not be such an available tool or solution in south-west Virginia. The use of cars as a sole means of transportation has become so deeply embedded into the public psyche that the existence of a bus service does not necessarily mean that it will be *used*. In fact, unless such a service arose from a concerted community campaign, it is unlikely that such a physical and practical connection would enable any actual flow. In which case, it is useless.

The lesson from this is that connections need to be situated within the Bergsonian (2004) cones of memory of local people, or they need to be able to resonate with how the general population understand their worlds, and their lives within it. Where public transportation would be a good way to activate mobilities in SWVA, and turn potentialities into realities, is with regard to long-distance rail connections. Bristol City Council (2019) already has done a report into the viability of a rail line connecting the far south of SWVA with the railhead in Roanoke, 150 miles northeast. They found that new intercity services and the new rail links outside of SWVA, but near enough to be relevant, have exceeded expectations in terms of passenger numbers. What this indicates though is that there is considerable support for greater connectivity *out* of the region into wider assemblages, and we will talk more about this later.

But from a Cornwall perspective, improved public transportation is an important way of facilitating better flows of people throughout the region. We know that it is a solution that people both use and want. But that there are three factors which inhibit more widespread flows through this important connector. First, bus services may be too remote from the community to be able to function well. Here, we hear about people who need a lift to the bus stop if they are to be able to use it at all, which clearly is a severe limitation on use. The connection might exist, but it is practically unusable. Second, we heard how services can be far too expensive for regular use by the most vulnerable who, by definition, are often the persons who need to use them the most. Third, existing bus services can take so long to get to the places that they are going, that they end up being functionally useless for all but the most vulnerable. As a consequence, we end up with a self-replicating cycle whereby the services that exist there are underutilised and so liable to be reduced.

For regional policy, this requires a total rethink in how important connectors are imagined. We can go back here to the phrase *the bottom line* mentioned by one of the SWVA participants. This signals a set of perspectives that is rooted in a market individualism which is based on profitability. But some businesses offer a public service, the externalities of which are potentially societally destructive. Public transport is one of these services. As we have mentioned above, the *in*ability to physically move to other parts of the region assemblage wastes talent which could contribute to regional flourishing. Even worse, it exposes the region assemblage – and the other assemblages with which it is immediately connected to the costly consequences of poverty, such as ill health, substance abuse, and criminal activity (See Alcock, 1997). This is not only about working people. Mandy, in particular, raised very significant concerns about the appalling impacts on older people when they are no longer able to drive. Loneliness, isolation, and ill health cause significant personal distress, but it also uses up available care resources the cost of which may outweigh the costs of better transportation. In other words, good public transportation may be a market failure in rural areas, and as such it may be expensive to maintain, but its lack may actually *not* be an efficient use of available resources. Consequently, it is essential if the region is to adapt and evolve as best it can. The benefits of having a system whereby people are able to physically get themselves to the opportunities and services that exist nearby is one of these extremely important amplificatory spaces, which benefits the area beyond all proportion.

For the south west of Virginia, the key connectivity gap is with regard to access to the internet. Annie and Otis discussed how the key problem was about getting internet connectivity the final mile, or final 5 miles, from main networks. We should also remember that the experiences being discussed here relate not only to not having fibre or high-speed broad band connectivity via a land-based connection. This also relates to not being able to get satellite internet connectivity on your mobile phone. Whilst the rest of the world talks about being able to access 5g mobile internet, people such as Otis are barely able to send an old school text from their homes. Of course people have found ways around this, such as driving to spots where signal is available, or saving internet use for when in town. But when most of the Western world (and some parts of the global south) have, over the past few decades, come to see the internet as a basic necessity, not having access to it at home is a significant lack.

As was shown in the chapter, this is not just about being able to access online popular culture, this is also about being able to connect to the different types of information-sharing networks that the internet brings, as well as being able to find and operationalise new opportunities. Chapter 6 mentioned the loss of the country store as a place where information could be shared and exchanged. Clearly this is a facility that was not very well adapted to the twenty-first-century socio-economic practices, but its connecting function still has a strong utility. To a limited degree, the church seems to provide some of this role in terms of face-to-face interactions. However, if inhabitants of the region are to be able to keep abreast of the broader socio-cultural developments and environments in assemblages beyond their immediate locality, then they need to be able to access the tools that this information can be shared on. As Dana's and Annie's stories illustrate, people in the region are already imagined through some deeply unflattering stereotypes by persons in other parts of the United States. Not being able to keep up with contemporary American cultural developments can only reinforce 'backwards' types of stereotypes and social exclusions.

But this is also a significant challenge to how people are able to do business in the area. We already know that unlike in Cornwall, there is a (more recent) tradition of large industries providing jobs in the locality. Big companies that can employ hundreds of persons. However, we also know that currently SWVA has a strong level of business start-ups and that 20 per cent of all job creation is by young companies. This outstrips current U.S. averages (GOVA, 2019). However, we know from Dana and Rashid that running business with only patchy cell signal and no fibre at home is a challenge that automatically puts local enterprises on the back foot compared to their counterparts in better connected localities.

This is the time to revisit Marsha's claim about small victories rather than big wins. Marsha's point is that a lot of *elan vital* is being overlooked because of a focus on headline projects. That if attention were to be refocused on how to improve the operating environment, and support for the small businesses that are trying to work out how to make a living doing what they love, then this will have a stronger spill over into a regional recovery. Certainly, we also know about the strong thread of independence and self-reliance that is infused into contemporary culture through the history of settlement in SWVA. In many respects, this could provide a fertile ground for a dispersed recovery. But we also know that such a dispersed mobilisation needs fuel, or the energy will dissipate. There needs to be adequate structural and individual support to allow this to flourish. Internet connectivity available to all is one of these structures that need to be put in place. Partially, of course, this is about the practicalities of running a business, from connecting to clients, communicating with suppliers, and advertising products and services. But it is also about *knowing* the region and how it is adapting and responding to contemporary challenges. This is vital if enterprises are to know the locality well enough in order to be able to follow market opportunities. In the light of what we have talked about above and drawing on Amy and the 'tinkerers' from earlier, it goes without saying that business support programs need to find ways to talk to and work with business owners from across the social spectrum.

Of course, the importance of the internet is not limited to businesses but is also about the ways that people find out about what job opportunities are available and what kinds of training is required. These are searches that *should* be able to be completed whilst at home, if connectivity allows it. But we also know that merely having technologies available is not sufficient on its own (Raisanen and Tuovinen, 2020). Partially, this is about having both the skills and equipment in order to be able to get online and use it effectively. But there are other ways that regional planners can help to connect individuals with the opportunities that are available. One of these is with regard to finding better ways to share information about where the opportunities are for jobseekers or for those wishing to retrain. This is something that SWVA currently does, with programs that work with young people through the school system to help them to consider the kinds of careers that they might have in the locality and the skills that they would need to join these careers (United Way, 2020). There is also a way for members of the public to access information on the kinds of jobs that have been hired in the past year, which allows a rudimentary knowledge about skills gaps for the tenacious searcher (New River/Mount Rogers Development Board, 2018). The Local Enterprise Partnership in Cornwall has begun to work with young people about the careers that can be found in the region. However, currently there is no way for even a determined member of the public to find out the industries that are hiring in the locality or any data around skills gaps or what sectors have been recruiting recently.

These are vital pieces of information that need to be readily available to any jobseeker, of any stage in their career. There needs to be freely flowing conduits between the public, businesses, and training providers. At present, it is as if the economic life of these complex adaptive regional assemblages is fragmented into many pieces with few bridges between them. We hear that there are skills gaps which mean that businesses are unable to evolve and flourish in the ways that they would like, but we don't know definitively what they are. Or we might find out what they are *not* when we make a leap into the labour market and begin searching for local work. Moreover, for a small business or for an individual that is starting to develop a small business idea, a world of big data *should* be able to provide some form of freely avail-able and easily accessible public information hub, to be able to explore more about local markets and economies. Such a facility should also be able to connect together the skill-set of an interested inquirer and opportunities that are currently available in the locality. Or we hear both Amy and Marsha dis-cuss how they know that there are the kinds of work that they are qualified for out there, but they just don't know how to find out about them. These kinds of open and flowing conduits are essential if the region is to flourish in its evolution.

There is an additional function that improved knowledge flows could have for SWVA in particular, although this is connected to Cornwall too. We know that through tourism in particular, Cornwall has a strong place in the British popular imagination. That although it is a coherent and strong assemblage in its own right, and no matter the kinds of contestations over how it is rep-resented (Willett, 2016; Dickinson, 2008) it is also enfolded within, but not engulfed by phenomena assembled around 'Britain'. There might be debate around the extent that flows of information are reciprocal or whether or about the kinds of power relationships and knowledge relationships between the assembled 'Britain' and 'Cornwall'. However, it is still a strong relationship facilitated by knowledge flows through media and online and through physi-cal travel.

This is different for SWVA. Although within the region there is a strong sense of territorialised place, culture, shared history, shared present, and of course, landscape, SWVA bleeds into East Tennessee (the city of Bristol straddles the border between each) or North Carolina, Kentucky, or West Virginia. Part of the southern Appalachian mountain range, and dissected into small planning districts, counties, or cities. In the Bristol/East Tennessee area, it is part of the Tri-Cities region (not to be confused with the Tri-Cities part of Virginia, around Richmond, well to the north) SWVA only *really* exists as a stand-alone entity as a Go-Virginia area. And yet ideationally, it has already extended far beyond state boundaries into national assemblages, through popular creatives such as Barbara Kingsolver or Adriana Trigliani, the Smithsonian Birthplace of Country Music museum, or Pulitzer-Prize-winning Bristol Herald newspapers.

Although Cornwall offers a cautionary tale about the problems of (over) tourism, it remains one very effective means through which places can become known about, loved, and folded into a broader popular imagination. If the rail link can be extended into the depths of the region, it will go a long way towards making it more accessible to the casual visitor. It will also make it easier for individuals to extend themselves into assemblages outside of the immediate region, accessing new knowledges, processes, and ideas which might foster new spaces of possibility.

But as one Cornwall participant noted obliquely, the story that visitors are exposed to during their stay has important implications for how it is later narrated elsewhere. Whilst visitors have the potential to act as ambassadors for the region and what it has to offer, this cannot function effectively if the story that is narrated is about life on a remote sea cliff, where you won't see another person for a week if you don't want to. The curated visitor's consumption of space needs to include some aspect of pointing them towards the vibrant economies that the region sustains. No tourist wants to spend their vacation in an industrial estate, but coming away from Cornwall knowing that there is a really interesting, nascent aerospace industry, home-grown international clothing brands, and a thriving digital tech sector would be useful take-home points. In many respects, holiday-makers are conduits for regional advertising, connecting a possibly remote or 'sheltered' place, with the outer world. Perhaps it is time for a rethink of a visitor model that is largely extractive, to one that could potentially be productive and informative, highlighting that there are more facets to the locality than the visitor experience (See also Pine and Gilmore, 2019).

This is one of those spaces of possibility that COVID-19 has opened up rather than closed down. The pandemic has changed working practices to the extent that many jobs that previously required an office base are currently, as I write in latter 2020, being done from home. Culturally in Britain, this has led to significant speculation around the possibilities that this presents with regard to (finally) making it viable for workers to move to other parts of the country which they find more attractive, but had been unable to find the kind of work that they wanted or at the salary level which they were used to. Although tele or digital home-working has been discussed as a site of potentiality for rural workers since at least the early 1990s (Perry, 1993), the COVID-19 Pandemic has led to a widespread decoupling of work from space which might finally make it possible for many more of us than before. There is the possibility that such a decoupling might even go some ways towards collapsing the employment differences between urban and rural places. This offers an enormous space of opportunity for rural areas and which makes better-paid positions suddenly accessible to rural and peripheral assemblages. But there is also an enormous potential challenge and risk of expanding inequalities.

As we have seen already in the Cornwall example, the general trend for pre-COVID homeworking tended to be that an individual had got their job, and risen in their career, through working outside of the region. This might be that a young person has left the region and chosen to return later in their lives, or like Sophie and her husband, it might be that an individual or family made the conscious decision that this was where they want to make their home. Perhaps this was facilitated by an agreement with their employers, or perhaps as a self-employed person or free-lancer, they were able to take their client list with them and work remotely. The digital nomad is not a new phenomenon. The thing that links these differing examples, however, is that their roles, their careers, or their business arose from having left the region and moved away for several years or decades. This implies, however, that in order to be able to take advantage of the digital nomad jobs, which offer better pay and career choices than positions more firmly rooted in peripheral complex adaptive assemblages, requires a level of social capital and networks that cannot be found within the region. Instead, an individual *must* have left in order to be able to participate in homeworking opportunities which are disconnected from spatiality.

The consequences of this was raised by a number of participants in Cornwall, who noted the inequalities that occur because of the higher purchasing power of inward migrants on account of their access to better-paid job opportunities. We have also seen in chapter 4 how this has decoupled the link between house prices and average incomes in Cornwall, where average house prices are 9 times average incomes. It must also be remembered that there are many good reasons why people choose to remain in their communities rather than leave (Stockdale et al., 2018), and Mandy reminds us that it would be extremely undesirable societally to expect that 'to get on, you have to get out'. But the upshot is that persons like Amy are made extremely vulnerable through housing precariarity, which negatively impacts on her ability to flourish and fully contribute to the on-going development of the complex adaptive assemblage. Additionally, we know from Jeff that contrary to suppositions of the counter-urbanisation literature (Bosworth and Bat Finke, 2019), inward migrants do not necessarily share their social capital and networks but can hoard it, entrenching and perpetuating existing inequalities.

A more sustainable solution would be for regional or national policy to create a nodal point for finding information about remote working opportunities at all stages in one's career. The point is that there needs to be an easily accessible location for job seekers and job providers, nation-wide and potentially globally, to disseminate and find opportunities. Local government can then work with training providers to ensure that necessary training and skills are put in place for persons to be able to access remote-working job opportunities. Obviously though for such a scheme to work, the digital infrastructure needs to be in place and accessible throughout the region, not just up to the final mile.

CONCLUDING THOUGHTS: POWER

It would be insufficient to say that complex adaptive region assemblages uniformly disperse power throughout the collected phenomenon of which they are comprised. As we have seen, there are hierarchies within the system. There are some spaces which exert more of an influence at some points in time than at others. There are also some spaces that provide more amplificatory 'bounce' than others, and some of the suggestions put forward in this chapter could be read as ideas for better connecting assembled nodal points, in order to better facilitate amplificatory bounce. Many of the ideas discussed here have also related to creating the spaces and connectivities for individuals to better flourish within the environments in which they find themselves. This might be imagined as being about helping power to better flow outwards, towards radically dispersed nodal points. But what we also see, particularly with regards to support for persons to access the knowledges required for flourishing in the changing regional environment, is that this support needs to be accessible. For this to happen, it needs to be knowable and visible. People need to know where they can turn to for information than can help them to navigate what might be unfamiliar conduits. To take the final example offered in this chapter, a facility-offering information about remote-working careers, connecting rural job seekers with employers in other regions, needs to have the visibility of its own, defined and connected assemblage. It needs to be a nodal point that disperses connections within and throughout much larger assemblages.

Chapter 8

Conclusion

In this book, I ask what we see if we look at rural peripheral regions as complex adaptive assemblages and use this as a basis to consider how complex adaptive regional assemblages might evolve. I began this journey by relating a story about a piece of research that myself and Garry Tregidga led, considering why regions in Britain, with the highest levels of European Union structural funds, voted disproportionately to Leave the EU in the 2016 referendum on Britain's relationship with the EU. I mentioned in the outset that this helped us to question the relationship between inhabitants of the regions receiving economic development support and the aims and priorities of the programmes that were devised by those charged with delivering development. In short, we questioned whether local satisfaction ought to be introduced as an outcome measure for success and whether members of the public should be surveyed for their qualitative experiences of investment initiatives, alongside more 'objective' indicators. From this jumping-off point, exploring a version of regional development that centres the lives and lived experience of residents rather than an abstract assessment of economic gain or productivity is a logical progression.

The response of this book is to take this observation and use it to propose an entirely new ontological perspective for our analysis and treatment of regions. In so doing, I wanted to conduct a detailed and systematic account of the complex, adaptive, regional assemblage in order to develop a model that can help analysts and practitioners be more inclusive. This was not intended as a claim that the ways that we have previously understood space, place, and economies have no merit. On the contrary, chapter 1 journeyed through a wide range of the perspectives and tools through which regions and their economies are examined, diagnosed, and treated. Much of this research holds important merits as practices and tools in the ongoing quest to flatten out spatial economic inequalities.

For example, the Peripheralisation literature helps us to consider the processes through which regions become more or less peripheral and alerts us to the tight linkages between the ways that regions are imagined and discursively constructed, and also economic potentiality (see for example, Burke et al., 2012; Gormar and Lang, 2019; Meyer, 2016). We get to understand what is meant by terms like 'rural' and the symbolic repertoire that is attached to this characterisation and what this means for individuals and communities that inhabit places of dispersed population density (DeSouza, 2018; Lowe, 2012; Shucksmith, 2012). This brings us to important questions around what is meant by 'innovation', asking too if this something that predominantly happens in the metropole and on the converse is absent from rural spaces (Shucksmith and Brown, 2016; Kleinschmit and Clausen, 2012). Contemporary research examines policies that are enacted on a local, national, and supranational level and the impacts that these have on the rural development that is pursued (High and Nemes, 2007; Canete et al., 2018; Dominguez Garcia et al., 2013). We hear too about some of the specific characteristics of regions, such as the importance of internet connectivity to contemporary living, and some of the challenges that rural dwellers face in order to get online (Raisanen and Tuovinen, 2020; Strover et al., 2020; Bowen and Morris, 2019). We also encounter conceptual tools such as social capital (Putnam, 2000) which act as a shorthand to a range of phenomena through which we understand the levels and types of skills held by persons in a territorial space (Atterton, 2007), and how these skills might best be acquired and transmitted amongst the broader population (Shortall and Warner, 2012).

All of these kinds of studies are important and tell us valuable things through which we can come to better understand contemporary society. However, what the complex adaptive regional assemblage offers is a way of appreciating how these different aspects connect up together, shape each other, and move towards a shared future. Its rhizomatic structure and understanding that power is dispersed throughout assembled phenomena can also help us to understand something else. Deleuze and Guattari (2004) flag this when they call *A Thousand Plateau's* a 'rhizome book' and tell the reader that the introduction is just a one-entry point into the volume and that the reader may choose to start anywhere they desire. Deleuze and Guattari are pointing out amongst other things that we don't have to begin our inquiries in the same place. In this book, through the mechanism of the complex adaptive assemblage, we are beginning an old inquiry in a different starting point to usual. By centring this study on the lives of normal, regular members of the public, we encounter the notion that spatial development *looks* different when viewed from the position of the public. In practice, such an inquiry can be begun from the positionality of any part of the region assemblage. This might include different social groupings or categorisations of individuals, or, like Jones et al.'s (2019) article about the global wool assemblage, might be from the position of a particular industry sector or, by extension, set of institutions.

I argued in the previous chapter that for regional analyses, decentering the positionality of our subjects expands our perspectives on the region. Moreover, it helps to make clear hitherto hidden spaces of possibility and the mobilities, fluidities and connectivities between people, ideas and things in the regional economy. But from a position of theoretical development, it does more than this. It shows us how the different topics, through which we have traditionally examined regional development, are connected. To some extent, the literature on resilience has been doing this (Boschma, 2015; Bristow and Healey, 2014), as has evolutionary economic geography (Martin and Sunley, 2007; Boschma and Frenken, 2011). However, what the concept of the affective assemblage does is help us to better consider the flows and connectivities within the region assemblage. As a consequence, we see from this type of analysis that development is about infinitely more than isolated measures designed to support some aspects of rural assemblages. Instead of being fragmented and siloed modes of inquiry and policy tools, development questions are all intimately and deeply connected.

So for example, *can* we talk about social capital or innovation without considering each other, internet connectivity, the creative industries (Florida, 2002), and commercial counter-urbanisation (Bosworth and Bat-Finke, 2019)? I argue that you cannot, and that instead seemingly disparate assemblages intersect and collide. To illustrate, in Cornwall, we see that the bus and rail networks are related to innovation in ways that are not immediately apparent. Here, the connection is that it is not only about being able to physically get to a job, but that it is also about being able to get to a job that makes the best use of your talents and interests and therefore is able to unlock an individual's capacity and help them to flourish. Public transportation is a vital way of ensuring that people are able to physically get to the places where they will be able to hone their talents, flourish, and so put something back. Similarly, in SWVA, we notice the intersection between assemblages around local histories and assemblages around small business development. We might imagine the retrospective, backwards focus of history to be completely opposite to the forward march of progress of small businesses. However, we find that these assemblages actually intersect through the self-reliance and determination that is hard-wired into local DNA and which was an essential characteristic from the times of settler communities. The weight of this historical memory, transmitted into present generations, presents a space of possibility, which with adequate care and attention could be nurtured into flourishing.

We saw over the course of this book, that these connectivities and intersections are one of the strengths of imagining the region as a complex adaptive assemblage. It helps us to see *how* things connect, how they *should* connect, and what work needs to be done if we are to be able to build strong regions in the future. And of course, it also helps us to consider how these connections and connectivities might need to change either now or in the future. To draw from Bedau and Humphries (2008) and Smith and Jenks (2006), this is about the relationship between parts and wholes. Between individual assemblages, the assemblages of which they are constituted, and the assemblages of which they are a part of. We were able to see this in SWVA, and the historical example of how poor rural families would use the fine cotton cloth from sacks of flour to make clothing. But we also note how this was not a set of memories that was isolated to this region only, but that it was part of much broader rural histories across the United States. For this book, this became a metaphor for how deeply entangled the local and the national are. Cornwall's experience here is a different one, which in the preceding pages I narrate in terms of the popularity of the region as a tourist destination for people from across the United Kingdom but particularly from the urban core. This stretches the idea of Cornwall and popular experience of it, well beyond its territorial boundaries. It means that the assemblage 'Cornwall' holds a place in the hearts of people from across Britain, who have fond memories of happy holidays, as children or adults.

In the book, I talked about these things as deterritorialising factors – aspects of regional assemblages which extend assemblages outwards and blur their boundaries. This deterritorialisation and blurring of boundaries are highlighted through Jones et al. (2019)'s discussion of the global assemblages around the wool industry. Here, we see that the economies of which regions are a part of materially extend the locality beyond destination markets, but also into other localities which form a part of its practical, emotional, and ideational supply chain. SWVA has done this through (but not limited to) coal, tobacco, and country music. Cornwall through (but not limited to) the supply of minerals, the visitor industry, and we could also have talked about communications, referencing its historic role in transatlantic and satellite technologies.

This reminds us of the truism that all matter that we use was originally either mined or grown. These activities, this natural capital, are gifts from the rural. What I am trying to say here is that regional assemblages, and indeed all assemblages, have more than just a symbiotic relationship with each other. Instead, they form part of the same organism, which in turn forms a part of other organisms. Ultimately, our complex adaptive, regional assemblages all form part of a universal whole which incorporates all human, animal, and ecological assemblages on our planet. Like Cornwall and SWVA, many rural areas are post-industrial places, which before becoming known for their amenity value, were known for their natural capital. The minerals to be mined, or an abundance of food, or other materials to be grown. Natural capital may well be an important asset as we start to consider the rural periphery with a more critical eye. Complex, adaptive, regional assemblages may help to do this as they allow us to better trace interconnectedness and interdependencies. That said, we also need to ask why both of our case study regions were left so vulnerable when their natural capital-based industries changed into something else.

This raises another important contribution of this book. Its role in understanding regional change and how to manage that change better. Both of the case studies here had been experiencing this and over recent decades had seen their old, familiar economy become replaced by something different. But by centering on personal experiences, what we see in both examples is that individuals are struggling to be able to navigate these changes. Perhaps this is because they don't know what new things and activities have replaced the old ones that they have lost, or perhaps they physically and practically do not know how they might be able to access important parts of the new socio-economic environment that they find themselves in. What the complex adaptive regional assemblage helps us to do is to trace the spaces where connections and linkages have broken down and consider where and how new ones could be developed. This is about diagnosing and prescribing tools to enable better regional adaptation to the inevitable changes that regions encounter.

We are not talking here about some kind of 'failure' of some regions to 'keep up' with contemporary modernity. Communities grew up at specific moments in time, in response to specific socio-economic and cultural conditions. Some communities have adapted over the decades and centuries to become large and vibrant. But as we can see from the example of some of Germany's 'shrinking cities' (see, for example, Burke et al., 2012), this question affects communities of any size. The ability to navigate change is a crucial question for all regions, rural or urban. This is especially the case as we move through a new era of global change from the inevitable social and economic revolutions that will follow the COVID-19 pandemic and climate change. The new perspective of the complex adaptive regional assemblage provides an important tool for evening out inequalities which blight our communities and regions as they adapt to the uncertain future that awaits all of us. In this, the complex adaptive regional assemblage becomes a theory of change through which to consider contemporary society and, as we saw in the previous chapter, it also helps us to spot the sites of untapped or underutilised energy – or *elan vital* – which will be vital to regional adaptation in the uncertain years moving forward. We also see how motivating a commitment to place and a love of one's locality can be, together with the desire to be able to make a life in a certain location despite the challenges that may be faced. This helps to provide energy which is a crucial underpinning of adaptive change. But this is also a space where policy (and funding) has an important role to facilitate and help to direct that energy in ways that will fit well within the particular assemblages of the time and place.

But if assemblages collect together and slide into much bigger assemblages, then it raises a further question. If regions and the socio-economic and cultural assemblages are so deeply interconnected, why split them into discrete, assembled parts for our analysis? To some extent, this question is answered in the call for decentering the positionality of our inquiry into regional development. Starting with certain discrete assemblages helps to make the processes, institutions, practices, meanings, and activities within them more visible to the outside world. Sometimes, we need to make global questions feel smaller and more manageable if they are to be more readily tackled. It is from this point of particular inquiry that we can then extend outwards to ensure that their fluidities, mobilities, organisations, and interconnections are operating in a way that better facilitates adaptation to the global challenges that we all face. In short, and moving through a new era of extreme uncertainty, we need to adopt a much more fluid understanding of what the region is, what it does, and how it does it.

References

Ahmed, Sara. 2004. *The Cultural Politics of Emotion*. Edinburgh: Edinburgh University Press.

Alcock, P. 1997. *Understanding Poverty*. Hampshire: Palgrave.

Ali, C., & Duemmel, M. 2019. The Reluctant Regulator: The Rural Utilities Service and American Broadband Policy. *Telecommunications Policy* 43: 380–392.

Angarrack, J. 1999. *Breaking the Chains*. Camborne: Cornish Stannary Publications.

Antonietti, R., & Gambarotto, F. 2018. The Role of Industry Variety in the Creation of Innovative Start-Ups in Italy. *Small Business Economics*. https://doi.org/10.1007/s11187-018-0034-4.

Appalachian Regional Commission. 2020. *Subregions in Appalachia*. https://www.arc.gov/research/mapsofappalachia.asp?MAP_ID=31. Accessed 27 April 2020.

Argent, N. 2016. Demographic Change: Beyond the Urban-Rural Divide. In M. Shucksmith & D. Brown (Eds.), Routledge Handbook of Rural Studies. London: Routledge.

Armstrong, H., & Taylor, J. 2000. *Regional Economics and Policy* (3rd ed.). Oxford: Blackwell.

Askegaard, S., & Kjeldgaard, D. 2007. Here, There and Everywhere: Place Branding and Gastronomical Globalization in a Macromarketing Perspective. *Journal of Macromarketing* 27(1): 138–149.

Atterton, J. 2007. The Strength of Weak Ties: Social Networking by Business Owners in the Highlands and Islands of Scotland *Sociologia Ruralis* 47(3): 228–245.

Bache, I., & Scott, K. 2017. Wellbeing in Politics and Policy. In I. Bache & K. Scott (Eds.), *The Politics of Wellbeing: Theory, Policy and Practice* (pp. 1–22). London: Palgrave.

Bajpai, O., Dutta, V., Singh, R., Chaudhary, L., & Pandey, J. 2020. Tree Community Assemblage and Abiotic Variables in Tropical Moist Deciduous Forest of Himalayan Terai Eco-Region. *Proceedings of the National Academy of Sciences, India Section B* 20200101: 1–11.

Barke, M., & Newton, M. 1997. The EU LEADER Initiative and Endogenous Rural Development: The Application of the Programme in Rural Areas of Andalusia, Southern Spain. *Journal of Rural Studies* 13(3): 319–341.

Bauman, Z. 2000. *Liquid Modernity*. Oxford: Blackwell.

BBC. 2013. *Does Lead Poisoning Make You Violent?* https://www.bbc.co.uk/news/health-20961241. Accessed 2 April 2020.

BBC. 2014. *A Craze for Loom Bands*. https://www.bbc.co.uk/news/magazine-2797 4401. Accessed 26 October 2019.

BBC. 2017. How Much of Your Area is Built On? https://www.bbc.co.uk/news/uk -41901294. Accessed 26 May 2020.

Bedau, M., & Humphries, P. 2008. Introduction *and* Introduction to Philosophical Perspectives on Emergence. In M. Bedau & P. Humphries (Eds.), *Emergence: Contemporary Readings in Philosophy and Science*. Cambridge: MIT Press.

Bell, D., & Jayne, M. 2010. The Creative Countryside: Policy and Practice in the Rural Cultural Economy. *Journal of Rural Studies* 26(3): 209–218.

Bennett, J. 2010. *Vibrant Matter: A Political Ecology of Things*. Durham: Duke University Press.

Bergson, H. 1944. *Creative Evolution*. New York: Random House.

Bergson, H. 2004 [1908]. *Matter and Memory*. Mineola: Dover Publications.

Black, N., Scott, K., & Shucksmith, M. 2018. Social Inequalities in Rural England: Impacts on Young People Post 2008. *Journal of Rural Studies* 68: 264–275.

Blackley, D. J., Halldin, C. N., & Laney, A. S. 2018. Continued Increase in Prevalence of Coal Workers' Pneumoconiosis in the United States, 1970–2017. *The American Journal of Public Health* 108(9): 1220–1222.

Blumer, H. 1969. *Symbolic Interactionism; Perspective and Method*. California: University of California Press.

Bodenhamer, A. 2016. King Coal: A Study of Mountaintop Removal, Public Discourse, and Power in Appalachia. *Society & Natural Resources* 29(10): 1139–1153.

Boschma, R. 2015. Towards and Evolutionary Perspective on Regional Resilience. *Regional Studies* 49(5): 733–751.

Boschma, R., & Frenken, K. 2011. The Emerging Empirics of Evolutionary Economic Geography. *Journal of Economic Geography* 11: 295–307.

Bosworth, G., & Bat Finke, H. 2019. Commercial Counterurbanisation: A Driving Force in Rural Economic Development. *Environment and Planning A: Economy and Space* 52(3): 654–674.

Bosworth, G., & Willett, J. 2011. Embeddedness or Escapism? Rural Perceptions and Economic Development in Cornwall and Northumberland. *Sociologia Ruralis* 51(2): 195–214.

Boulding, K. 1981. *Evolutionary Economics*. London: Sage.

Bourdieu, P. 1991. *Language and Symbolic Power*. Boston: Harvard University Press.

Bowen, R., & Morris, W. 2019. The Digital Divide: Implications for Agribusiness and Entrepreneurship: Lessons from Wales. *Journal of Rural Studies* 72: 75–84.

Bramwell, A., Nelles, J., & Wolfe, D. 2008. Knowledge, Innovation and Institutions: Global and Local Dimensions of the ICT Cluster in Waterloo, Canada. *Regional Studies* 42(1): 101–116.

Bristol City Council. 2019. The Economic Impact of Restoring Passenger Rail to Bristol, VA/TN, February 2019.

Bristow, G., & Healey, A. 2014. Building Resilient Regions: Complex Adaptive Systems and the Role of Policy Intervention. *Raumforsch Raumordn* 72: 93–102.

Bristow, G., & Healey, A. 2018. Innovation and Regional Economic Resilience: An Exploratory Analysis. *Annals of Regional Science* 60: 265–284.

Brooks, S. 2019. Brexit and the Politics of the Rural. *Sociologia Ruralis.* https://doi .org/10.1111/soru.12281. Accessed 26 May 2020.

Bruckmeier, K., & Tovey, H. 2008. Knowledge in Sustainable Rural Development: From Forms of Knowledge to Knowledge Processes. *Sociologia Ruralis* 48(3): 313–329.

Bruneau, I., Mischi, J., & Renahy, N. 2018. *Les Gilets Jaunes en Campagne – Une Ruralite Politique.* AOC. https://aoc.media/analyse/2018/12/13/gilets-jaunes-camp agne-ruralite-politique/. Accessed 26 May 2020.

Bürk, T., Kühn, M., & Sommer, H. 2012. Stigmatisation of Cities: The Vulnerability of Local Identities. *Raumforschung und Raumordnung* 70(4): 337–347.

Burnham, P., Gilland, K., Grant, W., & Laylon-Henry, Z. 2004. *Research Methods in Politics.* Basingstoke: Macmillan Palgrave.

Calzada, I. 2018. 'Algorithmic Nations': Seeing Like a City-Regional and Techno-Political Conceptual Assemblage. *Regional Studies, Regional Science* 5(1): 267–289.

Canavan, C. 2018. *New Year's Resolutions: I Gave Up Plastic for a Whole Year and You Can, Too.* https://www.huffingtonpost.co.uk/entry/i-gave-up-plastic-for-a-year -and-you-can-too_uk_5c1a2d6ee4b08db9905990d5?guccounter=1&guce_referrer =aHR0cHM6Ly93d3cuZ29vZ2xlLmNvbS8&guce_referrer_sig=AQAAAFtIBtt vNJCqleMiska0p_sO99FNxzYBJjFK7bDttdhRoAlYvXUACxlpk_eZlp13WgO GVaVyJkH77sJRom5r-B251wxNLKWGUfjrV0uuWPVANzbkQBvFrQzHO8 tmMKSO0ez8IrugXeuYIp9Tsys2Vy21ru9MI6dC16g-QQUbUxUp. Accessed 26 October 2019.

Canete, J., Navarro, F., & Cejudo, E. 2018. Territorially Unequal Rural Development: The Cases of the LEADER Initiative and the PRODER Programme in Andalusia (Spain). *European Planning Studies* 26(4): 726–744.

Casey, T., & Christ, K. 2005. Social Capital and Economic Performance in the American States. *Social Science Quarterly* 86(4): 827–846.

Castells, M. 2000. *The Rise of the Network Society: Information, Age, Economy, Society and Culture v.1 (Information Age Series).* Oxford: Blackwell.

Census. 2017. *One in Five Americans Live in Rural Areas.* https://www.census.gov/li brary/stories/2017/08/rural-america.html. Accessed 11 May 2020.

Champion, T. 2001. The Appropriation of the Phoenicians in British Imperial Ideology. *Nations and Nationalism* 4: 451–465.

Chancy, R. 2013. Straightening the Crooked Road. *Ethnography* 14(4): 387–411.

Charmaz, K. 2006. *Constructing Grounded Theory: A Practical Guide Through Qualitative Analysis.* London: Sage Publications.

Clausen, T. H. 2020. The Liability of Rurality and New Venture Viability. *Journal of Rural Studies* 73: 114–121.

Cloke, P., & Edwards, G. 1986. Rurality in England and Wales 1981: A Replication of the 1971 Index. *Regional Studies* 20(4): 289–306.

Coal River Mountain. 2017. *Newsy.* https://www.youtube.com/watch?v=uBDKdlGL p9U.

Connolly, W. 2002. *Neuropolitics: Thinking, Culture, Speed.* Minneapolis: University of Minnesota Press.

Connolly, W. 2008. *Capitalism and Christianity, American Style.* Durham, NC: Duke University Press.

Connolly, W. 2011. *A World of Becoming.* Durham, NC: Duke University Press.

Cooke, P. 2002. *Knowledge Economies, Clusters, Learning and Cooperative Advantage.* London: Routledge.

Coole, D., & Frost, S. (Eds). 2010. *New Materialisms: Ontology, Agency and Politics.* Durham: Duke University Press.

Cornwall and Isles of Scilly Local Enterprise Partnership CIOS LEP. 2017. *Cornwall and Isles of Scilly Vision 2030.* https://www. cioslep.com/vision/vision-2030. Accessed 28 April 2020.

Corradini, C. 2017. Location Determinants of Green Technological Entry: Evidence from European Regions. *Small Business Economics.* https://doi.org/10.1007/s 11187-017-9938-7.

Crabtree, J. 2016. A Different Path for Rural America. *American Journal of Economics and Sociology* 75(3): 605–622.

Crescenzi, R., Cataldo, M., & Rodriguez-Pose, A. 2016. Government Quality and the Economic Returns of Transport Infrastructure Investment in European Regions. *Journal of Regional Science* 56: 555–582.

Crone, M., & Roper, S. 2001. Local Learning from Multi-National Plants: Knowledge Transfers in the Supply Chain. *Regional Studies* 36(6): 535–548.

Crow, P. 2007. *Do, Die, Or Get Along: A Tale of Two Appalachian Towns.* Athens and London: University of Georgia Press.

Dabrowski, M. 2012. Shallow or Deep Europeanisation? The Uneven Impact of EU Cohesion Policy on the Regional and Local Authorities in Poland. *Environment and Planning C: Government and Policy* 30: 730–745.

Daily Mail. 2020. *Turn Around and F*** Off! Angry Locals in Devon and Cornwall Slam Holidaymakers as Hoardes of Caravans Descend on Beauty Spots After Travel Ban Was Lifted.* https://www.dailymail.co.uk/news/article-8493693/Angry-locals-slam-holidaymakers-hordes-caravans-descend-Cornish-beauty-spots.html. Accessed 1 December 2020.

Daily Mirror 2014. *Winning Bidder for £170,000 eBay Loom Band Dress Doesn't Want to Pay Up.* https://www.mirror.co.uk/news/uk-news/winning-bidder-170000-ebay-loom-3895935. Accessed 26 October 2019.

Damasio, A. 2004. *Looking For Spinoza.* London. Vintage.

Dargan, L., & Shucksmith, M. 2003. Leader and Innovation. *Sociologia Ruralis* 48(3): 275–291.

Darwin, C. 1910. *The Origin of the Species By Means of Natural Selection.* London: John Murray.

Dawley, S., Pike, A., & Tomaney, J. 2010. Towards the Resilient Region? *Local Economy* 25(8): 650–667.

Day, G. 2002. *Making Sense of Wales: A Sociological Perspective.* Cardiff: Cardiff University Press.

De Souza, P. 2017. *The Rural and Peripheral in Regional Development.* London: Routledge.

Delanda, M. 2011. *A New Philosophy of Society: Assemblage Theory and Social Complexity.* London: Continuum.

Deleuze, G. 1991. *Bergsonism.* New York: Zone Books.

Deleuze, G., & Guattari, F. 2004. *A Thousand Plateaus.* London: Continuum.

Deller, S., Kures, M., & Conroy, T. 2019. Rural Entrepreneurship and Migration. *Journal of Rural Studies* 66: 30–42.

Department for Environment, Food and Rural Affairs (DEFRA). 2020. *Rural Population and Migration Statistics.* https://www.gov.uk/government/publications /rural-population-and-migration/rural-population-201415. Accessed 26 May 2020.

Dickinson, R. 2008. Changing Landscapes of Difference; Representations of Cornwall in Travel Writing. In P. Payton (Ed.), *Cornish Studies Sixteen.* Exeter: University of Exeter Press.

Dominguez Garcia, D., Horlings, L., Swagemakers, P., & Fernandez, X. F. 2013. Place Branding and Endogenous Rural Development: Departure Points for Developing an Inner Brand of the River Minho Estuary. *Place Branding and Public Diplomacy* 9(2): 124–140.

Donner, M., Horlings, L., Fort, F., & Vellema, S. 2017. Place Branding, Embeddedness and Endogenous Rural Development: Four European Cases. *Place Branding and Public Diplomacy* 13(4): 273–292.

Dovey, K. 2010. *Becoming Places: Urbanism/Architecture/Identity/Power.* London: Routledge.

Dovey, K. 2012. Informal Urbanism and Complex Adaptive Assemblage. *International Planning Development Review* 34(3): 371–389.

Drabenstott, M. 2001. New Policies for a Rural America. *International Regional Science Review* 24(1): 3–15.

Dunstan, S., & Jaeger, A. J. 2016. The Role of Language in Interactions With Others on Campus for Rural Appalachian College Students. *Journal of College Student Development* 57(1): 47–64.

Durkheim, E. 2002 [1897]. *Suicide: A Study in Sociology.* Abingdon: Routledge.

Elcock, H. 2008. Regional Futures and Strategic Planning. *Regional and Federal Studies* 18(1): 77–92.

Eriksson, M. 2008. (Re)Producing a 'Peripheral' Region – Northern Sweden in the News. *Geografiska Annaler: Series B, Human Geography* 90(4): 369–388.

Evans, J., & Jones, P. 2011. The Walking Interview: Methodology, Mobility and Place. *Applied Geography* 31: 849–858.

Evans, M., & Synett, S. 2007. Generating Social Capital? The Social Economy and Local Economic Development. *European Urban and Regional Studies* 14(1): 55–74.

Evans, N., Morris, C., & Winter, M. 2002. Conceptualising Agriculture: A Critique of Post-Productivism as the New Orthodoxy. *Progress in Human Geography* 26(3): 313–332.

Fabricant, N., & Fabricant, M. 2018. Cognitive Fracture: How Disposeable Bodies and Toxic Status Quo Led to the Rise of Trump in Appalachia. *Journal of Land, Labour and Society* 22: 187–195.

Faulkner, J., Murphy, E., & Scott, M. 2019. Rural Household Vulnerability a Decade After the Great Financial Crisis. *Journal of Rural Studies* 72: 240–251.

Fenwick, J., McMillan, J., & Elcock, H. 2009. Local Government and the Problem of English Governance. *Local Government Studies* 35(1): 5–20.

Florida, R. 2002. *The Rise of the Creative Class.* New York: Basic Books.

Foster, G., & Hummel, R. 1997. Wham, Bam, Thankyou Sam: Critical Dimensions of the Persistence of Hillbilly Caracatures. *Sociological Spectrum* 17(2): 157–176.

Foucault, M. 1998. *The History of Sexuality Vol 1 – The Will to Knowledge.* London: Penguin.

France 24. 2017. *Seven Years After Arab Spring Revolt, Tunisia's Future Remains Uncertain.* https://www.france24.com/en/20171217-tunisia-seven-years-after-arab-spring-revolution-protests-economic-uncertainty. Accessed 7 May 2019.

Galliano, D., Goncalves, A., & Triboulet, P. 2019. The Peripheral Systems of Eco-Innovation: Evidence from Eco-Innovative Agro-Food Projects in a French Rural Area. *Journal of Rural Studies* 72: 273–285.

Gaventa, J. 2019. Power and Powerlessness in an Appalachian Valley – Revisited. *The Journal of Peasant Studies* 46(3): 440–456.

Gest, J. 2016. *The New Minority: White Working Class Politics in an Age of Immigration and Inequality.* New York: Oxford University Press.

Giesbrecht, K., Varela, D., Wiktor, J., Grebmeier, J., Kelly, B., & Long, J. E. 2019. A Decade of Summertime Measurements of Phytoplankton Biomass, Productivity and Assemblage Composition in the Pacific Arctic Region from 2006–2016. *Deep Sea Research Part II: Topical Studies in Oceanography* 16(1): 93–113, 121.

Gleick, James. 1987. *Chaos.* London: Abacus.

GO Virginia Region One. 2019. *Growth and Diversification Plan.*

Goffman, E. 1959. *The Presentation of the Self in Everyday Life.* Middlesex: Penguin Books.

Görmar, F., & Lang, T. 2019. Acting Peripheries: An Introduction. *ACME: An International Journal for Critical Geographies* 18(2): 486–495.

Hallerod, B., & Larson, D. 2008. Poverty, Welfare Problems and Social Exclusion. *International Journal of Social Welfare* 17: 15–25.

Hantrais, 2009. *International Comparative Research: Theory, Methods, Practice.* Basingstoke: Palgrave Macmillan.

Hechter, M. 1975. *Internal Colonialism: The Celtic Fringe in British National Development.* California: University of California Press.

Heilman, E. 2004. Hoosiers, Hicks, and Hayseeds: The Controversial Place of Marginalized Ethnic Whites in Multicultural Education. *Equity & Excellence in Education* 37(1): 67–79.

Herkus-Ozturk, H. 2018. Related Variety and Innovation: Evidence from the Tourism industry. *Journal of Economic and Social Geography* 109(2): 256–273.

Herrschel, T. 2010. Growth and Innovation of Competitive Regions: The Role of Internal and External Connections. *European Planning Studies* 18: 1169–1172.

Herslund, L. 2012. The Rural Creative Class: Counterurbanisation and Entrepreneurship in the Danish Countryside. *Sociologia Ruralis* 52(2): 235–255.

Hewitt-Dundas, N., Andreosso-O'Callaghan, B., Crone, M., & Roper, S. 2005. Knowledge Transfers from Multinational Plants in Ireland: A Cross Border Comparison of Supply Chain Linkages. *European Urban and Regional Studies* 12(1): 23–43.

Higgens, V., Potter, C., Dibden, J., & Cocklin, C. 2014. Neoliberalising Rural Environments. *Journal of Rural Studies* 36: 386–390.

High, C., & Nemes, G. 2007. Social Learning in LEADER: Exogenous, Endogenous, and Hybrid Evaluation in Rural Development. *Sociologia Ruralis* 47(2): 103–119.

Hill, S., Pritchard, C., Laugharne, R., & Gunnell, D. 2005. Changing Patterns of Suicide in a Poor, Rural County Over the 20th Century. *Social Psychiatry, Psychiatry Epidemiology* 40: 601–604.

Honadle, B. 2011. Rural Development Policy in the United States: A Critical Analysis and Lessons from the "Still Birth" of the Rural Collaborative Investment Program. *Community Development* 42(1): 56–69.

Huttlinger, K., Schaller-Ayers, J., & Lawson, T. 2004. Health Care in Appalachia: A Population-Based Approach. *Public Health Nursing* 21(2): 103–110.

Ivaldi, G., & Gombin, J. 2015. The Front National and the New Politics of the Rural in France. In D. Strijker, G. Voerman, & I. Terluin (Eds.), *Rural Protest Groups and Populist Political Parties*. Wageningen: Wageningen Academic Publishers.

Jansson, D. 2003. Internal Orientalism in America: W.J. Cash's the Mind of the South and the Spatial Construction of American National Identity. *Political Geography* 22(3): 293–316.

Jenkins, T. N. 2000. Putting Postmodernity into Practice: Endogenous Development and the Role of Traditional Cultures in the Rural Development of Marginal Regions. *Ecological Economics* 34: 301–314.

Jensen, L., Tickmayer, A., & Slack, T. 2019. Rural-Urban Variation in Informal Work Activities in the United States. *Journal of Rural Studies* 68: 276–284.

Johnston, R., Rossiter, D., Manley, D., Pattie, C., Hartman, T., & Jones, K. 2018. Coming Full Circle: The 2017 UK General Election and the Changing Electoral Map. *The Geographical Journal* 184(1): 100–108.

Jones, L., Heley, J., & Woods, M. 2019. Unravelling the Global Wool Assemblage: Researching Place and Production Networks in the Global Countryside. *Sociologia Ruralis* 59(1): 137–158.

Kalantaridis, C., Bika, Z., & Millard, D. 2019. Migration, Meaning(s) of Place and Implications for Innovation Policy. *Regional Studies* 53(12): 1657–1668.

Kaufman, S. 1995. *At Home in the Universe: The Search for the Laws of Self-Organisation and Complexity*. Oxford: Oxford University Press.

Kim, J. 2008. Making Sense of Emergence. In M. Bedau & P. Humphries (Eds.), *Emergence: Contemporary Readings in Philosophy and Science.* Cambridge: MIT Press.

Kleinschmit, J., & Clausen, A., 2012. Rural Development, Energy, and Conservation in the Farm Bill. *American Planning Association: Planning & Environmental Law* 64(4): 9–13.

Kneafsey, M. 2000. Rural Tourism and Identity, Stories of Change and Resistance from the West of Ireland and Brittany. In A. Hale & P. Payton (Eds.), *New Directions in Celtic Studies.* Exeter: University of Exeter Press.

Kok, 2006. *Facing the Challenge, the Lisbon Strategy for Growth and Employment. OECD Policy Brief, Reinventing Rural Policy.* Paris: OECD.

Land Registry. 2020. *House Price Index.* https://landregistry.data.gov.uk/app/ukhpi /browse?from=2019-03-01&location=http%3A%2F%2Flandregistry.data.gov.uk %2Fid%2Fregion%2Funited-kingdom&to=2020-03-01. Accessed 28 April 2020.

Lang, T. 2012. Shrinkage, Metropolitization and Periperhalization in East Germany. *European Planning Studies* 20(10): 1747–1754.

Latour, B. 2005. *Reassembling the Social: An Introduction to Actor Network Theory.* Oxford: Oxford University Press.

Lavender-Stott, E. S., Grafsky, E. L., Nguyen, H. N., Wacker, E., & Steelman, S. M. 2018. Challenges and Strategies of Sexual Minority Youth Research in Southwest Virginia. *Journal of Homosexuality* 65(6): 691–704.

Laviolette, P. 2003. Landscaping Death: Resting Places for Cornish Identity. *Journal of Material Culture* 8(2): 215–240.

Lee, J., Arnason, A., Nightingale, A., & Shucksmith, M. 2005. Networking Social Capital and Identities in European Rural Development. *Sociologia Ruralis* 45(4): 269–283.

Lovelock, J. 2000. *The Ages of GAIA: A Biography of Our Living Earth.* Oxford: Oxford University Press.

Lowe, P., Marsden, T., Murdoch, J., & Ward, N. 2012. *The Differentiated Countryside.* London: Routledge.

Mackinnon, K. 2002. Cornish at Its Millenium: An Independent Study of the Language Undertaken in 2000. In P. Payton (Ed.), *Cornish Studies 10.* Exeter: Exeter University Press.

Macpherson, H. 2016. Walking Methods in Landscape Research: Moving Bodies, Spaces of Disclosure and Report. *Landscape Research* 41(1): 425–432.

Macy, B. 2015. *Factory Man: How One Furniture Maker Battled Offshoring, Stayed Local, and Helped to Save and American Town.* Basingstoke: Pan Books.

Macy, B. 2018. *Dopesick: Dealers, Doctors, and the Drug Company that Addicted America.* New York: Hachette.

Malerba, F., & McKelvey, M. 2018. Knowledge-Intensive Innovative Entrepreneurship Integrating Schumpeter, Evolutionary Economics, and Innovation Systems. *Small Business Economics.* https://doi.org/10.1007/s11187-018-0060-2.

Mamonova, N., & Franquesa, J. 2020. Right Wing Populism in Rural Europe: Introduction to the Special Issue. *Sociologia Ruralis* 60(4): 702–709.

Margarian, A. 2013. A Constructivist Critique of the Endogenous Development Approach in the European Support of Rural Areas. *Growth and Change* 44(1): 1–29.

Markey-Towler, B. 2018. A Formal Psychological Theory for Evolutionary Economics. *Journal of Evolutionary Economics*. https://doi.org/10.1007/s00191 -018-0566-4.

Marsden, T. K., Murdoch, J., Lowe, P., & Ward, N. 2003. *The Differentiated Countryside*. Abingdon: Routledge.

Martin, R., & Sunley, P. 2006. Path Dependence and Regional Economic Evolution. *Journal of Economic Geography* 6: 395–437.

Martin, R., & Sunley, P. 2007. Complexity Thinking and Evolutionary Economic Geography. *Journal of Economic Geography* 7: 573–601.

Marx, K. Grundrisse. 2005 [1858]. In D. Mclellan (Ed.), *Karl Marx, Selected Writings*. Oxford: Oxford University Press.

Marz, S., Friedrich-Nishio, M., & Grupp, H. 2006. Knowledge Transfer in an Innovation Simulation Model. *Technological Forecasting and Social Change* 73(2): 138–152.

McFarlane, C. 2011. The City as Assemblage: Dwelling and Urban Space. *Environment and Planning D: Politics and Space* 29(4): 649–671.

Mead, G. 1934. *Mind, Self and Society*. Chicago: University of Chicago Press.

Meekes, J., Buda, D., & De Roo, G. 2017. Adaptation, Interaction and Urgency: A Complex Evolutionary Economic Geography Approach to Leisure. *Tourism Geographies* 19(4): 525–547.

Merleau-Ponty, M. 2002. *A Phenomenology of Perception*. London: Routledge.

Meyer, F., Miggelbrink, J., & Schwarzenberg, T. 2016. Reflecting on the Margins: Socio-Spatial Stigmatisation Among Adolescents in a Peripheralised Region. *Comparative Population Studies* 41(3–4): 285–320.

Moreno, R., Paci, R., & Usai, S. 2005. Spatial Spillovers and Innovation Activity in European Regions. *Environment and Planning A* 37: 1793–1812.

Morgan, C., & Sheperd, J. 2020. *Land of Opportunity: England's Rural Periphery*. London: New Local Government Network.

Mulholland, H. 2011. Boris Johnson Unveils Redesigned Routemaster Bus for London. *The Guardian*. https://www.theguardian.com/uk/2011/dec/16/boris-j ohnson-routemaster-bus-london. Accessed 2 April 2020.

Nakano, T. 2007. Alfred Marshalls Economic Nationalism. *Nations and Nationalism* 13(1): 57–76.

Nathan, M. 2005. *The Wrong Stuff: Creative Class Theory, Diversity and City Performance*. Discussion Paper 1, London: Centre for Cities, Institute of Public Policy Research.

New River/Mount Rogers Workforce Development Board. http://nrmrwib.org/. Accessed 3 July 2018.

NOMIS. 2020. *Total Population – Time Series*. https://www.nomisweb.co.uk/reports/ lmp/la/1946157349/subreports/pop_time_series/report.aspx? Accessed 28 April 2020.

NOMIS. 2020b. *Earnings By Residence – Time Series*. https://www.nomisweb.co.u k/reports/lmp/la/1946157349/subreports/asher_time_series/report.aspx? Accessed 28 April 2020.

NOMIS. 2020c. *Labour Market Profile*. https://www.nomisweb.co.uk/reports/lmp/la /1946157349/report.aspx? Accessed 28 April 2020.

Nuvolari, A. 2004. Collective Invention During the British Industrial Revolution: The Case of the Cornish Pumping Engine. *Cambridge Journal of Economics* 28: 347–363.

Paniagua, A. 2013. Farmers in Remote Rural Areas: The Worth of Permanence in the Place. *Land Use Policy* 35: 1–7.

Payton, P. 2002. Introduction. In P. Payton (Ed.), *Cornish Studies 10*. Exeter: Exeter University Press.

Pearson, G. 1983. *Hooligan: A History of Respectable Fears*. London: Palgrave.

Pendlebury, J. 2013. Conservation Values, the Authorised Heritage Discourse and the Conservation-Planning Assemblage. *International Journal of Heritage Studies* 19(7): 709–727.

Perry, R. 1993. Economic Change and Opposition Economics. In P. Payton (Ed.), *The Making of Modern Cornwall, Cornwall Since the War*. Redruth: Institute of Cornish Studies.

Pike, A., Rodriguez-Pose, A., & Tomaney, J. 2006. *Local and Regional Development*. Abingdon: Routledge.

Pine, J., & Gilmore, G. 2019 (Revised Edition). *The Experience Economy: Competing for Customer Time, Attention, and Money*. Boston: Harvard Business Review Press.

Pluymers, K. 2016. Atlantic Iron: Wood Scarcity and the Political Ecology of Early English Expansion. *The William & Mary Quarterly (Project Muse)* 73(3): 389–426.

Politico. 2019. *2016 Virginia Election Results*. https://www.politico.com/2016-elect ion/results/map/president/virginia/. Accessed 25 October 2019.

Poudyal, N., Hodges, D., & Cordell, K. 2008. The Role of Natural Resource Amenities in Attracting Retirees: Implications for Economic Growth Policy. *Ecological Economics* 68: 240–248.

Powe, N. 2018. Non-Amenity Business Growth and Small Town Revival. *Journal of Rural Studies* 62: 125–133.

Polyakova, A. & Fligstein, N. 2016. Is European Integration Causing Europe to become More Nationalist? Evidence from the 2007–9 Financial Crisis. *Journal of European Union Public* Policy 23(1): 60–83.

Prigogine, I., & Stengers, I. 1985. *Order Out of Chaos: Man's Dialogue with Nature*. London: Flamingo, Harper Collins.

Putnam, R. 2000. *Bowling Alone: The Collapse and Revival of American Community*. London: Simon Schuster Paper Backs.

Pye, J., & Alexander, A. T. 2018. *Cornwall Marine and Maritime Growth and Innovation Report*. University of Exeter Business School in Cornwall. http://hum anities.exeter.ac.uk/history/research/centres/ics/research/economy/maritime_grow th/. Accessed 1 December 2020.

Quiller-Couch, A. 1898/9. *The Cornish Magazine, Vols 1 and 2*. Truro: John Pollard.

Raisanen, J., & Tuovinen, T. 2020. Digital Innovations in Rural Micro-Enterprises. *Journal of Rural Studies* 73: 56–67.

Reed, P. 2018. The Importance of Appalachian Identity: A Case Study in Rootedness. *American Speech* 93(3–4): 409–424.

Reimer, A., Han, Y., Goetz, S., Loveridge, S., & Albrecht, D. 2016. World Networks in US Rural Policy Discourse. *Applied Economic Perspectives and Policy* 38(2): 215–238.

Roberts, E., & Townsend, L. 2015. The Contribution of the Creative Economy to the Resilience of Rural Communities: Exploring Cultural and Digital Capital. *Sociologia Ruralis* 56(2): 197–219.

Roddern, J. 2019. *Why Cities Lose: The Deep Roots of the Urban Rural Political Divide*. Hachette.

Rodriguez-Pose, A., & Crescenzi, R. 2008. Research and Development, Spillovers, Innovation Systems and the Genesis of Regional Growth in Europe. *Regional Studies* 42: 51–67.

Roggenkamp, K. 2008. Seeing Inside the Mountains: Cynthia Rylant's Appalachian Literature and the "Hillbilly" Stereotype. *The Lion and the Unicorn* 32(2): 192–215.

Russell Hochschild, A. 2016. *Strangers in their Own Land*. New York: The New Press.

Said, E. 2003. *Orientalism*. London: Penguin Books.

Salva, J., Bivens, R., Roberto, K., & Blieszer, J. 2019. Where Your Age Matters: Individual and County-Level Predictors of Formal and Informal Care in Rural Appalachia. *Journal of Aging and Health* 5: 837–860.

Sampaio, D., & King, R. 2019. 'It's Not Everybody that Wants to Stay on a Remote Island': Understanding Distinction in the Context of Lifestyle Migrants Growing Older in the Azores. *Journal of Rural Studies* 72: 186–195.

Satterwhite, E. 2005. That's What They're All Singing About: Appalachian Heritage, Celtic Pride and American Nationalism at the 2003 Smithsonian Folklife Festival. *Appalachian Journal* 32(5): 302–338.

Satterwhite, E. 2015. *Dear Appalachia: Readers, Identity, and Popular Fiction Since 1878*. Kentucky: The University Press of Kentucky.

Shand, W. 2018. Urban Assemblage, Street Youth and the Sub-Saharan African City. *City: Analysis of Urban Trends, Culture, Theory, Policy, Action* 22(2): 257–269.

Shortall, S. 2004. Social or Economic Goals, Civic Inclusion or Exclusion? An Analysis of Rural Development Theory and Practice. *Sociologia Ruralis* 44(1): 109–124.

Shortall, S., & Warner, M. 2012. Rural Transformations: Conceptions and Policy Issues. In M. Shucksmith, D. Brown, S. Shortall, J. Vergunst, & M. Warner (Eds.), *Rural Transformations and Rural Policies in the US and the UK*. Abingdon: Routledge.

Shucksmith, M. 2018. Re-Imagining the Rural: From Rural Idyll to Good Countryside. *Journal of Rural Studies* 59: 163–172.

Shucksmith, M., & Brown, D. (Eds.). 2016. *Routledge International Handbook of Rural Studies*. Abingdon: Routledge.

Shucksmith, M., Brown, D., Shortall, S., Vergunst, J., & Warner, M. (Eds.). 2012. *Rural Transformations and Rural Policies in the US and UK*. Abingdon: Routledge.

Shucksmith, M., & Chapman, P. 1998. Rural Development and Social Exclusion. *Sociologia Ruralis* 38(2): 225–242.

Smith, A. 1991. *National Identity*. Oxford: Blackwell.

Smith, J., & Jenks, C. 2006. *Qualitative Complexity: Ecology, Cognitive Processes and the Re-Emergence of Structures in Post Humanist Social Theory*. Routledge: Oxon.

Software Cornwall. 2020. *Cornwall's Fast-Growing Tech Sector Highlighted in National Tech Nation 2018 Report*. https://www.softwarecornwall.org/cornwal ls-fast-growing-tech-sector-highlighted-in-national-report-technation-wearetechn ation-technation/. Accessed 28 April 2020.

Spatz, B. 2017. Embodied Research: A Methodology. *Liminalities: A Journal of Performance Studies* 13(2): 1–31.

Spinoza, B. 1996. *Ethics*. London: Penguin Books.

Spooner, D. 1972. Industrial Movement and the Rural Periphery: The Case of Devon and Cornwall. *Regional Studies* 6: 197–215.

Stecker, C., & Debus, M. 2019. Refugees Welcome? Zum Einfluss der Fluchtlingsunterbringung auf den Wahlerfolg der AfD bei der Bundestagswahl 2017 in Bayern. *Politische Vierteljahresschrift* 60: 299–233.

Stockdale, A., Theunissen, N., & Haartsen, T. 2018. Staying in a State of Flux: A Life Course Perspective on the Diverse Staying Processes of Rural Young Adults. *Population, Place and Space* [e2139]. https://doi.org/10.1002/psp.2139.

Stoyle, M. 2002. *West Britons*. Exeter: Exeter University Press.

Strauss, A., Corbin, J., & Corin, J. 2008. *Basics of Qualitative Research: Techniques and Procedures for Developing Grounded Theory* (2nd ed.). Thousand Oaks: Sage Publications.

Strover, S., Whitacre, B., Rhinesmith, C., & Schrubbe, A. 2020. The Digital Inclusion Role of Rural Libraries: Social Inequalities Through Space and Place. *Media, Culture and Society* 42(2): 242–259.

Szabova, L., Brown, K., & Fisher, J. 2020. Access to Ecosystem Benefits: More Than Proximity. *Society and Natural Resources* 33(2): 244–260.

Thanem, T., & Knights, D. 2019. *Embodied Research Methods*. London: Sage.

Thiede, B., Lichter, D., & Slack, T. 2018. Working But Poor: The Good Life in Rural America? *Journal of Rural Studies* 59: 183–193.

Thompson, D. 2006. Searching for Silenced Voices in Appalachian Music. *Geojournal* 65: 67–78.

Thornton, G., & Deitz-Allyn, K. 2010. Substance Abuse, Unemployment Problems, and the Disparities in Mental Health Services in the Appalachian Southwest Region. *Journal of Human Behavior in The Social Environment* 20(7): 939–951.

Townsend, P. 1979. *Poverty in the United Kingdom: A Survey of Household Resources and Standards of Living*. Harmondsworth: Penguin.

Tregidga, G. 2000. *The Liberal Party in South West Britain Since 1918: Political Decline, Democracy, and Rebirth*. Exeter: Exeter University Press.

Trozzo, K., Munsell, J., Niewolny, K., & Chamberlain, J. 2019. Forest Food and Medicine in Contemporary Appalachia. *Southeastern Geographer* 59(1): 52–76.

Tuitjer, G., & Steinfuhrer, A. 2019. The Scientific Construction of the Village: Framing and Practicing Rural Research in a Trend Study in Germany, 1952–2015.

Vachelli, E. 2018. *Embodied Research in Migration Studies*. Bristol: Policy Press.

Verghese, A. 2016. *My Own Country: A Doctor's Story of a Town and Its People in the Age of AIDS*. Scribner.

Willett, J. 2013. National Identity and Regional Development: Cornwall and the Campaign for Objective 1 Funding. *National Identities* 15(3): 297–311.

Willett, J. 2016. The Production of Place: Perception, Reality, and the Politics of Becoming. *Political Studies* 64(2): 436–451.

Willett, J. 2019. The Periphery as a Complex Adaptive Assemblage: Local Government and Enhanced Communication to Challenge Peripheralising Narratives. *ACME* 18(2).

Willett, J., & Giovannini, A. 2014. The Uneven Path of UK Devolution: Top-Down Vs. Bottom-Up Regionalism in England – Cornwall and the North-East Compared. *Political Studies* 62: 343–360.

Willett, J., & Lang, T. 2018. Peripheralisation: A Politics of Place, Affect, Perception and Representation. *Sociologia Ruralis* 58(2): 258–275.

Willett, J., Tidy, R., Tregidga, G., & Passmore, P. 2019. Why Did Cornwall Vote for Brexit? Assessing the Implications for EU Structural Funding Programmes. *Environment and Planning, C: Politics and Space* 37(8): 1343–1360.

Williams, J. A. 2002. *Appalachia: A History*. Chapel Hill: University of North Carolina Press.

Williams, M. 2003. Why is Cornwall Poor? Poverty and In-Migration since the 1960's. *Contemporary British History* 17: 55–70.

Williams, M., & Harrison, E. 1995. Movers and Stayers: A Comparison of Migratory and Non-Migratory Groups in Cornwall 1981–1991. In P. Payton (Ed.), *Cornish Studies Three*. Exeter: Exeter University Press.

Witt, U. 2008. What is Specific About Evolutionary Economics? *Journal of Evolutionary Economics* 18(5): 547–575.

Young, S. 2017. Wild, Wonderful, White Criminality: Images of "White Trash" Appalachia. *Critical Criminology* 25(1): 103–117.

Young-Powell, A. 2019. New Zealand Unveils New 'Well-Being Budget' with Focus on Mental Health Over Economic Growth. *The Independent*, 31 May. https://www.independent.co.uk/news/world/australasia/new-zealand-budget-wellbeing-mental-health-jacinda-ardern-economy-a8938226.html.

Zcni, J., Perez-Mayorga, M., Roa-Fuentes, C. A., Brejao, G., & Casatti, L. 2019. How Deforestation Drives Stream Habitat Changes and the Functional Structure of Fish Assemblages in Different Tropical Regions. *Aquatic Conservation: Marine and Freshwater Ecosystems* 29(8): 1238–1252.

Zwonitrer, M., & Hirschberg, C. 2004. *Will You Miss Me When I'm Gone? The Carter Family and their Legacy in American Music*. New York: Simon Schuster.

Index

Abingdon, 90, 112, 114
actants, 102, 103
Actor Network Theory, 21, 25, 26
affective: assemblage, 21, 22, 27,
    40, 68, 107, 161; attachment, 67;
    economy, 25, 30, 34, 68; impacts,
    23, 25, 32, 33, 49, 62, 132;
    interactions, 19, 55; relationships, 48,
    132; responses, 34, 49, 148
agglomeration, 59, 135
Ahmed, 18, 22, 25, 34, 67
Alcock, 15, 52, 159
Ali and Duemmel, 16
amenity, 18, 117, 163
amplification, 147; amplificatory, 32,
    38, 52, 126, 151, 157, 163; amplified
Angarrack, 78
Anomie, 44, 52, 53, 102, 133, 148
anthropocentric, 10, 25
Antonetti and Gambarotto, 55, 60
Appalachia, 73–75, 87, 88, 90, 92, 96,
    103, 104; Regional Commission, 73;
    trail, 73
Argent, 118
Aristotle, 32, 38
Armstrong and Taylor, 7, 44
Arzrout and Wojcieszak, 44
Askegaard and Kjeldgaard, 37
assembled communities, 29, 31, 59

atomised, 1, 4, 88, 135
attachment to place, 36, 75, 147
Atterton, 17, 160

Bache and Scott, 7
bachelor's degree, 71, 79
backwards, 13, 33, 80, 103, 118, 141,
    152; backwardness, 14, 15, 106
Bait, 119, 137
Bajpai, 4
Barke and Newton, 1, 15
bartering, 43, 90, 91
Barter Theatre, 90
Bauman, 29, 36, 51
becoming, 5, 6, 8, 16, 19, 22, 35, 38, 43,
    47, 53, 63, 65, 93
Bedau and Humphries, 48, 49, 56, 162
Bell and Jayne, 46, 114
Bennett, 5, 10, 18, 22, 25, 27, 34, 112
Bergson, 5, 23, 24, 27, 33, 34, 45,
    52, 57, 67–69, 102, 110, 125, 146;
    Bergsonian, 33, 37, 52, 56, 83, 150
Big Stone Gap, 89, 111
biodiversity, 94, 95
Birthplace of Country Music, 111, 154
Black, 7, 11, 74
Blackley, 74
Blacksberg, 72, 97
Blumer, 67

Bodenhamer, 74
bonding capital, 16–17, 38
Boschma, 6, 54, 55, 63, 102, 161; and Frenken, 6, 55, 102, 161
Bosworth: and Bat Finke, 17, 142, 156, 161; and Willett, 17, 69
bottom up, 1, 2, 66, 69
Bouazizi, 23, 31, 32
Boulding, 54, 57, 59, 61, 63
boundary conditions, 5, 50, 51
Bourdieu, 37
Bowen and Morris, 16, 160
Bramwell, 59, 60
branding (place), 15, 46
Brexit, 1, 4
bridging capital, 16, 17, 38
Bristol: Bristol City Council, 72, 150; Bristol Herald Courier, 111, 154; Bristol Sessions, 92, 111
Bristow and Healey, 6, 49, 54, 55, 60, 63, 161
Brooks, 12
Bruckmeier and Tovey, 14
Bruneau, 12
Burke, 13, 17, 33, 160, 163
Burnham, 69
butterfly effect, 31–32

Calzada, 5
Canavan, 40
Canete, 1, 15, 160
Carrico, 75
Carter Family, 87, 91, 111
Casey and Christ, 60
cash economy, 90, 91
Castells, 36, 51
causality, 32, 46, 49
Champion, 79
Chaney, 73
change, 5, 6, 22, 28, 37, 41, 45, 46, 49, 50–52, 64, 98, 99, 106, 108, 112, 113, 119, 136, 138, 145, 146, 149, 163; adaptive, 5, 28, 38, 57, 61, 164; anomie and, 102; facilitate, 100; navigating, 6, 110, 125, 143, 147,

163; perception of, 100; rapidity of, 51, 52, 86, 87, 96, 124, 125
chaos, 50, 51, 53
Charmaz, 69
China Clay, 79, 122
church, 89, 152
civic organisations, 22
cloaking effect, 25, 69, 70, 83, 133, 142
Cloke and Edwards, 10
closed system, 17, 37, 46, 55, 89, 93, 98, 99
cluster, 59, 60, 72, 77, 78
coal, 72, 74, 89, 96, 97, 101–3, 107, 111, 112, 123, 162; Coal River Mountain, 96; miners, 74
coastal communities, 28, 29, 119, 120
college: college education, 87, 88, 94, 103, 104, 129, 131
commodities, 48, 57–58
community: activism, 75, 82, 118, 135; participation, 15, 37, 38
comparative advantage, 17
competitiveness, 47, 59
complex adaptive assemblage, 3, 19, 53, 56, 62, 65, 66, 69, 80, 115, 120, 130, 131, 143, 148, 156, 159, 160, 162; complex interactions, 25, 27; complexity, 4, 5, 32, 39, 48, 54, 63, 142; region assemblage, 4, 15, 16, 18, 19, 65, 67, 121, 129, 131, 143, 146
cone of memory, 21, 24, 33, 39, 47, 52, 56
Connolly, 5, 18, 22, 23, 27, 33, 34, 44, 46, 47, 49, 51–53, 58, 102
Cooke, 47, 60
Coole and Frost, 45
core areas, 7, 10
Cornish: cornishness, 116, 122, 144; identities, 79, 125; magazine, 125
Cornwall and Isles of Scilly Local Enterprise Partnership, 77
Council of Europe, 116
counter-urbanisation, 17, 18, 156, 161
country bumpkin, 103

countryside, 10, 12, 13, 18, 33, 60, 93, 95, 105, 128
Covid-19, 6, 11, 18, 64, 76, 82, 118, 143, 145, 146, 150, 155, 163
Crabtree, 14
creative: class, 46, 48; economy, 9; industries, 8, 77, 161
Crescenzi and Rodriguez-Pose, 59, 60
Crone and Roper, 47
Crooked Road, 73
crops, 25, 86, 88, 89, 100
Crow, 95, 96, 101, 102
cultural: landscape, 73; melting pot, 87

Dabrowski, 1
Daily Mail, 118
Daily Mirror, 39
Damascio, 23
Dante, 101–3
Dargan and Shucksmith, 48
Darwin, 54, 58, 61
Dawley, 54, 55, 60, 63, 102
Day, 35
decline: community, 32, 122, 125, 136, 139; economy, 7, 72, 74, 79, 102, 109, 122; population, 17, 71, 109; young people, 34
Delanda, 4, 5, 18, 22, 34–36, 38, 46
Deleuze, 5
Deleuze and Guattari, 3, 4, 18, 22, 23, 27, 31, 35, 38–40, 47, 53, 85, 146, 149, 160
Deller, 10, 15, 17, 18, 71, 142
democratic pluralism, 51
Department for the Environment, Food, and Rural Affairs, 9
De Souza, 9, 59, 160
deterritorialisation, 35–37, 92, 93, 99, 112, 115–18, 120, 136, 141, 162
dialect, 36, 78, 118
Dickinson, 80, 154
digital economy, 77, 141
digital tech sector, 76, 77, 126, 149, 155
discourse, 11, 27, 40, 51, 75
disposability, 91

Dolly Parton, 111
Dominguez Garcia, 15, 160
Donner, 15
Dovey, 5, 28
downward causation, 49, 61, 81
Drabenstott, 11
Dunstan and Jaeger, 74
Durkheim, 44, 51–53, 102, 133, 148
dynamic: entrepreneurs, 46; interconnectedness, 62

earthworm, 25
ecological, 4, 25, 26, 50, 57, 162
economic: dynamism, 59; growth, 7, 47, 63, 149
economies of scale, 59, 141
eco-systems, 21, 22, 26, 29, 39; entrepreneurial, 72
Elan Vital, 47, 50, 110, 111, 113, 114, 146–49, 152, 163
Elcock, 78
embeddedness, 15
embodied research, 80–82
emergence, 5, 6, 19, 27, 44, 45, 47, 49–51, 53, 54, 56, 58, 63, 65, 67, 85
employment: growth, 71, 79; precariarity, 3, 108, 109, 113, 145, 148; skills, 60, 107, 129; statistics, 61, 72, 74, 76, 77; underemployment, 134; work, 113, 114, 127, 141
endogenous: development, 1, 2, 14, 15; growth, 15, 59, 142
entropy, 5, 21, 37, 100
Epicurus, 22, 26
Eriksson, 13, 18, 33, 60
ethnography, 19, 66
Evans, 97
Evans and Jones, 81
Evans and Synett, 48, 60
evolution: evolutionary Economic Geography, 6, 54, 161; evolutionary economics, 54, 55, 57; evolving, 4, 5, 27, 57, 63
exogenous, 15, 48
Experience Economy, 120

exteriority, 36–39, 100

Fabricant and Fabricant, 74
Factory Man, 89, 112
family ties, 75
farming, 29, 79, 82, 86, 89–91, 93, 126
Faulker, 10
feedback loop, 34, 41, 44, 48, 52, 55,
  56, 63, 102, 115, 121, 126, 129
Fenwick, 78
fishing, 28, 29, 78, 79, 94, 119
Florida, 8, 46, 52, 161
flows (information and knowledge), 3,
  5, 6, 15–17, 19, 22, 30, 38, 39, 41,
  46, 57, 61, 63, 67, 102, 106, 109,
  113, 118, 128, 132, 136, 140, 149,
  150, 153, 154, 161
fluidities, 5, 8, 9, 21, 22, 26, 34, 37, 38,
  89, 117, 128, 132, 143, 145, 149,
  161, 164
fold, 26, 67, 91, 95, 115, 154
forest, 75, 89, 93, 100
Foster and Hummel, 74
Foucault, 27, 33
Framework Convention for the
  Protection of Minorities, 116
France 24, 23

Galliano, 14
Gaventa, 74, 75
General Education Diploma, 107
geological, 28, 29, 31, 96, 112
Gest, 44, 53
Giesbrecht, 4
Gilet's Jaunes, 12, 13
Gleick, 4, 31
global: assemblages, 7, 8, 162;
  economic environment, 30, 62, 119,
  123, 124
Goffman, 24, 67, 80
Gormar and Lang, 7, 8, 60, 160
GOVA, 71, 72, 152
GO VA Region One, 9, 19, 72, 109, 154
green technology, 126
Grounded Theory, 69

growth paths, 55

Hallerod and Larson, 44
Hantrais, 66
Harvey, 4
Hechter, 78
Heilman, 74
heritage, 5, 73, 87, 116, 120, 144
Herrschel, 59
Herslund, 46, 114
Hewitt-Dundas, 47
Higgens, 18
High and Nemes, 15, 160
higher education, 72, 75
hiking, 73, 82, 94
hillbilly, 74, 92, 100
Hill et al, 4
histories, 22, 23, 28, 35, 55, 61, 65, 66,
  73, 83, 87, 92, 103, 116, 144, 145,
  161, 162
Holler, 87, 90, 92, 94, 100, 104
Honadle, 11
hospitality industry, 121, 127
Hoyvarde Clausen, 11
hunting, 29, 96
Huttlinger, 74

identities, 1, 14, 15, 35, 36, 53, 55, 56,
  63, 78, 79, 125, 144
Independence of Spirit, 88, 112
inequalities, 1, 7, 10, 12, 18, 44, 47, 53,
  56, 59, 60, 103, 113, 134, 142, 153,
  155, 156, 160, 163
information technology, 46, 72
infrastructure, 30, 41, 56, 59, 96, 103–5,
  113, 128, 132, 136, 141, 156
innovation: adaptation, 15, 31, 57;
  business, 7, 72; clusters, 57,
  60; economy, 77, 78, 121, 161;
  knowledges, 14, 16, 55; rural, 7, 33,
  160; systems, 55, 61
Institute of Cornish Studies, 78
interconnectivities, 4, 21, 30, 31, 38,
  41, 164
interiority, 37, 38, 89, 93, 98, 99

internal colonialism, 78, 80
interpretive, 24, 25, 30, 40, 56, 83, 108, 115, 125
inward investment, 59
inward migration, 18, 48, 79, 142, 144, 156
Ivaldi and Gombin, 12

Jansson, 13, 35, 60
Jenkins, 14
Jensen, 11
job creation, 72, 152
Johnston, 12
Jones, 5, 37, 161, 162

Kalantaridis, 17
Kaufman, 46, 50, 51
Kernow, 79
Kim 2008, 48
Kingsolver, 111, 154
Kleinschmit and Clausen, 11, 14, 160
Kneafsey, 37
knowledge: flows, 17, 63, 106, 154; systems, 55, 60; transfer, 60
Kok, 47

Lang, 7
Latour, 5, 9, 10, 18, 21–22, 25–27, 30
Lavender-Stott, 75
Laviolette, 125
LC King, 90, 111
LEADER, 9, 15
Lee, 46, 59, 60, 114
Lefebvre, 4
libraries, 16, 110, 115
linearity, 19, 44, 50, 55, 56, 63, 85, 118
line of flight, 39, 40, 53, 63, 119
local economies, 15, 17, 26, 70, 89, 125, 136
Lovelock, 4
Lowe, 12, 18, 60, 120, 160
lumber, 89, 90

Mackinnon 2002, 78
Macpherson, 81

Macy, 89, 90, 102
Main Street, 110
Mamonova and Franquesa, 12
manufacture, 8, 15, 72, 79, 89, 108
Margarian, 15
Markey and Taylor, 55
Marlerba and McKelvey, 55, 60
Martin and Sunley, 6, 54, 55, 102, 161
Marx, 54, 68
Marz, 47
Massey, 4
McFarlane, 4
Mead, 24, 33, 67
meanings: cultural, 3, 22, 36, 115
Meekes, 54, 55
memory: cloaking effect of, 68, 70, 83; cone of, 24, 33, 39, 47, 52, 56, 61, 68, 150; cultural, 33, 34, 67, 92, 150; interpretive, 24, 25; pathway, 127; resonance, 33
Merleau-Ponty, 33, 47, 69
metropolitan, 7, 9, 10, 12–14, 32, 33, 59, 60, 69, 118, 142
Meyer 2016, 13, 160
mining, 29, 58, 72, 74, 78, 79, 89, 95, 96, 102, 120, 123, 125
mobilities, 26, 30, 35, 38, 89, 117, 128, 132, 145, 150, 161, 164
money, 2, 11, 23, 58, 86, 87, 90, 105, 109, 112, 113, 123, 127, 131, 138, 140
Moreno, 55
Morgan and Shepherd, 9, 11
Mountain Valley Pipeline, 97, 112
Mount Rogers Planning District Commission, 72, 153
Mulholland, 36
Murdoch, 33
mutation, 58, 62

NAFTA, 107
narrative, 2, 17, 33–34, 35, 69, 74, 75, 79, 85, 93, 97, 108, 109, 110, 116, 117, 122, 125, 139, 142, 147
Nathan, 46, 114

nation, 7, 23, 29, 31, 41, 44, 74, 92, 100, 156; nation state, 12, 32, 37, 66
National Teacher Hall of Fame, 112
Native American, 73, 87
neighbours, 87, 99, 120
neoclassicism, 54, 61
neoliberal, 145
networks, 2, 3, 10, 14, 15, 17, 18, 21, 22, 28, 31, 37, 38, 41, 55, 88, 130–32, 134, 135, 138–41, 147, 149, 151, 152, 156, 161
Niche, 50, 54, 57–62, 65, 72
NOMIS, 76, 77, 119, 137, 142, 146, 147
non-human, 22, 25, 26
normlessness, 52, 53, 102
nostalgia, 34, 51, 122, 125, 148
Nuvolari, 58, 79

older people, 18, 135, 151
ontology, 50, 54
open system, 46, 64
organism, 25, 26, 40, 41, 47, 54, 57–59, 61–63, 110, 113, 124, 162
outsider, 99, 103, 106
outward migration, 18, 119, 125, 135, 140
Ozturk, 55

Paniagua, 11, 14
pastoral, 12, 60, 100
path dependencies, 51, 52, 55, 69, 102, 103, 109, 117, 142
patterns, 5, 12, 17, 28, 45, 51–53, 55, 56, 91, 96, 102, 109, 119, 136
Payton, 78
Pearson, 34, 51
Pendlebury, 13
performance, 16, 48, 81, 92, 120
peripheral, 7–9, 14, 19, 45, 49, 55, 56, 59–62, 66, 69, 142, 155, 156, 159, 160; peripheralisation, 7, 13, 160; peripheralised, 106; peripheralising, 8, 15, 17, 18; peripherality, 77
phenomenological, 23, 39–40, 67
Pike, 55, 59

Pine and Gilmore, 120
plateau, 31–32, 39, 41, 43, 53, 54, 59–61, 63
Pluymers, 73
polarisation (political), 12
policy: policy and social programmes, 10; policy discourse, 11; policy initiatives, 8; policy-makers, 11, 69
Politico, 97
Polyakova and Fligstein, 44
popular culture, 92, 104, 122, 152
populist, 12, 13
poverty, 7, 11, 13, 44, 53, 58, 71, 72, 75, 80, 121, 122, 130, 140, 143, 151
Powe, 18
precariarity, 107, 108, 139, 156
predictability, 5, 45, 47, 50
Prigogine and Stengers, 4, 5, 23, 37, 45, 46, 49–53, 55, 56
production of place, 5
productivist, 18, 97
productivity, 47, 55, 77, 102, 134, 147, 159
public transportation, 66, 81, 128, 129, 131, 134, 150, 151, 161
pure perception, 70
Putnam, 16, 22, 30, 37–38, 48, 134, 135, 138, 160

quality of life, 3, 7, 17, 46, 122
Quiller-Couch, 125

rail, 72, 87, 100, 113, 150, 154, 161
Raisanen and Tuovinen, 15, 16, 141, 153, 160
rapid changes, 51, 52, 86, 87, 96, 124, 125
realities, 18, 121, 122, 150
regional inequality, 7, 10, 11, 32, 44, 53, 65, 147
regionalism, 78
regional studies, 4, 5
Reimer, 9, 11
relations of exteriority, 36–39, 100
repeatability, 5, 45–46, 48–49

resilience, 6, 11, 40, 54–55, 143, 147, 161
resonance, 23–24, 33, 39–40, 61, 63,
  81, 90, 92, 95–96, 107, 109, 115,
  121, 122, 127, 133, 150
retail, 71, 76, 127
reverberated, 92, 120, 122, 125
rhizome, 39–41, 85, 160
ripples, 32, 87, 89, 132
Roberts and Townsend, 16, 103
Roddern, 12
Rodriguez-Pose and Crescenzi, 59, 60
Roggenkamp, 74, 75
root, 1, 11, 14, 15, 35, 39–41, 74, 79,
  85, 94, 96, 147, 151, 156
rupture, 53, 90, 93, 114
rural: areas, 9–19, 33, 71, 104, 134,
  135, 141–43, 151, 155; culture, 12,
  88; economies, 60, 131, 143; idyll,
  12, 13, 17, 18, 60, 76, 120, 121;
  stigmatisation, 13, 80; urban divide,
  10, 12, 19

Salva, 75
Sampaio and King, 18
Satterwhite, 73, 75, 103
seasonal employment, 79, 118, 127,
  128
self: employment, 76, 156; organised,
  51; reliance, 88, 145
sentient, 22, 25, 26
settlement, 73, 87, 128, 136, 152
settler, 73, 74, 87, 88, 95, 114
Shand, 5
sheltered, 71, 92, 94, 155
shortall, 48, 59; and Warner, 10, 16, 160
shrinking cities, 7, 163
Shucksmith, 12, 65, 160; and Brown,
  14, 160; and Chapman, 44
sites of possibility, 6, 19
skills, 4, 16, 26, 43, 59, 60, 76, 77, 80,
  92, 97, 113, 124, 125, 127, 139,
  141–44, 148, 149, 153, 156, 160
small-town, 18, 28, 93, 95, 131
Smith and Jenks, 4, 5, 45, 46, 162

social capital, 2, 16, 17, 30, 37, 38, 48,
  60, 89, 93, 98, 105, 134, 138, 142,
  156, 160, 161
socio economic, 54, 71, 74, 100, 134,
  152, 163, 164
Southern Appalachia, 74, 88, 92, 96,
  103, 104
spaces of possibility, 38–40, 47, 55, 60,
  63, 103, 110, 145–55, 161
spatial redistribution, 15
Spatz, 80
Spinoza, 22, 26
Spooner, 79
Stam, 114
Stecker and Debus, 12
stereotype, 13, 74, 99, 100, 103, 146, 152
stigmatising, 13, 74, 80
Stockdale, 17, 156
Stoyle, 78
St Paul, 101, 102, 113
St Piran, 78
Strauss, 69
Striker, 16
Strover, 16, 106, 160
structural funding, 1, 2, 15, 77
subjective position, 1
subsistence farming, 86, 91
survival of the fittest, 58, 61
sustainable, 6, 18, 69, 127, 156
Szabova, 80

talent, 8, 109, 148, 151
Talley, 112
temporality, 5, 19, 21, 33, 44–46, 53,
  55, 90, 93, 96, 100, 104, 115
territorialisation, 34–36, 39, 89, 92–94,
  99, 112, 115–20, 122, 139, 141, 154
Thanem and Knights, 80
Thiede, 11
Thompson, 73
Thornton and Deitz-Allyn, 75
threads, 85, 86, 96, 147
tobacco, 86, 100, 162; Commission, 72,
  104

topography, 28, 94
totalising, 34, 35
tourism: tourist industry, 29, 76, 79; visitor assemblages, 121, 122; visitor economy, 117, 119, 120, 122, 126, 127
town centre, 110, 126
Townsend, 44
trade, 5, 28, 31, 43, 76, 78, 89, 90
transport, 18, 58, 59, 100, 128–31, 134, 150, 151
travel, 36, 70–72, 89, 93, 128, 130–32, 135, 148, 150, 154
Tregidga, 78, 159
Trevithick, 58, 59
Trigliani, 111, 154
Trozzo, 75
Trump, 97, 107
Tuitjer and Steinfuhrer, 14

underemployment, 77, 108, 109
unpredictability, 47, 50, 51, 62, 65
utility, 27, 32, 37, 91, 92, 152

Vachelli, 80

Verghese, 98–99
virtual communities, 29
vital impetus, 110, 112
vulnerability, 10, 53, 107, 130, 134, 145

wages, 15, 71, 76, 80, 109, 129, 137, 144
Washington County Economic Development Team, 71, 101
Willett, 2, 4, 9, 13, 14, 33, 44, 46, 53, 60, 69, 76, 79, 106, 114, 154; and Giovannini, 78; and Lang, 13, 17, 18, 35, 69, 106; and Tredinnick-Rowe, 37
Williams, 14, 75, 79; and Harrison, 17
windfarms, 126
Witt, 54
wool, 5, 161, 162

younger people, 11, 17, 18, 71, 89, 129
Young-Powell, 63

Zeni, 4
Zwoniter and Hirschberg, 87, 92

www.ingramcontent.com/pod-product-compliance
Lightning Source LLC
Chambersburg PA
CBHW022316280326
41932CB00010B/1125